PLANTED EVIDENCE

The Story of the Trump-Russia Collusion Debacle

Dale Rowe

Lulu Press, Inc.
Lulu.com

ISBN 978-1-7166-6466-3

Dedication

To my wife Marty for her moral support and her shared knowledge of the Intelligence Community from years of working with the CIA, DIA, NSA, DEA, CND, FBI and Secret Service.

Marty's personal knowledge of the competitive spirit between agencies helped in the understanding of how the FBI wouldn't necessarily know that the CIA was planting evidence for them to find.

CONTENTS

PREFACE

WHAT MAKES THIS BOOK DIFFERENT?

Over twenty books have been inspired by the Trump-Russia collusion narrative. These books all address the process of investigating the evidence of collusion.

This book is different. It examines the real crime – the creation and planting of phony evidence of Trump-Russia collusion. The crime that was "investigated" was the alleged crime of collusion. It started with a pile of phony evidence. After nearly three years and $30 million, both the FBI and Mueller teams concurred, there was no crime of collusion. The evidence was bogus. The real crime was committed by those who created and planted the phony evidence of collusion. The real crime was committed by persons who hated Trump and did not want him elected or if elected wanted him impeached.

This book is different. It documents that the "evidence" was <u>created</u> by just two people, Joseph Mifsud and Christopher Steele, both with UK ties. It identifies John Brennan, his CIA and his UK intelligence buddies as the culprits responsible for recruiting Joseph Mifsud to create the evidence of collusion and maneuver the unsuspecting George Papadopoulos to plant it and the FBI to investigate it.

This book is different. It documents that the FBI team; James Comey, Andrew McCabe and Peter Strzok were fundamentally good talented FBI professionals whose egos and biases allowed them to willingly get sucked into investigating Brennan's planted evidence and prolong the investigation because of their documented, shared hatred of Donald Trump.

This book is different. It documents that the Lisa Page/Peter Strzok relationship was simply an embarrassing office romance but provided the best insight into why Strzok took the actions he did and did not take.

This book is different. It demonstrates that the whole collusion debacle was not a planned coordinated attack on Trump, but it developed into one with the common thread being a shared dislike of Trump by CIA and FBI leadership – the unofficial "deep state".

This book is different. It examines the Trump-Russia collusion debacle from the unique perspective of just an average American, but one who knows firsthand that the CIA is entirely capable of creating and planting evidence for the FBI to find.

REVELATIONS

- John Brennan knew Joseph Mifsud going back to 1998 and helped select him to plant evidence of Trump-Russia collusion,
- Christopher Steele was not hired to find dirt against Donald Trump, he was hired to create and plant evidence against Trump,
- The FBI knew the dossier was garbage from the start. Even in July 2016, what Christophe Steele felt was "a matter of US National security", the FBI didn't even consider when deciding to open an investigation even though they possessed the first three Steele dossier reports.

ABOUT THE AUTHOR

Dale Rowe is an average 82-year-old retired American. He considers himself one of those "American people who want to know" that are used as an excuse for every Congressional hearing.

Dale Rowe is not active in politics. He watches the news and reads the paper and generally keeps up on political, scientific, sports and social developments. Aside from being an average Joe, Dale does take an interest in controversial topics and researches them until he understands them. The Trump-Russia collusion episode is one of those topics.

Born and raised on a dairy farm in Oconomowoc, Wisconsin, Dale graduated from the one-room Brown Street school in 1952 and in 1956 graduated from Oconomowoc High School. He attended the University of North Dakota (UND) and in 1960 graduated with a degree in Mechanical Engineering and a commission in the US Army. At UND Mr. Rowe was awarded the Distinguished Military Graduate honor.

Mr. Rowe served on activity duty with the Army and spent seven years in the Army Reserve. He was employed by General Electric as an engineer and senior manager for 28 years. He started his first company, Gescan International. Inc. in 1988 producing the first search engine. His initial customers, the only ones with huge textual databases at the time, were the intelligence agencies.

Working with all agencies and their intel data for years, Dale and his wife, Marty had simultaneous Top Secret, compartmentalized SCI clearances in all intelligence agencies and understand that it is entirely possible for the CIA to plant evidence for the FBI to discover. As described in *"Planted Evidence,"* when all the dots are connected, that is what likely resulted in the Trump-Russia collusion investigation.

PART I

PLANTING THE EVIDENCE

JANUARY 2016 TO JULY 31, 2016

JOHN
BRENNAN

JOSEPH
MIFSUD

CHRISTOPHER
STEELE

Chapter 1: Introduction – The Bottom Line

On July 31, 2016 sufficient "evidence" of Trump-Russia collusion existed to start an investigation. After \$30 million and nearly three years of investigating, the FBI and Mueller's team found no evidence of collusion. How could that be? There is an obvious answer. The initial "evidence" was phony and planted. Here is how that happened.

CIA and UK Intelligence Were Responsible for Creating, Planting & Leaking Collusion Evidence.

John Brennan, Director of the Central Intelligence Agency (CIA) did not want Trump to be president. Brennan, with the help of Joseph Mifsud, the mysterious Maltese professor and Christopher Steele, the ex-head of the Russian Desk of the United Kingdom's (UK) Intelligence MI6, created and planted evidence of Trump-Russia collusion right in the laps of the Federal Bureau of Investigation (FBI). The process occurred on two different tracks; (1) the Mifsud Track and (2) the Steele Track. Chapters 2 and 3 connect the dots for both tracks.[1] The Mifsud track yielded a paper and electronic communication trail of collusion evidence consisting of (1) "attempts" to set up a back door channel to arrange a nn-Trump meeting and (2) collusion between the Russians and the Trump campaign to hack and release Clinton and Democratic National Committee (DNC) emails. The Steele track yielded a dossier consisting of seventeen reports containing evidence of Trump-Russia collusion and potentially blackmail opportunities for the Russians. Additionally, the Steele track yielded strategic leaking of evidence of collusion and sex-capades to the press. The two tracks are illustrated in Figure 1-1.

Brennan didn't need the evidence to be real. He just needed it to be created, planted and leaked. Leaking to the media was expected to sufficiently damage Trump's chance of being elected at best or at worse

---

[1] **Papadopoulos** was George Papadopoulos, the unsuspecting unpaid advisor to the Trump campaign. **Downer** was Alexander Downer an Australian diplomat who fed the FBI rumors of dirt from Papadopoulos. **Simpson** was Glen Simpson the person who was hired by the DNC to get dirt on Trump. Simpson subcontracted part of that to Christopher Steele. **Ohr** was Bruce Ohr the Associate Deputy Attorney General who was an unofficial backdoor information conduit between the FBI, Christopher Steele and Glen Simpson.

form the basis for a Special Prosecutor being named leading to impeachment.

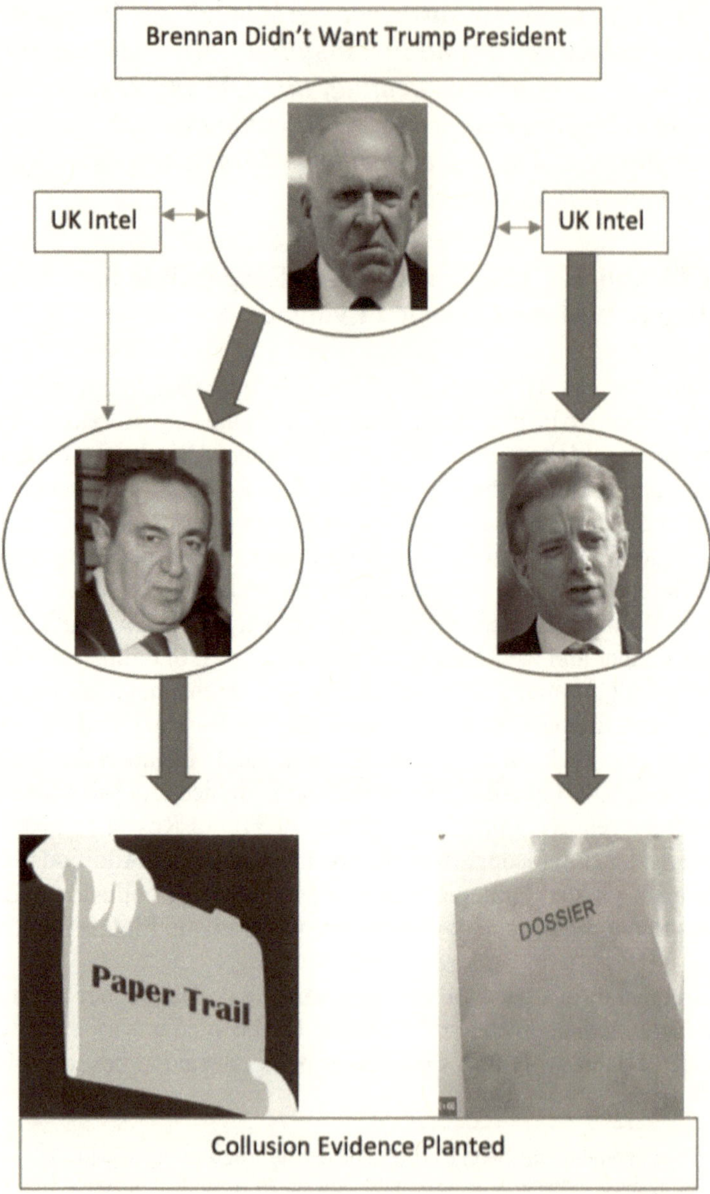

Figure 1-1 Connecting the Dots – Two Tracks to Interfere with Trump Presidency Using Planted Evidence of Collusion

FBI Egos and Bias Were Responsible for Prolonging the Investigation

The FBI discovered the obvious – the data they investigated was phony. There was no credible evidence. How could this happen? How could they waste so much time and money and find nothing? Even with all that money and time they failed to adequately follow up on how the phony evidence was created and who was responsible. In short, the FBI didn't finish the job. They didn't pursue the real criminals who planted all the disinformation it took them three years and $30 million to discredit.

All of the planted evidence of collusion came from just two sources, Joseph Mifsud and Christopher Steele. UK-based Mifsud was the sole source for Track 1. UK-based Steele was the sole source for Track 2. This fact alone should have prevented the start of a full investigation into Trump-Russia collusion until some vetting was performed. After all, the FBI still have no idea who Mifsud is or who he was working for. They knew Steele was being paid by Trump's political enemy to find dirt. Two factors prevented the vetting of the planted evidence before it led to an investigation, (1) Comey's ego and (2) FBI's bias. Chapter 4 connects the dots between the planted Mifsud "evidence" and finding that no evidence existed. Chapter 5 connects the dots between planted Steele "evidence" and the finding that no evidence existed.

The evidence of collusion and of Trump's sex romp in Moscow in 2013 turned out to be non-factual hearsay – some of it planted as a deliberate effort by the Russians to provide disinformation to Steele. The Mifsud "evidence" was shown to be just rumors that he himself had created. The Steele "evidence" was shown to be just speculation that even the sources later disavowed. The logical question is, "how could there be so much evidence to start with and then after two years of investigating find nothing?" The logical conclusion is that the planted "evidence" was fabricated. The logical conclusion is that it was fabricated and intentionally planted to incriminate Donald Trump.

Trump-Russia collusion was investigated by three teams; (1) Crossfire Hurricane FBI team (pre-Mueller investigation), (2) Mueller team and (3) Horowitz team.

The FBI agents comprising the Crossfire Hurricane team were not Trump fans. There were agents with documented anti-Trump biases. Even with the known biases the FBI could not find evidence of collusion.

5

In no way could the FBI's efforts be considered a "whitewash." There simply was no "there" there.

The agents comprising the Mueller investigation found no evidence of collusion. The Mueller team was composed solely of democrats. The Mueller team members were not Trump fans. Most of them had documented anti-Trump biases. This was not a team picked from a set of Trump supporters.

The Horowitz investigation found no evidence of collusion. Although the Horowitz team didn't investigate the collusion narrative per se, they did look into misconduct of any kind on the part of those doing the investigating into collusion. Both Democrat and Republican law makers respected Horowitz. The Horowitz team found no biases or misconduct that would suggest that anyone was trying to "whitewash" evidence of collusion. To the contrary, the Horowitz investigation uncovered evidence that FBI personnel had falsified data, omitted exculpatory evidence and displayed personal bias against Trump and his associates. All 17 cases of errors and omissions (FISA warrants) would have provided more evidence of innocence if the errors had been corrected or the omissions included. Based on the errors and omissions, Horowitz found that the FBI and Mueller investigations were highly flawed.

The Horowitz investigation found that despite the use of witness entrapment, blackmail and other questionable coercion techniques available to the FBI, they were unable to ferret out any evidence of collusion.

When all the dots are connected in Chapter 2 and 3 it shows that (1) John Brennan was the lead conspirator, (2) Comey's FBI got sucked into becoming co-conspirators and (3) the FBI under James Comey embarrassed itself, trampled on innocent people, and totally missed looking at real perpetrators of wrongdoing all because of their ego and bias. It has been a sad three years for the reputation of the FBI and Department of Justice (DOJ).

Chapter 2: Planting Evidence of Collusion – Track 1

Connecting the Dots – Track 1 The Mifsud Track: These dots are well known; (1) Brennan hated Trump, (2) Brennan had access to UK Intelligence and personnel, (3) Brennan had a long-term connection to Mifsud, (4) George Papadopoulos was the perfect "patsy" and (5) Alexander Downer and Erika Thompson were available to serve as a backup for delivery of collusion evidence. Connecting these dots from motive to planted evidence defines "Track 1". Figure 2-1 illustrates the connection of the dots.

Brennan Had the Motive: It is no secret that Brennan did not like Trump.[2] He did not want him elected. If somehow, Trump got elected, Brennan wanted him removed from office. Brennan did not like Trump.[3] Brennan had a motive.

Brennan Was Well Connected with British Intelligence: The Guardian reported on April 13, 2017 that UK Intelligence Agency Government Communications Headquarters (GCHQ) started reporting suspicious communications between figures connected to Trump and known or suspected Russian agents, a source close to UK intelligence said.[4] According to one account, "GCHQ's then-head, Robert Hannigan, *was the origin of the Trump-Russia collusion investigation.* He passed his suspicions on to Brennan. This is unusual because Hannigan's direct counterpart in the United States (US) was Mike Rogers, head of the National Security Agency (NSA), GCHQ's Five Eyes intelligence-sharing partner. The problem for Hannigan was that Mike Rogers would ask tough questions before embarking on spying on Trump's team. John Brennan was different. He hated Trump. He would investigate Donald Trump without proper predication.

There is only one missing piece to this track that can only be filled in by further investigation into the Brennen-UK intelligence connection in late 2015 and early 2016. Specifically, what "troubling" intelligence was so sensitive that it had to be shared directly between Robert Hannigan

---

[2] See Appendix A, *"Evidence That Brennan Did Not Like Donald Trump"*

[3] The Hill, *"17 times Brennan has torched Trump"* Emily Birnbaum , August 15, 2018

[4] The Guardian, *"British spies were first to spot Trump team's links with Russia"* - Luke Harding, Stephanie Kirchgaessner and Nick Hopkins, April 13, 2017

and John Brennan?   Was it real? Or, was it some of Steele's disinformation?

Figure 2-1 Connecting the Dots – Track 1 Brennan & UK Intelligence to Planted Trump-Russia Collusion Evidence

That material was delivered in the summer of 2016 directly to the CIA Director, John Brennan.[5] The matter was deemed so sensitive it was handled at 'director level'. *It is significant that Brennan's relationship with GCHQ head, Robert Hannigan was the start of the ill-fated investigation.*

British Intelligence Had Ties to Joseph Mifsud, The Source of The Planted Evidence – It is well established that British intelligence had ties to Christopher Steele, one source of evidence of Trump-Russia collusion. Steele was the ex-head of the Russian Desk at MI6.

It is less well established that British Intelligence as well as US Intelligence had ties to Joseph Mifsud, the other source of evidence of Trump-Russia collusion. These ties are less well established because the FBI failed to explore them. This failure was likely due to FBI bias toward finding evidence of collusion, not on objectively investigating if there was collusion.

Ties between Joseph Mifsud and British Intelligence are defined in Appendix B.

John Brennan Had Ties to Joseph Mifsud - John Brennan had a connection with Joseph Mifsud going back to 1998 when Brennan was CIA's chief of station in Riyadh, Saudi Arabia. The connection is through Nawaf Obaid and Prince Truki, Ex-Saudi intelligence chief. Nawaf Obaid interfaced with Brennan in Riyadh.

In 2016, Joseph Mifsud introduced George Papadopoulos to Nawaf Obaid.[6] Nawaf Obaid is an ex-Saudi intelligence analyst and Visiting Fellow for Intelligence and Defense Projects at Harvard Kennedy School's Belfer Center for Science and International Affairs.[7] (Where Ashton Carter, ex-Secretary of Defense also teaches.) The close relationship between Harvard and the CIA is well known.[8] Brennan may have used Nawaf Obaid in 2016 to check up on Mifsud's progress with coopting George Papadopoulos.

---

[5] Tablet Magazine, *"How CIA Director John Brennan Targeted James Comey"*, Lee Smith

[6] Lawfare, *"Transcript of George Papadopoulos Interview with House Judiciary and Oversight Committees"* Mey 26, 2019, page 178

[7] *"The Looming Tower – Al-Qaeda and the road to 9/11"*, Lawrence Wright Random House 2006, PP448.

[8] *"Spy Schools"*, Daniel Golden, Henry Holt & Company, 2017

Brennan served as the agency's chief of station in Saudi Arabia (1996–99). Prince Turki told the Associated Press (AP) on Oct 17, 2003 that he had given the names of two of the eventual 9/11 hijackers to the CIA (Brennan) in 1999. Nawaf Obaid, a security consultant for the Saudi government confirmed that Turki had given the names to the CIA station chief in Riyadh, John Brennan.[9] Obaid knew John Brennan very well.

Nawaf Obaid also knew Joseph Mifsud very well. So did Prince Turki. Mifsud has been associated with Prince Turki since his days at the London Academy of Diplomacy where Mifsud trained his intelligence officers.

Nawaf Obaid courted Mifsud and tried to get him a cushy job working with CNN's Freedom Project at Link Campus in Rome.[10]

Brennan was comfortable with having Joseph Mifsud on "the team."

It Is No Mystery Why Joseph Mifsud was Selected to Create Bogus Evidence of Trump-Russia Collusion - There is no direct evidence that Mifsud worked for John Brennan and/or UK intelligence to plant evidence of Trump-Russia collusion. The main reason this direct evidence isn't available is because the FBI didn't bother to look for it. However, when the dots are connected, there is little doubt that Mifsud was an agent of Western intelligence and an acquaintance of John Brennan. There is little reason to think he was a Russian agent. Why was he recruited to create the false evidence of collusion?

- Mifsud was a bonified shady character, totally capable of creating false evidence and manipulating a "patsy" to plant it. Mueller politely called Mifsud "mysterious" instead of calling him "shady." Appendix C documents his shady dealings.
- Mifsud was a documented "con man." Joseph had a track record of luring people, even prominent people, into doing things they wouldn't normally do. He stiffed two universities for over a $100,000. Getting Papadopoulos to plant a paper trail of collusion was a "piece of cake" for Dr. Mifsud. Appendix B documents how Mifsud's associates,

---

[9] "The Looming Tower – Al-Qaeda and the road to 9/11" Lawrence Wright Random House 2006, PP448.

[10] Zero Hedge, *"Death of Russiagate? Mueller Team Tied to Mifsud's Network"*, *Dyler Durden, 1/22/2019*

employers, students, and "friends" determined that he was a con man.

- Mifsud was known by Brennan.
- Mifsud was known by UK intelligence.
- Mifsud was likely a long time Confidential Human Source (CHS) for UK Intelligence and/or the CIA.
- The CIA had established channels to covertly pay for Mifsud's services using an array of university "affiliations" as enumerated in Appendix C.

In short, Joseph Mifsud was the ideal Brennan resource for creating evidence and manipulating an inside "patsy" to plant it.

George Papadopoulos Was a Godsend for Brennan – the Perfect Patsy to Unknowingly Plant the Bogus Evidence of Collusion Created by Mifsud. - Brennan needed a paper trail of Trump-Russia collusion planted and recoverable inside the Trump campaign. A seasoned political campaign veteran would process gossip and act on it without a  whole lot of emails asking for approval or convincing co-workers to pursue the gossip.

George Papadopoulos was not that seasoned veteran. He was not empowered to set up meetings between Putin and Trump, but if he could, Papadopoulos would be a hero in the campaign. George needed to be a hero.

Appendix D details how George was driven to be important, to make a mark. It establishes how he was driven by the need to rub elbows with important people and to get credit for making a difference. George could be counted on to plant the evidence that Mifsud created. George needed to be "important."

Mifsud delivered two pieces of incriminating evidence for Papadopoulos to unwittingly plant in the Trump campaign. - The two pieces of incriminating evidence Mifsud, his employer (CIA) and Mifsud's handler decided that Papadopoulos would deliver to the campaign were;
- Evidence of attempts to set up a secret meeting between Trump and Putin, and

- Evidence that the Trump campaign and the Russians were conspiring together to hack the DNC computer and to develop and leak dirt on the Clinton campaign.

Mifsud's scheme to plant evidence of efforts to secretly set up a Putin -Trump meeting. - This is the biggest joke of the whole evidence planting scheme. Mifsud used two scenarios and two Russians in this scheme. The Russians were (1) Olga Polonskaya and (2) Ivan Timofeev.

The first Russian Mifsud introduced George to was Olga Polonskaya, "Putin's niece." This occurred on March 24, 2016 in London. Except Olga Polonskaya was not Putin's niece, she was a liquor store manager in Moscow. Seriously, FBI, does this sound like something that a <u>Russian</u> agent would do to gain long term access to the Trump campaign? Dress up a liquor store manager and present her as Putin's niece? That doesn't make any sense. What does make sense is that Mifsud was a CIA operative and was trying to plant evidence of an attempt by the Trump campaign to secretly set up a Trump-Putin meeting. The hope was that Papadopoulos would report back to the Trump campaign of his meeting with Putin's niece and that a meeting between the two leaders was being planned. It worked. That is exactly what Papadopoulos did. And, what do you know? The FBI found that e-communication trail. Hard evidence of Trump-Russia collusion! (By the way, no meeting was ever set up!)

The second Russian Mifsud introduced to Papadopoulos was Ivan Timofeev. Of course, just as with Putin's niece, no meeting ever got set up, but plenty of evidence of trying was planted. And again, Mifsud never tried to set up a meeting, he just advised Papadopoulos how to go about it. That way, the e-communication trail would show that the Trump campaign was colluding with Russia. That is exactly what happened.

On April 18, Mifsud introduced Papadopoulos by email to Ivan Timofeev, who was program director at the Russian International Affairs Council. Timofeev suggested a meeting in Moscow or London.[1] Papadopoulos notified the Trump campaign. Over the next several weeks, Papadopoulos and Timofeev had multiple conversations over Skype and email about setting "the groundwork" for a "potential" meeting between the Campaign and Russian government officials.

On May 4, 2016, Papadopoulos forwarded to Lewandowski an email from Timofeev raising the possibility of a meeting in Moscow, asking Lewandowski whether that was "something we want to move forward with." The next day, Papadopoulos forwarded the same Timofeev email to Sam Clovis, adding to the top of the email "Russia update." He included the same email in a May 21, 2016 message to senior Campaign official Paul Manafort, under the subject line "Request from Russia to meet Mr. Trump," stating that Russia has been eager to meet Mr. Trump for quite some time and had been reaching out to me to discuss.[11] Lewandowski, Clovis, and Manafort never responded to the emails from Papadopoulos

Mission accomplished. Mifsud had planted evidence of Trump-Russia collusion using the unsuspecting George Papadopoulos. There was no follow-up and no meeting. Mifsud was 2-for-2.

Mifsud's scheme to plant evidence of Trump campaign colluding with the Russians to hack Hillary's emails and dig up dirt on her. It was suspected that the Russians were responsible for hacking the DNC computers and that they had secret dirt on Hillary Clinton. Mifsud and his cronies reasoned that if there was evidence that the Trump campaign was in on the hacking it would be huge for the collusion case against Trump and Russia.

The opportunity presented itself when Mifsud returned after a two-week trip to Russia (Mifsud attended an annual meeting of the Valdia Discussion Club in Moscow on April 19, 2016). Joseph and George met up for breakfast at the Andez Hotel in London on April 26, 2016, the day after Mifsud got back. George expected Joseph had an update on arrangements for the Trump-Putin meeting. Instead, Joseph Mifsud passed the "bombshell" information that, **"THE RUSSIANS HAD DIRT ON HILLARY CLINTON AND THOUSANDS OF EMAILS."**

The problem was, George wasn't that interested. To Mifsud, knowledge of Russian possession of dirt on Hillary AND thousands of her emails was just the kind of thing that investigations into collusion are made of. This was the ultimate plant of incriminating information passed from Mifsud to Papadopoulos. If a paper trail of this knowledge was found in possession of the Trump campaign, it would be hard evidence that Trump and Russia were really colluding.

Much to the chagrin of Mifsud, Papadopoulos didn't think that was a big deal. Mifsud had to hatch a new plan to plant the evidence. As hard as the FBI tried, they could find no incriminating e-communication

---

[11] The Mueller Report, page 91

between the campaign and Papadopoulos about Hillary dirt or email. A perfectly good evidence planting scheme gone to waste.

An alternate path to delivery of the Hillary dirt was required. If George wasn't going to share his knowledge of dirt on Hillary with the Trump campaign, the FBI couldn't find that bit of evidence of collusion. Mifsud, his sponsor, (CIA) and handler (MI6 Agent 1) needed an alternate route to get the evidence to the FBI. It was too late to develop an alternate patsy inside the Trump campaign. The decision was to simply get George to orally share his juicy gossip on Hillary dirt with a third party and have that third party deliver it to the FBI.

Mifsud and crew had to select a trusted third party and stage a "George encounter" with that "trusted person" who could draw this rumor out of George and relay it to the FBI directly.

Selecting the right third party to draw the story about the existence and access to Hillary dirt from Papadopoulos was key. - The "trusted person" had to have several attributes;

- He/she had to have legitimate access to the FBI,
- He/she could not be "suspicious" to George,
- He/she had to be "trusted" by Mifsud's employer, the CIA and
- He/she had to be "legitimate" and unconnected to any relevant investigation if the scheme was uncovered.

Mifsud, his employer and his handler came up with the ideal person, Alexander Downer, High Commissioner (Ambassador) to the United Kingdom. Downer lived in London. He had established access to the FBI. He was trusted by Mifsud's sponsor (CIA), and he had no prior connection to the investigation.

Downer wasn't that thrilled with his proposed "volunteer assignment." Downer didn't know Papadopoulos. How would the introduction occur? What if Papadopoulos got suspicious? Was Papadopoulos more-savvy than he was being portrayed? Downer had to protect himself from getting played. He wanted an independent assessment of Papadopoulos before he committed.

Mifsud's employer, the CIA, had access to a couple of ex-Defense Intelligence Agency (DIA) guys (Terrance Dudley and Gregory Baker) in the US embassy in London that could check out Papadopoulos for Downer. They could get a good read on whether it was safe for Downer to take on the role he was being asked to perform. Dudley and Baker met with George on May 7, 2016 in London. They gave the CIA and Downer a "thumbs up." Yes, Papadopoulos was naïve.

The only box to fill was how to arrange an unsuspicious meeting between Downer and Papadopoulos. That didn't take long. Between the CIA and Downer they learned that the Australian intelligence person in the embassy, Erika Thompson was dating a friend of George's, Christian Cantor, an intelligence person in the Israeli embassy in London. Christian agreed to introduce Erika to George.

The stage was set. The history of what transpired is a matter of record.

The Downer-Papadopoulos-Thompson meeting got set up without raising any suspicions - On May 3, 2016 George got a call from his friend at the Israeli embassy saying he wanted to introduce George to his girlfriend, Erika Thompson. The three of them met for dinner that evening.

On May 6, 2016 Erika contacted George and set up a date for her, George and her boss at the Australian embassy, Alexander Downer to get together for a drink. That "get together" was scheduled for May 10, 2016. That date is well established. It has been confirmed by both George and Alexander and their calendars.

The date is further evidenced by the fact that Papadopoulos noted in his book that it was raining hard the night they met at the Kensington Wine Rooms, a ten minute walk from his apartment.[12] (A check on the weather record for London on May 10, 2016 confirms it was raining that evening. It also confirms that it wasn't raining on May 6, 2016, the day that the Mueller Report said the information about dirt was transmitted to "a representative of a foreign government".)

The reason the date is significant is the Mueller report[13] says, "*...on May 6, 2016, Papadopoulos suggested to a representative of a foreign government the Trump Campaign had received indications from the Russian government that it could assist the Campaign through the anonymous release of information that would be damaging to candidate Clinton.*"

---

[12] "*Deep State Target*", Op. Cit. page 73
[13] "Mueller Report" Op. Cit. page 81

May 6 is NOT May 10. Either Mueller got the date wrong or the *"representative of a foreign government"* was Erika Thompson, not Alexander Downer and the information was passed on May 6 when she set up the Downer meeting. It is likely that George told Erika when she called on May 6, 2016 to set the date for their meeting with Downer that, *"he (Papadopoulos) had received indications from the Russian government that it could assist the Campaign through the anonymous release of information that would be damaging to candidate Clinton".* This is the most logical interpretation since (1) the Mueller document has never been amended to "correct the error in dates", (2) both Papadopoulos and Downer downplay what was said at their May 10, 2016 meeting, (3) both Downer and Papadopoulos say their meeting occurred on May 10, 2016, and (4) Downer's belligerent attitude was not designed to "draw-out" rumors of Hillary dirt from George.

According to the Horowitz report, it was Erika Thompson's meeting with a USG official on July 26, that triggered the Crossfire Hurricane investigation - It is well established that Mifsud told Papadopoulos *"The Russians have dirt on Hillary Clinton. Emails of Clinton, he says. They have thousands of emails."*[14] Mifsud denies that he told Papadopoulos anything about "dirt" on Hillary but that is likely a lie to protect himself and his employer, Brennan's CIA.

Here is what the excerpt of what the Horowitz report (with redactions) said concerning information passed from the FFG (Australians) to US Intelligence on July 26, 2016 that led to opening Crossfire Hurricane five days later on July 31, 2016:

On July 26, 2016, the FFG official spoke with a U.S. government (USG) official in the European city about an "urgent matter" that required an in-person meeting. At the meeting, the FFG official informed the USG official of the meeting with Papadopoulos. The FFG official also provided **XX*XXXXXXXXXXXXXXXXXXX* XXXXXXXXXXX** *information from* **XXXXXXX** *FFG officials* **XXXXXX.** *following the May 2016 meeting.* **XXX XXXXXXXX** *stated, in part, that Papadopoulos suggested the Trump team had received some kind of suggestion from Russia that it could assist this process with the anonymous release of information during the campaign that would be damaging to Mrs. Clinton and President Obama.*

---

[14] "Deep State Target" Op. Cit. page 60

Here is that excerpt with the words inserted with the information that matches the character count of the redactions. The inserted words are bolded. The words in parentheses are added for clarification:

> *On July 26, 2016, The FFG official (Erika Thompson) spoke with a U.S. government official in (London) about an "urgent matter" that required an in-person meeting. (That meeting was held that day, July 26, 2016.) At the meeting, the FFG official (Erika) informed the USG official of the meeting (May 6th) with Papadopoulos. The FFG official also provided* **Terrance Dudley & Gregory Baker** *information from* **several** *FFG officials* **the day** *following the May (6), 2016 (Papadopoulos) meeting (i.e. May 7, 2016).[15]* **Ms. Thompson** *stated, in part, that Papadopoulos suggested the Trump team had received some kind of suggestion from Russia that it could assist this process with the anonymous release of information during the campaign that would be damaging to Mrs. Clinton and President Obama."[16]*

On July 27, 2016 the USG official called the FBI Legal Attache' and the ***Deputy Chief of Mission in London (Elizabeth Dibble)*** and provided her with the FFG information.[17] The FBI opened Crossfire Hurricane on July 31, 2016, just four days after its receipt of the information provided by the FFG official.[18] The Australian sourced information corroborated information already provided by Christopher Steele and thus was considered adequate predication for opening the full investigation, code-named "Crossfire Hurricane".

According to the Horowitz Report, *"We (Inspector General's Office (IGO)) did not find information in FBI or Department ECs, emails, or other documents, or through witness testimony, indicating that any information other than the FFG information was relied upon to predicate the opening of the Crossfire Hurricane investigation.[19]*

---

[15] "Horowitz Report, Op. Cit. page 51 (the highlighted names and words replaced the redacted names and words, matching the letter count of the redacted words and names.)

[16] Horowitz Report, Ibid. Page 51

[17] "Horowitz Report", Ibid.. Page 52 (the highlighted name replace the redacted name matching the letter count of the redacted name.

[18] Horowitz Report, Ibid. Page II

[19] Horowitz Report, Ibid. Page II

Obviously, the above quote from the Horowitz Report cannot be taken literally. The FBI was already aware of collaborating data from a variety of sources. But the timing of the Wikileaks release of "dirt" and the Papadopoulos bragging about having access to Clinton "dirt" supposedly made the Papadopoulos incident the tipping point to opening a formal investigation.

That is the starting point, but everyone has a different understanding of what was passed to the "agent of the foreign government," when it was passed, to whom, how long they sat on it and when it was released to the US government and to whom. The FBI "can't find that communication."

The most likely scenario, introduced above, is that George Papadopoulos told Erika Thompson on May 6, 2016 when she was arranging the meeting with Alexander Downer for May 10, 2016. Based on the Horowitz report, it is also likely that she relayed that to Downer, and to Dudley and Baker the next day.

It is also likely that Baker and Dudley then reported to Brennan's CIA that the planted evidence of collusion had been received and that Australian Intelligence could attest that they had the evidence. The Downer meeting really wasn't needed because the rumor of dirt on Hillary was already passed to the CIA. The meeting was held anyway, but with no real agenda. When Brennan needed to pull the trigger to start the investigation on collusion it would be portrayed as a result of an independent, friendly foreign government, not the CIA that notified the FBI of the incriminating evidence of collusion. Mifsud took a step to the side, but he achieved his goal of planting the evidence by adding Downer and Thompson in the chain. The timing of the release of the evidence to the FBI was likely directed by the CIA. To date, neither the FBI nor the Australian's have provided the text of that communication despite being asked for it. According to the IG report, the FBI says, "we lost it."

This scenario answers these questions;

- Why did the Mueller report say that the message of dirt on Hillary was passed to a "representative of a foreign government" on May 6, 2016? (Answer: It was because on May 6, 2016 Papadopoulos passed it to Erika Thompson. Ms. Thompson was the "representative of a foreign government.")

- Why did Mueller change Papadopoulos's description of the information he was given by Mifsud **from**: *"The Russians have dirt on Hillary Clinton. Emails of Clinton. They have thousands of emails"* **to:** *"he (Papadopoulos) had received indications from the Russian government that it could assist the Campaign through the anonymous release of information that would be damaging to candidate Clinton."* (Answer: It was because this description implies that the campaign was trolling for information (colluding with the Russians) that could damage the Clinton campaign.)

- Why was Downer confrontational with George (as reported both by Downer and Papadopoulos) at the meeting in the bar if Downer was supposed to be drawing out information from Papadopoulos on the Russian possession of dirt and emails? (Answer: Because George had already passed that rumor on to Erika two nights before.) Downer had no agenda. He was just venting.

- Why was there a nearly three-month delay in the relay of the information about dirt on Hillary Clinton to the recognition by the FBI that they had received it? Downer said that even though he and Papadopoulos did not discuss "dirt" on Hillary Clinton that he relayed the "troubling information" from Papadopoulos to "Canberra" **the next day**. (Answer: The CIA and Australian Intelligence elected to "sit on it" until it could be considered important enough by the FBI to trigger opening a formal investigation. That was on July 26, 2016. They could tie it to the Wikileaks release of Clinton's emails.)

The FBI was played by Brennan again. - Because of FBI bias and Comey's ego the FBI was eager to run with the totally manufactured evidence. This is an indictment of the FBI and their actions being influenced by bias.

Brennan's Mission Accomplished – Brennan's hatred of Trump had been transformed into evidence to be found by the FBI. The dots are connected.

*(**The above scenario varies from that described by others in that it directly ties Brennan and the CIA into the evidence planting scheme. It***

---

also puts Alexander Downer in a "reluctant participate" role, elevates the role of Erika Thompson, and paints the FBI as being manipulated by Brennan.)

Chapter 3: Planting Evidence of Collusion – Track 2 (Through July 31, 2016)

The FBI maintains that they opened the Crossfire Hurricane investigation based on the rumor of Trump and Russia colluding to hack the DNC emails and collect dirt on Hillary from an Australian source. To an average American this doesn't seem likely, particularly given that the FBI had three perfectly good reports of collusion from Christopher Steele at the time. Let's give the FBI credit for reading the reports that Christopher Steele found so troublesome that his assessment was that the national security of the United States rested on the data in those reports. The FBI either "blew-off" the documents as trash, didn't read them, or didn't want to admit they used them to kick off a full investigation. No matter the reason, it reflects poorly on the FBI.

It is well documented that the three Steele reports were in the hands of the FBI prior to opening the investigation on July 31, 2016. They were planted in the FBI using Steele's handler, Michael Gaeta. It is not credible that they were judged by Steele to be critical to the national security of the US when in turn, the FBI treated them as immaterial and not worthy of investigation at that time. The three reports were simply planted to damage Trump. They were NOT reports documenting investigative work done on contract with the FBI. They were reports gathered by Steele's network to satisfy Steele's contract with the Clinton campaign and the DNC to find and document dirt on Trump. Planting them in the FBI was part of Steele's job. Why else would he take a DNC authored report (Report 112) and hand it the FBI?

Connecting the Dots – Track 2: The Steele Track: These dots are well known; (1) The Clinton campaign and the Democratic National Committee (DNC) wanted dirt on Trump. (2) The Clinton campaign and DNC hired the law firm of Perkins Coie to launder a payment of $1.2 M[20] to opposition research firm, Fusion GPS (headed by Glen Simpson) to do the digging for Trump dirt. (3) Glen Simpson, in turn, hired Ex-MI6 agent Christopher Steele for $168,000 to dig up Russian-unique dirt on Trump campaign-Russian connections and plant it in the FBI. A mutual hate for Trump plus money was the initial motivation for Simpson and Steele. (4) Steele enlisted a "Primary Sub-source" to engage "Unnamed" Russians

---

[20] Wikipedia, *"Steele Dossier"*

to serve as sources of "evidence." (5) The unvetted, unedited "evidence" was assembled into three reports (Report 80, 86, and 94) and delivered to Michael Gaeta, Steele's FBI Handler. (6) There were more reports to

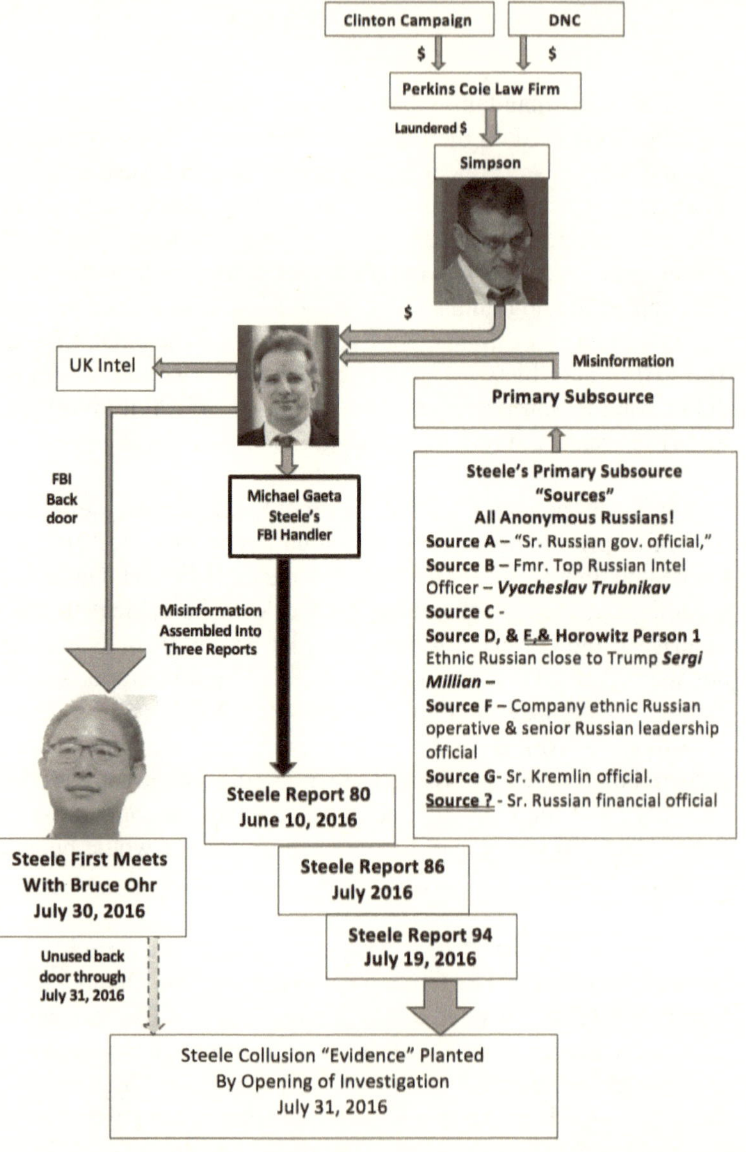

Figure 3-1 Connecting the Dots – Track 2 Clinton Campaign - to Planted Trump-Russia Collusion Evidence

come after the investigation was opened, so to ensure all the reports got delivered to the right people in the FBI, Mr. Steele, in parallel, developed a back-up route into the FBI using old friend and US Associate Deputy Attorney General at the Department of Justice (DOJ), Bruce Ohr just in case his primary route failed to plant his collusion evidence. Connecting these dots from motive to planted evidence defines "Track 2". Figure 3-1 illustrates the connection of the dots.

The Clinton Campaign and DNC Had the Motive: It is no secret that the Clinton campaign and DNC did not like Trump. Neither organization wanted Trump elected. They had a motive to plant dirt on Trump with the FBI. They hired Fusion GPS and Christopher Steele to do that. They were successful.

The FBI got the evidence of collusion for free. The Clinton campaign and DNC paid for it. The FBI got what they paid for – nothing.

The Clinton Campaign and DNC Had Contacts with Glen Simpson: The origin of the Steele Dossier can be traced to Paul Singer. Paul Singer was a rich "never-Trumper" Republican. He was aware that Glen Simpson had started his own investigation into Trump's business dealings and in particular with Russia back when Simpson was with the Wall Street Journal.

Singer funneled money through the Washington Free Beacon to hire Fusion GPS to get dirt on Trump. When Trump won the Republican nomination, Glen Simpson, CEO of Fusion GPS, shopped the deal to the Clinton campaign and the DNC. They bought in.

When Trump won the General Election on November 9, 2016, the DNC and Clinton Campaign suspended their funding of Steele and Fusion GPS. Fusion GPS continued the investigation using their own funds. Obviously, unlike Glen Simpson, the democrats didn't give a damn about the huge threat Trump posed to national security, their only interest was beating Trump. When Trump won, they lost interest in funding any more Trump dirt. Glen Simpson, on the other hand, disliked Trump so much he was willing to spend his own money to "get" him.
-

Glen Simpson Had Ties to Christopher Steele – According to the Horowitz report[21], in May 2016, Simpson met Steele at a European airport and inquired whether Steele could assist in determining Russia's actions related to the 2016 U.S. elections, whether Russia was trying to achieve a particular election outcome, whether candidate Donald Trump had any personal and business ties in Russia, and whether there  were any ties between the Russian government and Trump. Steele further stated that, by late July 2016, Steele had met with Simpson and an attorney from Perkins Coie.

According to Simpson[22] he turned to Steele, a former spy who had left his position as the head of MI6's Russia desk to co-found Orbis, a private-investigation firm in London, and whom Simpson had known and trusted from previous engagements. Coincidentally, Simpson and his partner Fritsch disclosed that just weeks before they tapped Steele, Steele had reached out to them regarding a different investigation.

Christopher Steele had engaged Fusion GPS to help Steele get money due his client, Oleg Deripaska from Paul Manafort. - Steele was working on behalf of the Russian oligarch Oleg Deripaska. Deripaska was a hugely rich associate of Putin with a cloudy reputation. He had hired an American law firm, which in turn hired Steele, to help them track down millions  of dollars that the oligarch believed had been stolen from him by Paul Manafort. Paul Manafort was a former business associate of Deripaska and was about to become the manager of Trump's Presidential campaign.

Oleg Deripaska was Steele's client and at one time was thought to be Steele's Primary Sub source for the dossier. Oleg Deripaska is a key guy in the whole Trump-Russia collusion narrative. Significantly, Oleg;

- Knew Paul Manafort and was pursing him to get back $10 million that Manafort had allegedly stolen from Oleg,
- Knew Christopher Steele and had engaged him to pursue Manafort, and

---

[21] Horowitz Report, Op. Cit.

[22] The New Yorker, "*The Inside Story of Christopher Steele's Trump Dossier*", June Mayer, November 26, 2019

- Was a personal friend of Putin and had been married to Yeltsin's stepdaughter (Yeltsin picked 46-year old Vladimir Putin to serve as Russia's Prime Minister in 1999)

It has since been determined that another Russian, Igor Danchenko was Steele's "Primary sub source" [23].

Igor Danchenko and Christopher Steele selected and activated their cadre of sources. - Igor was well connected in Russia and could informally meet with key people in the government and solicit "dirt" on Trump just as part of a normal interaction. He did that, took notes and reported back to Steele who assembled them into his first three reports. The cadre of sources consisted of:

Source A	Senior Russian Foreign Ministry figure,
Source B	Former top-level Russian intelligence officer **Vyacheslav Trubnikav,**
Source C	
Source D	Close associate of Trump, **Sergei Millian**. Also "Person 1" in Horowitz Report,
Source F	Female staffer at the Ritz Carlton hotel,
Source E	Ethnic Russian close to Trump associate **Felix Sater**.
Source F	Company ethnic Russian operative, and
Source G	Senior Kremlin official, **Vladislav Surkov.**

---

[23] Washington Examiner, "*Primary source for Christopher Steele's anti-Trump dossier identified*", Jerry Dunleavy, July 25, 2020

The dirt these sources dug up was significant on the surface but as detailed in Chapter 5 was mostly proven to be planted disinformation that either was false or unsupportable.

The Trump dirt provided to Igor Danchenko by the cadre of sources was relayed to Christopher Steele and documented in three reports, Report 80, 86 and 94. –

Report 80 documented three unsupported claims which to this day remain unsupported;

- *According to **Source A - Senior Russian Foreign Ministry figure and Vyacheslav Trubnikav, a former top-level Russian intelligence officer;-*** "Russian authorities" had cultivated Trump "for at least 5 years," and that the operation was "supported and directed" by Putin. *(Evidence of "cultivation of Trump")*
- *According to **Source A - Senior Russian Foreign Ministry figure and confirmed by** Sergei Millian;* Trump accepted a regular flow of intelligence from the Kremlin, notably on his political rivals. (Evidence of *conspiracy, co-operation, and back channel communication.)*
- *According to* **Sergei Millian -** Trump employed a number of prostitutes to perform a urination show in front of him at the Moscow Ritz hotel. Reportedly a female staffer at the hotel, source F, confirmed this. **According to Vyacheslav Trubnikav,** the alleged incident from 2013 was reportedly filmed and recorded by the FSB as compromising material and as a result Trump was vulnerable to blackmail from Russian authorities for paying bribes and engaging in unorthodox and embarrassing sexual behavior over the years and that the authorities were "able to blackmail him if they so wished." ((*Evidence that Trump could be blackmailed.)*

To an average American reading Report 80, it reads more like a cheap set of rumors lifted from the National Enquirer than it does being information "so concerning, that it raises questions about our national security." It is easy to see how the FBI blew this off as gossip. It is really hard to see why Steele thought it was a national emergency situation.

Report 86 documented a synopsis of Russian state sponsored and other cyber offensive (criminal) operations and is unrelated to the Trump collusion activity narrative.

Report 94 contained information about Carter Page and a "secret" meeting he had in Russia in late July 2016. There are no "sources" attributed to this Report. What it revealed was a meeting in Russia attended by Carter Page that could be interpreted as a step to conspire with the Russians.

- Page was informed by Igor Divyekin, a senior Kremlin Internal Affairs official, "that the Russians had compromising information on Clinton and Trump, and allegedly added that Trump 'should bear this in mind'." (*Evidence of collusion.*)

- Page met secretly with Igor Sechin, Chairman of Russian energy conglomerate Rosneft and close associate of Putin, to discuss future cooperation and the lifting of Ukraine-related sanctions against Russia; and with Igor Divyekin, a highly-placed Russian official, to discuss sharing with the Trump campaign derogatory information about Clinton (Report 94[24]); Sechin confided the details of a secret meeting with Page; Sergei Ivanov confided in a compatriot that Divyekin had met secretly with Page. (*Evidence of collusion.*)

- Report 94 was one of 4 reports the FBI relied upon to support the probable cause in the Carter Page FISA applications.[25]

To an average American reading it, Report 94 could, on the surface, be legitimate evidence. As reported in Chapter 5, there was a meeting but it was not "secret" and Igor Divyekin and Carter Page have never met, much less had a meeting.

These three reports comprised the full extent of the evidence of collusion planted directly into the FBI for the FBI to investigate. The information contained in them was gathered from Vyacheslav Trubnikav, Sergei Millian and an unnamed source (Source A). They transmitted the information to Igor Danchenko who in turn handed his notes to Christopher Steele. Steele packaged them up and handed them to his FBI handler, Michael Gaeta.

Steele had successfully planted evidence of Trump-Russia collusion right in the laps of the FBI agents.

The Clinton Campaign/DNC had partially achieved their mission and got their evidence planted inside the FBI. The Democrats had hired Steele to dig up dirt on Trump from Russian sources. By July

---

[24] Horowitz Report Op. Cit. Page vii
[25] Horowitz Report Op. Cit. Page 98

31, 2016, Steele had delivered three reports containing dirt on Trump from those Russian sources. He managed to get evidence that Trump may be open to blackmail from the Russians. He managed to get some initial evidence on the Trump team's collusion with the Russians. As a bonus, Steele had planted this incriminating information inside the FBI. The only downside for Steele was that the FBI didn't seem to appreciate all Steele was doing to protect our national security.

(The above scenario varies from that described by others in that it characterizes Steele's sharing of his first three reports with the FBI as an "evidence planting" role, similar to what Mifsud's role was. It raises the question as to why the FBI didn't consider the three Steele reports they had in hand when they opened the Trump-Russia collusion investigation.)

PART II

FINDING THE EVIDENCE

JULY 31, 2016
TO
PRESENT

JAMES
COMEY

PETER
STRZOK

Chapter 4: Investigating Planted Evidence in Track 1

Connecting the Dots – Investigating Track 1 The Mifsud Track: These dots are well known, but their connections are still being debated. Starting with the "dot" identified as *"Mifsud's planted evidence of collusion"* and ending with the "dot" *"No evidence of collusion found by FBI"* there were legitimate covert and overt investigations into Papadopoulos but also failed attempts to plant more evidence on George. Additionally, there was a successful deliberate attempt to catch Papadopoulos in a lie, resulting in a two-week jail sentence for George. The dots consisted of four types, (1) covert investigation, (2) overt investigation, (3) entrapment, and (4) creation of an unrelated crime to make Papadopoulos pay for wasting the FBI's time. Figure 4-1 illustrates the connection of the dots.

4.1– Validation of Track I Evidence

The Evidence Existed: The Australians had handed the FBI evidence of Trump-Russia collusion consisting of Papadopoulos's brag to "a representative of an Australian (FFG) official" that George knew of the existence of DNC emails and Hillary Clinton dirt being held by the Russians. The FBI quickly looked at the e-communication between Papadopoulos and the Trump campaign and found evidence of Papadopoulos attempting to set up a meeting between Trump and Putin. This was the starting "dot" for the investigation of George Papadopoulos and for the entire collusion narrative.

The FBI begins to Investigate Papadopoulos: On July 31, 2016 the FBI legitimately started investigating George Papadopoulos, the guy who had "inside knowledge of the Russians having dirt and thousands of emails on Hillary Clinton.'

Between opening the investigation on July 31, 2016 and the first time they talked to Mr. Papadopoulos on January 27, 2017, the FBI had been looking into George, his life and his role on the Trump campaign. In the course of their investigation they would have looked at the record of e-communication and physical meetings between George, persons in the Trump campaign, any Russians and of course the source of the rumor about Clinton dirt and emails, Professor Mifsud. If they didn't, they wouldn't be doing their job and they wouldn't be doing an investigation of Papadopoulos. There is no way they would drop in on George on

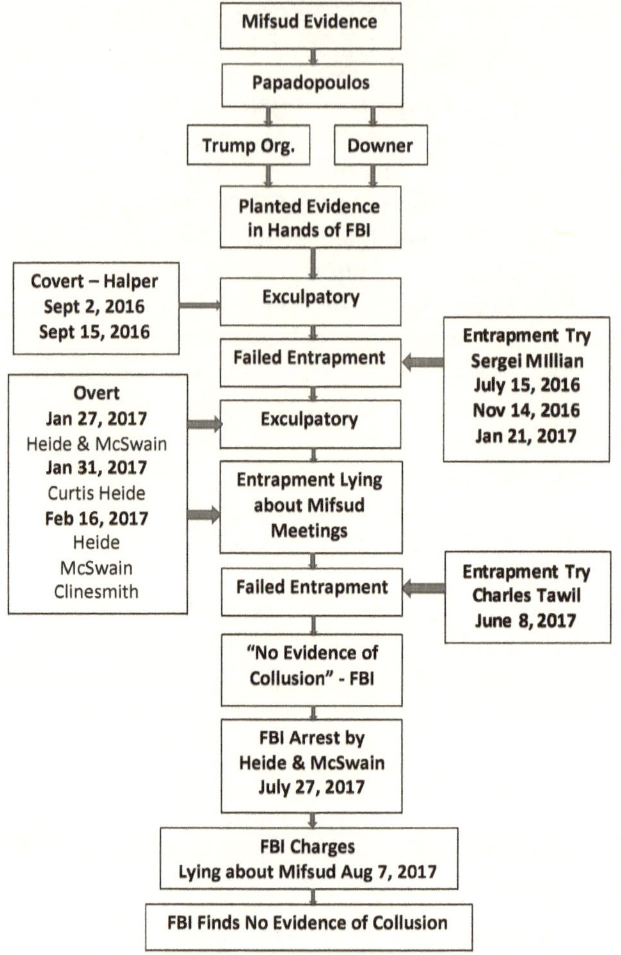

Figure 4-1 Connecting the Dots – Track 1 Investigation From Mifsud Evidence Creation to FBI's Conclusion that There Was No Evidence

January 27, 2017 and not know anything about the evidence against him. If the FBI did not know the dates of Papadopoulos's meetings, the content of his communication with the Trump campaign and Papadopoulos's contacts with Russians, the FBI would be the equivalent of the Keystone Kops. That is almost surely not the case.

It is known that the FBI started looking at e-communications between Papadopoulos and the Trump campaign to uncover any documented evidence of cooperation between Trump and Russia in an effort to accumulate dirt or hack emails. They found none. They did find, however, evidence that Papadopoulos was trying to set up "back door" meetings between Trump and Putin. Possibly "collusion in the making?"

The FBI Decided to Use Stephan Halper, a Confidential Human Source to Gain Intelligence on Collusion by Covertly Questioning Papadopoulos: A perfectly legitimate law enforcement tactic to gathering intelligence is to send in a "plant" to question a suspect under some legitimate guise, gain their confidence and start shifting the conversation to inadvertently get the "mark" to provide incriminating evidence of a crime. In the intelligence community, that "plant' is called a Confidential Human Source or (CHS). The FBI elected to use one of their "regulars" on George, Stephan Halper.

On Sept. 2 Stephan Halper, unsolicitedly contacted Papadopoulos. He offered to fly George to London for several nights to discuss writing this energy policy paper. George didn't know Halper from Adam, but, why not? He needed the money and exposure. But why London and why two days? Both Halper and Papadopoulos are in the US? Papadopoulos agreed to meet.

Law enforcement has a number of tricks they use to gain the confidence of a "mark." They like to use attractive females and lures of great business deals. Mifsud had his attractive female "assistant", Olga Polonskaya (Putin's "niece"), Downer had Erika Thompson, and Stephan Halper had "Azra Turk". Halper's business "guise" was an immediate

Stefan Halper

Azra Turk

$3,000 contract to write a policy paper about energy issues in Turkey, Cyprus and Israel. George could use the money. He hadn't had a real job for a while.

George flew to London for the meeting on September 15, 2016. After checking into the hotel he had a few drinks alone with Halper's "helper," the voluptuous Azra Turk. According to George, "Azra came onto him" and at the same time questioned him about the Trump campaign's interest in Russia. Nothing about the paper on energy that he is supposedly there to discuss.

As an FBI Confidential Human Source Halper Had "Real" Russian Ties.

Halper, a former Cambridge professor, rattled off the names of the Russians, Vyacheslav Trubnikov, Leonid Shebarshin, and Yuri Traughtoff, according to a transcript of the secretly recorded conversation released on April 16, 2020.

Halper was not bluffing about his friendship with at least one of the ex-Russian spies. He has collaborated with Trubnikov, the former head of Russia's foreign intelligence service, the SVR. Halper hosted Trubnikov at two intelligence seminars at Cambridge in 2015 and 2016 and interviewed the former Kremlin insider for a 2015 study on China-Russia relations he did for the Pentagon's Office of Net Assessment (ONA). Trubnikov, coincidentally was Steele's "Source B!"

The next day George met with Azra and Halper. Halper wanted to talk politics, not about the paper he's supposed to want from George.

It wasn't long into his conversation with George Papadopoulos that FBI confidential informant Stefan Halper mentioned his links to several retired Russian spies. "I have a lot of friends in Russia," Halper told Papadopoulos during their conversation, which occurred over drinks, and which the FBI recorded.[26] "My point is that," Halper said, "the Russians

---

[26] Daily caller, "*FBI Informant Bragged About Links To Russian Spies In Secret Recording Of Trump Aide*", Chuck Ross, April 19, 2020.

can be very helpful to us at this time and we've got some great information coming out."

Halper's goal in bringing up his Kremlin links was to get Papadopoulos to reveal whether he or the Trump campaign were working with the Russian government or were involved with the WikiLeaks release of Democrats' emails, according to the Justice Department inspector general's (IG) report on the FBI's Trump-Russia probe.

The meeting was over. The following day, Halper called George and wanted to have a "goodbye" drink. They met and Halper grilled George about the Hillary emails. George didn't engage. Halper was upset. The meeting ended.

Halper's Covert Investigation Yielded Only Exculpatory Evidence: The net result of Halper's attempt to get more evidence of George Papadopoulos's involvement in a Trump-Russia collusion scandal was instead more evidence that George was not involved. At no time during either meeting between Papadopoulos and Halper did Halper try to plant any evidence on George. He simply tried to extract damning evidence that might already exist. There wasn't any. At least to the FBI, George was looking less guilty.

Papadopoulos wrote the paper and delivered it in early October. He was paid $3,000 for the work. Days before making that payment, Halper had finalized a contract with the Office of Net Assessment, the Pentagon's think tank. Federal records show that Halper was paid $928,800 since 2012 for work on four "policy projects" for the Pentagon. No doubt $3,000 of that $928,800 was paid for George's "paper on energy policy."

In Parallel to Halper's Covert Investigation, An Apparent Second Attempt to Plant Evidence on Papadopoulos Was Tried. This time by Sergei Millian: While Stephan Halper and the FBI were clearing George Papadopoulos of any Trump-Russia collusion on the Hillary dirt and emails, a guy named Sergei Millian (and likely the CIA) attempted to plant more evidence of collusion. Sergei's approach to George was identical to Mifsud's approach to incriminating Papadopoulos with evidence of "secret" Russian contacts. Millian promised George names of Russian business contacts that could be very useful to him. If George bit, there would be evidence of collusion in e-communications between Papadopoulos and Russian "businessmen". As a fallback, in case the evidence of "secret meeting collusion" didn't pan out, Sergei also tried to set George up as an unregistered agent of a foreign government, just to "dirty him up" for working for Trump.

The contact from Millian started on July 15, 2016[27] at the same time Christopher Steele was writing his first report of the "Steele dossier," Report 80. Through a fifteen-minute phone call with Igor Danchenko or someone else in Igor's confidence, Sergei Millian relayed his "knowledge" of the Trump "romp" with prostitutes in Moscow among other things.

> *(It is interesting to note that Steele labels Sergei as a "close associate of Trump!" Some associate! He is providing dirt on Trump to Steele and at the same time, trying to set up Trump's Foreign Affairs Advisor as a non-registered agent of a foreign government. The fact that both Mifsud and Millian have "disappeared" lends credibility to the supposition that they were both working for the CIA and are stashed somewhere.)*

Between July 15, 2016 and January 21, 2017, Millian contacted Papadopoulos seven times;

- On July 22, 2016 Sergei arranged his first meeting with George. He told George, "I have a lot of Russian business leader connections. I could be a middleman for you." This sounded like a replay of the first Mifsud meeting with George.
- Within a week Millian emailed Papadopoulos an invitation to an energy conference in Moscow (George checked with Dearborn on Trump's staff who said, "don't waste your time.")
- In mid-August 2016, Millian and Papadopoulos met in NY. They went to dinner then took a drive when Millian suddenly stopped on the road and asked to take George's picture. Weird!
- In late-August 2016 they met again in the basement of the Andaz Hotel in New York. Millian started talking to Papadopoulos about introducing him to important Russians. Papadopoulos claimed he told him, no!
- On October 7, 2016 Papadopoulos got a call from Sergei. They set up a meeting in Chicago for October 15, 2016. At

---

[27] Mueller Report, Op. Cit.

the meeting, Sergei offered to pay Papadopoulos $30K/month to work as a PR consultant. The funding source was "a former Russian Energy minister." Sergei did not identify this person by name. Sergei conditioned the offer on the premise that George would be working for Trump if he was elected. George claimed he told Sergei he was not interested.

- On November 5, Papadopoulos got a strange email from Millian saying, "beware of men in black."
- On January 21, 2017 the day after the inauguration. Sergei arranged to meet George in Washington, D.C. The meeting goes nowhere because George isn't involved in the Trump administration.

The job prospect with Sergei's contacts was a dead issue. George didn't bite and his value was diminished because George had yet to land a job in the Trump Administration. But George continued to try with the Trump administration. George scheduled phone interviews with persons charged with staffing the new administration. Nothing worked out. The good news - the Millian entrapment scheme failed.

The FBI has been unable to close the loop on Sergei Millian because he has been "out of the country" and the FBI has been unable to locate him for an interview. The FBI has also been unable to close the loop on Joseph Mifsud. Perhaps another item on Christopher Wray's "to-do" list should be to initiate agent training on how to find people who don't want to be found!

Since the FBI was investigating Trump-Russia collusion and apparently Mr. Millian did not play a role in that caper, the FBI had no real reason to try very hard to locate Sergei. It is troubling though that the FBI's curiosity regarding who was trying to set up the Trump team didn't exist. The reason has to be either; (1) the FBI was just lazy, (2) the FBI's anti-Trump bias prevented them from looking at anything that detracted from uncovering evidence of Trump team guilt because it was just "noise," or (3) the FBI knew or suspected that the CIA was behind the Millian evidence planting scheme and that was best left alone.

There is a fourth possibility for not pursuing the Millian involvement with Papadopoulos and that is the FBI was part of the attempt to plant evidence. The one coincidence that supports this possibility is the timing of the overt investigation of George Papadopoulos. Just one week after George's last meeting with Sergei, the FBI swooped in on George.

The Case Against Papadopoulos was Slipping. The FBI Finally Initiated its Overt Investigation of George.

Starting on January 27, 2017, less than a week after Papadopoulos' last meeting with Millian, the FBI paid a visit to George. According to George, in the first interview, agents Curtis Heide and Michael McSwain questioned him about his lifestyle, a little about Millian, a little about Russians, a little about Israelis and then about Russian hacking of Clinton emails.[28]

Of course, the hacking of Clinton emails came from the Australian-provided intelligence. According to Papadopoulos, the FBI knew about the Millian encounters and point blank asked George if "Millian was attempting to cultivate him," but they clearly were not interested in following up on the Millian connection, because they likely knew who Millian was and what he was up to either because they were part of it or because they had been tailing him and eavesdropping on his conversations. The FBI dropped the Millian connection questioning. The FBI pair showed some interest in George's Israeli connections, but soon dropped that also.   The FBI's main interest was George's Russian connections.[29]

According to the Mueller report, FBI agents Heide and McSwain characterized the meeting a little differently. They said that they informed George that, *"the interview was part of the investigation into potential Russian government interference in the 2016 presidential election."* They did not mention Millian or George's alleged ties to the Israelis as part of their investigation.

According to the FBI, during the interview, Papadopoulos lied about (1) the timing, extent, and nature of his communications with Joseph Mifsud[30] and (2) his contact with Olga Polonskaya and, Ivan Timofeev, two Russians introduced to George by Mifsud.

With respect to the first "lie" about the timing, extent and nature of his communications with Mifsud, Papadopoulos acknowledged that he had met Mifsud and that Mifsud told him the Russians had "dirt" on Clinton in the form of "thousands of emails." But Papadopoulos stated

---

[28] "Deep State Target" Op. Cit.

[29] Ibid.

[30] According to Heide and McSwain, *Papadopoulos also made false statements in an effort to minimize the extent and importance of his communications with Mifsud.*

multiple times that those communications occurred before he joined the Trump Campaign and that it was a "very strange coincidence" to be told of the "dirt" before he started working for the Campaign. This account was false.[31] The Hillary "dirt" was passed to George by Joseph Mifsud on April 26, over a month AFTER George joined the Trump campaign. The timing was false, but George freely admitted that the rumor of dirt from Mifsud was true.

The FBI has since implied, and it is reasonable to assume, that the FBI had investigated George Papadopoulos during the six months between the opening of the investigation and January 27, 2017. Assuming they had, the trail of e-communication between George, Mifsud, Trump campaign staff, Millian, Polonskaya, Halper, Downer and Erika Thompson was all available to them. Also, they would have read Halper's report exonerating George. If they were half-way competent, Heide and McSwain already knew the names of the two Russians George had talked to and the dates and times of all the meetings with Mifsud, etc. etc. After all, they had been assigned to investigate George back in July 2016. The point is, Heide and McSwain knew on January 27, 2017 that Papadopoulos was misrepresenting the timing and nature of his communications with Joseph Mifsud. They also knew it was immaterial.

Given that nothing ever happened as a result of the Mifsud-Papadopoulos contact there was no reason for George to lie to hide guilt about the number and dates of those contacts. No covert Trump-Putin meetings were set up or even got close to being set up and no dirt or emails were ever uncovered by joint Russian-Papadopoulos hacking efforts because there weren't any. What could be the reason for George misrepresenting the extent and nature of his communications with Mifsud? It has since been revealed, George was ashamed of being duped and set up by Mifsud. The campaign had nothing to do with George's encounter with Mifsud. He didn't want to involve them in any way, particularly since he was still hoping to land a job with the Trump administration. This could be considered a "fib." If George had given Heide and McSwain exact dates and times it would not have affected their investigation in any way. They already knew the dates! Certainly, Heide and McSwain were intelligent enough to reach that conclusion.

Still addressing the first example of "lying" to the FBI, according to the Heide and McSwain report, Papadopoulos understood Mifsud to have substantial connections to high-level Russian government officials and

____

[31] Mueller Report, Op. Cit. Page 193

that Mifsud spoke with some of those officials in Moscow before telling Papadopoulos about the "dirt." In other words, according to Heide and McSwain, Papadopoulos held Mifsud in high esteem. But, when Papadopoulos was questioned about Mifsud, **"George lied"** when he stated on January 27, 2017, that *"[Mifsud]'s a nothing," that he thought Mifsud was "just a guy talking up connections or something," and that he believed Mifsud was "BS'ing to be completely honest with you."*

That statement is hardly lying! This questioning took place nine months after Papadopoulos had any contact of significance with Mifsud. Over this nine months, George had time to reflect on how Mifsud had set him up and how he had been used. After realizing what had happened, George came to the same conclusion that almost everyone who came in contact with Mifsud since 2012 had, "Mifsud is a complete charlatan."[32] To an average American, George was not lying to the FBI about Mifsud's importance, he was in-fact telling the truth about how he had sized up Mifsud by late January 2017. Surely the FBI realized this?

With respect to the second "lie" Papadopoulos told Heide and McSwain, it wasn't technically a lie; Papadopoulos had played down the contact with Olga Polonskaya, and never mentioned, Ivan Timofeev. On the surface it would appear that George was less than candid. But it was the same kind of "lie" that Heide and McSwain told when they failed to include in their report of their interview with Papadopoulos that they questioned him about George's Israeli contacts and about Millian. Since trying to set up a meeting is not illegal in itself, it is totally inconsequential.

But looking behind the obvious, by the time of the Papadopoulos interview with the FBI, George knew that Olga was not Putin's niece, but the manager of a wine store in Moscow posing as Putin's niece - not a likely candidate to be setting up a Trump-Putin meeting. Certainly, the FBI knew that too. Regarding Ivan Timofeev, his ability to set up a Trump-Putin meeting was no better than Olga's. No meeting ever got close to happening. It is another embarrassment for George. He had gotten sucked into a meaningless dialogue, certainly meant to plant evidence of collusion in the Trump campaign. George knew there wasn't any collusion. He knew he had not made a meaningful attempt at arranging a Trump-Putin meeting. Why embarrass himself further? Of course, he should not have misled the FBI, but on the other hand, anything that is said to the FBI, can and will be held against you. Unfortunately

---

[32] See Appendix C, *"Who is Joseph Mifsud?"*

for the FBI, and future investigations, we average Americans are now fully aware of the perils of saying anything. Had Papadopoulos not said anything about the extent and timing of his meetings with Mifsud, he would not have spent two weeks in jail. He was totally innocent but paid for it anyway. Surely the FBI realized this.

The second Papadopoulos investigative interview was with just Curtis Heide on January 31, 2017. In this interview Curtis asked George to wear a wire and meet with Mifsud. Somehow the FBI must have known that Joseph Mifsud was going to be in Washington DC on February 10, 2017. At least on the surface, this request indicated that the FBI still wasn't aware that Mifsud was most likely a CHS working for the CIA to plant evidence of collusion. Papadopoulos refused to participate. To an average American, this seemed to be an inconsistent position for George to take unless George just didn't want any more contact with this despicable character. Besides, cooperating with the FBI has its price.

The next FBI investigative interview was held with Professor Joseph Mifsud, in the lobby of the Mayflower hotel in Washington, D.C. on February 10, 2017. According to the account published in the Mueller report, here's what Mifsud told the FBI in the investigative interview;

- Mifsud admitted to knowing Papadopoulos. (That was true),
- Mifsud admitted to having introduced George to Polonskaya and Timofeev. (That was true),
- Mifsud denied that he had advance knowledge that Russia was in possession of emails damaging to candidate Clinton, (That was probably true since he had no real Russian connections. He did not say that he did or didn't tell George that he had heard that the Russians had Clinton emails),
- But, Mifsud falsely stated that he had not seen Papadopoulos since the meeting at which Mifsud introduced him to Polonskaya on March 24, 2016. (That is not true. Mifsud and Papadopoulos met again on April 26, 2016 when Mifsud returned from Russia.)
- In addition, Mifsud omitted that he had drafted (or edited) the follow-up message that Polonskaya sent to Papadopoulos following the March 24 meeting and that, as reflected in the language of that email chain ("Baby, thank you!"), Mifsud may have been involved in a personal relationship with Polonskaya at the time. (And of what relevance is either one of these "bombshells?")

According to Heide and McSwain, the false information and omissions in Papadopoulos's January 2017 interview undermined investigators' ability to challenge Mifsud when he made these inaccurate statements. First of all, Papadopoulos is not required to tell the FBI anything. The fact that he may have omitted information is irrelevant. He could have and should have omitted everything. By not doing so, he was convicted of a felony and spent two weeks in jail. The "false information" was also irrelevant. Mifsud created his own false information. He would have challenged any dates Papadopoulos might have provided and even under the highly unlikely event that the FBI didn't already know those dates, it would be at best, a "he said – he said" difference in recollection of what happened.

The third interview with Papadopoulos was on February 16, 2017. This interview was with a full contingent of FBI'ers including Heide and McSwain and also included Kevin Clinesmith. (Clinesmith is the same FBI lawyer who altered the FISA warrant application to say Carter Page was NOT a CIA source, when the e-communication from the CIA said he WAS a CIA source.) The line of questioning from Clinesmith had to do with who George told back in the campaign about the Hillary email remarks. Papadopoulos said that the "Russians had her emails" because Mifsud told him that. Clinesmith clearly wanted to tie the campaign to the leaked emails. Papadopoulos couldn't help him because he never told anyone in the campaign. According to Papadopoulos's book, this really pissed off Clinesmith and he stormed out. Clinesmith wanted evidence of collusion so badly he even altered documents to make the collusion case. Clinesmith had no interest in Mifsud, only what Papadopoulos did with his rumors. This is not a search for the truth, this is a witch hunt.

The three-week FBI overt investigation into Papadopoulos's collusion activities was pretty much a bust as investigations go. At this point, the FBI had no evidence of Papadopoulos being involved in anything illegal regarding his activities with the Trump campaign. Mid-February of 2017 is the last contact the FBI had with Papadopoulos for a while. But in the weeks ahead, George heard from friends that the FBI had been questioning them. All-in-all the FBI's overt interrogation yielded no evidence of Papadopoulos being involved in any collusion with the Russians. They learned nothing about Millian's activities that they didn't already know. They didn't learn anything about Mifsud. The average American has to believe that either the FBI (1) was lazy and didn't care about who and why Trump and his team were being set up, (2) the FBI bias for finding the Trump team guilty of collusion didn't allow them to examine any crime being committed against the Trump organization, or (3) they were "in on" the sting.

4.2 Salvage Something out of Track 1 Investigation.

The seven months of digging into Trump-Russia collusion through Papadopoulos's monitored actions had turned up nothing. The FBI was not ready to throw in the towel yet, however. If not nailing him for collusion, the FBI still had hopes they could nail him for some misdeed. After all, their investigation turned up some unexplainable facts; (1) George seemed to have money, but he hadn't really ever had a paying job long enough to have any money, (2) he had started an e-communication romance with a European hottie, Simona Manigiante, a gal he had never met. From an FBI viewpoint, both things were worthy of investigation because they involved unexplainable money and in Simona's case, another connection to Joseph Mifsud. Both things could be explained if George was getting funding from some foreign (Russian?) source interested in colluding with Trump or influencing Trump's actions as an insider and/or if Simona could provide a reestablishment to the Mifsud link which had all but evaporated.

Enter Simona Manigiante, and George's fatal trip to Europe to romance her. – Simona Manigiante entered George's life in a very unlikely way. George had worked for a couple of months at the mysterious London firm, the ***London Center of International Law Practice*** (LCILP) after he left the Carson campaign and before he started working on the Trump campaign in early March 2016. It was while working there that he was introduced to Joseph Mifsud. George left LCILP in April of 2016 to work full time on the Trump campaign.

Through a series of events, Mifsud, who was now again working for LCILP, hired Simona in September 2016. Simona had been working for a friend of Mifsud's in Rome. Simona moved to London to take the job and quickly realized that LCILP and Mifsud were facades. "Nobody there did anything!", was her description. The significance of this is that George was still getting news releases from LCILP and happened to see Simona's picture along with the notice she had joined the firm. George and Simona started chatting on Linkedin. Simona quit LCILP in October but kept in contact with George. George was smitten.

In April 2017, Simona had the opportunity to travel to the US to visit her aunt in NY. George flew to NY and picked her up at the airport and they spent a few days together and "bonded."

In mid-May, George decided to take 2 ½ months off (from what?) and spend it in Europe wining and dining Simona. He traveled to Greece, landing in Athens. Of course, the FBI was tracking his movements and continuing to wonder how he was paying for all this. The details of his two-plus months in Europe are documented in **Appendix D, *"Who is George Papadopoulos?"*** and are summarized here as it relates to the FBI's continued investigation into George Papadopoulos.

George bopped around Europe with Simona. He landed in Athens. He spent some time there with friends, then went to the isle of Mykonos, about 90 miles from Athens to meet up with Simona, who was at the Cannes film festival about 1400 miles away. The Cannes festival was over on May 28. 2017. They got together for a week. They partied and spent time at the beach.

The party was interrupted when Charles Tawil called George and wanted to get together and talk about a business proposition. On June 8, George left Simona to go to Tel Aviv, then on to Cyprus with Tawil. It is unclear why Tawil and Papadopoulos had to meet in three different countries to discuss one business arrangement. After the meeting, George flew to Thessaloniki, Greece on June 14 for a two-day energy summit.

He then went back to his family in Greece. George and Simona had 1 ½ months left before George was scheduled to return home. They spent time with her family in Naples. They partied on the Isle of Capri. They went back to Athens to meet George's family. George flew home on July 27, 2017

What doesn't make sense at this point is where did Papadopoulos get the money to spend 2 ½ months partying in Greece with Simona? He didn't have that kind of money. In the long run, the partying paid off for George. Seven months later he and Simona got married. Although this relationship could be what it appears, true love, or a Simona attempt to use George as her route to the US and a career in Hollywood, or a long-term international conspiracy plot, or ??? This question is never answered in this book. One thing is highly likely, it was NOT a scheme hatched by George. His whole life to this point would indicate he is not an effective plotter and schemer.

Charles Tawil, Entrapment 2 or Legitimate Attempt to Buy Influence in Trump Administration? - June 2017 to July 27, 2017

Just like the question raised above about Simona's motivation to get involved with George, the question about Charles Tawil's motivation to get involved with George is not answered in this book.

Unlike Joseph Mifsud, Stefan Halper and Sergei Millian, Charles Tawil had legitimate business reasons to cultivate George Papadopoulos. He actually was a business facilitator. One of his clients was Shai Arbel, a legitimate businessman who runs Terrogence, a company that has very good facial recognition software. Shai could use an "in" with the Trump administration if George actually ended up there. The US intelligence community uses his software.

Although the events leading up to the meeting in Tel Aviv are a little suspicious, as are the events following the meeting with Arbel, there is no clear way to connect the dots.

On June 7, 2017, Charles Tawil called George while he was partying with Simona on the isle of Mykonos. Charles said he wanted to meet with George. George agreed, probably thinking it would impress Simona as to how important he was. Besides, George needed a job!

Charles flew to Mykonos on June 8, 2017 and convinced George to go to Tel Aviv, Israel to talk business with Shai Arbel. Shai Arbel, in addition to being CEO of Terrogence, was an ex-Israeli intelligence officer. The meeting seemed to go okay. Charles Tawil and George went back to their hotel and they met in Charles' room.

What happened next is significant, but Charles and George differ on what actually went down. George said that Charles threw $10,000 cash down on the bed and told him to take it as a "down payment" for services.[33] Charles said George asked him for a $10,000 loan and he gave it to him. Charles said George was "desperate" to keep working with him.

Knowing that George didn't have any money before he traveled to Greece and he had been spending a lot wining and dining Simona, it is not hard to believe that George asked for a loan. That is unknown, however. Neither party disagrees that $10,000 was transferred from Charles Tawil to George Papadopoulos. Also no one disagrees that Papadopoulos did not have the $10,000 on him when he arrived back in the US on July 27, 2017.

---

[33] "Deep State Target", Op. Cit. page 162

What happened next is unexplainable also. Tawil and Papadopoulos flew together to Cyprus the next day, June 9, 2017. No reason for that trip is available.

George then went on to Thessaloniki, a Greek port city to attend an "energy summit" on June 14 —15 2017.[34] George said he dropped the $10,000 cash off with a lawyer acquaintance he had there in Thessaloniki. According to George he was suspicious that they were "marked bills" and could be traced as coming from a foreign entity and that could get him in trouble. George said he got a receipt. George never produced a receipt. He said after the fact that he would retrieve the bills from the lawyer and have the FBI check to see if they were marked. He never followed through on that retrieval. Certainly, his wining and dining would easily have cost him the $10,000.

Charles Tawil has denied this account. *"The guy is a pathetic liar,"* Mr. Tawil said of Mr. Papadopoulos. *"I met him when he was out of a job and offered him a job and I gave him, on his demand, a loan, cash as he requested because he did not have an account in Europe."* Mr. Tawil continued, *"I have copies of emails and WhatsApp communication with George that can prove that he is a liar. Instead of thanking me, he is trying to drag me in his mud."* He finished his denial by stating, *"He is coward and a liar and probably other things too."*

Papadopoulos could easily put this controversy to rest. He could show the receipt and/or the "marked" bills. It is looking more likely that he has neither.

George was greeted and arrested by FBI Agents Heide and McSwain when he got off the plane at Dulles airport in Washington DC. - As described above, George finished off his European vacation with Simona more smitten than ever. He got on a plane in Athens, headed for Munich then on to Dulles and then to Chicago. He got stopped in Dulles and was arrested by the FBI.

There were five FBI agents to greet George Papadopoulos when he got off the plane in Dulles including Agents Heide and McSwain. This time Heide and McSwain were working for the Mueller investigation, not the FBI. Obviously, the Mueller team thought that George was valuable to their investigation. They searched his stuff and he spent the night in jail.

---

[34] Ibid. page 163.

The next day he was charged with lying to an FBI agent and obstruction of justice. The FBI agent was Curtis Heide. The lie was that he told Heide that he didn't have contact with Mifsud in April when actually he had one email with him in April. The obstruction of justice charge was that George had deleted his Facebook account. George was held overnight again. The next day he was released. There was no explanation. He flew back home to Chicago.

Given that George was arrested when he got off the plane in Dulles on July 27, 2017, and the FBI searched his luggage, it is logical that the FBI was expecting to find something in the luggage. George claims they were looking for the $10,000 of "marked" money that he was paid for being a agent of a foreign government without being registered. The FBI has offered no explanation for their search. It is unknown at this time, if the FBI was looking for evidence, or just looking for the sake of looking.

Had George been carrying marked $100 bills, the FBI would have had evidence of George acting as an agent of a foreign entity. That charge or threat of charge was what the FBI used on General Flynn, Carter Paige and Paul Manafort, so it would be consistent with their mode of operation to entrap people who had the gall to support Trump. Entrapment is a tool available to the FBI to extract information from their "marks."

Court Hearing & Plea Bargain, Sentencing and Prison, July 30, 2017 – December, 7, 2017

On August 7, 2017 George met in Chicago with prosecutors for the first time. George agreed to cooperate with the investigation and was offered a plea deal. The plea deal was filed on October 5, 2017. George's plea deal was unsealed on October 31, 2017. Simona moved to Chicago and they spent the winter of 2017-2018 living with George's mom, Kiki.

On August 17, 2018 the sentencing memorandum was filed by Mueller. George's sentencing hearing was held a year later on Friday, September 7, 2018 at E. Barrett Prettyman Courthouse in Washington DC– Simona, and George's parents were there. His sentence was handed down; 14 days in jail, 200 hours of community service, 12 months of supervised release and a fine of $9,500.

The next thing we know George and Simona are in Los Angeles. After the sentencing hearing, George and Simona left for California.

They went back to Chicago in time to drive up to Oxford, Wisconsin to report to prison on November 26, 2018.

George spent twelve days in Oxford Prison, a medium security prison in central Wisconsin, about 200 miles northwest of Chicago. He felt he was treated well by both the inmates and the prison staff. His now wife, Simona drove up with him when he checked in and was there to pick him up when he was released on Friday. December 7, 2016 at around 10:00 AM.

There were no charges or even suggestion of charges against George Papadopoulos for colluding with the Russians on behalf of the Trump campaign or anyone else. He was convicted of lying about his meetings with Joseph Mifsud which even the FBI agreed had no relevance.

The FBI's investigation of the evidence planted by Mifsud in Track 1 was a complete waste of time. The persons who could answer the real questions are Joseph Mifsud, Sergei Millian and Charles Tawil. The FBI can't find them! It is too hard.

Chapter 5: Investigating Planted Evidence in Track 2

Connecting the Dots – Investigating Track 2, The Steele Track: These dots and their connections are well known and well documented in the Mueller Report. Starting with the "dot" identified as *"Steele reports 80, 86 and 94 available at the opening of Crossfire Hurricane investigation"*, adding *Steele reports 95, 97, 100, 101, 102, 105. 111, 112, 113, 130, 134, 135, 136, 137, and 166*, and ending with the "dot" *No evidence of collusion found by FBI"*, the investigation was marred with FBI altering evidence, and seventeen FBI introduced errors and omissions[35] that would have further exonerated Trump. The intermediate dots between the starting evidence "dot" from *Reports 80, 86 and 94"* available on July 31, 2016 and the ending dot defining, *"No evidence of collusion"* consisted of the clearing of Trump himself, Carter Page, Paul Manafort and Michael Cohen of any collusion as implicated by the initial 3 reports and the additional reports from Christopher Steele. Despite the effects of obvious bias, the investigation found no evidence of collusion. The bias exhibited by the FBI and Mueller investigative teams is well documented in the Horowitz report.

The FBI investigated all the leads provided by Christopher Steele. These consisted of evidence on Donald Trump, Carter Page, Paul Manafort and Michael Cohen. The FBI also investigated General Michael Flynn and Roger Stone.

The "dots" between *"opening the investigation"* and *"No evidence of collusion"* consisted of charges of collusion and misdeeds by Trump and his associates then the subsequent discrediting of those charges against (1)Trump himself, (2) Carter Page, (3) Paul Manafort", and (4) Michael Cohen. Steele had nothing to do with identifying the other "villains" General Michael Flynn or Roger Stone. The FBI managed to plant their own evidence on General Flynn.[36]

---

[35] Horowitz Report, Op. Cit. page xiii

[36] *"What's our goal? Truth/Admission or to get him (Michael Flynn) to lie, so we can prosecute him or get him fired?"* Priestap (Peter Strzok's boss) wrote in his notes. From CNN, *"Michael Flynn's lawyers seize on note showing how FBI official approached key interview in White House"*, Katelyn Polantz, David Shortell and Eva Perez, April 30, 2020

The investigation consisted of examining e-communications, documents and in the case of Carter Page, Paul Manafort and Michael Cohen questioning them and, in some cases, their accusers. Trump answered questions in written form.

5.1 Validation of the Track 2 Evidence

The evidence of collusion planted by Christopher Steele consisted of a series of seventeen reports comprising the Steele dossier. These reports implicated the four persons associated with the Trump campaign identified above and "suggested" collusion or "black-mailable" activities on the part of the four persons. Not all of the reports documented any misdeeds but simply described things the Russians were doing to interfere with our presidential election independent of the Trump campaign. A complete discussion of the Steele dossier including the sources used and a description of each of the seventeen reports is provided in Appendix "G". Figure 5-1 below shows a top-level view of the dots that were connected that led to the FBI's conclusion there was no evidence of collusion or black-mailable activities engaged in by any of the investigated individuals identified in the Steele dossier.

5.1.1 Validation of Steele evidence on Trump

As shown in Figure 5-1 the evidence against Trump was documented in Steele Reports 80, 94, 95, 97, 112, 137 and 166. With the exception of Report 112, these reports documented conversations that Steele's "Primary sub source", Igor Danchenko[37] had with others. All of Danchenko sources only reported "hearsay" from third parties.

The documentation found in the reports consisted of notes of the conversations that Mr. Danchenko provided to Christopher Steele. Report 112 was provided directly to Christopher Steele by Michael Sussmann, of Perkins Coie, the law firm that was paying Steele to find dirt on Donald Trump on behalf on the Clinton campaign and the DNC. In other words, the DNC and Clinton campaign were providing their own inputs into the dossier they were funding. This dossier wasn't for them. They already had this "dirt." The dossier was assembled to serve as planted evidence against Trump for the FBI to investigate!

---

[37] Washington Times, *"Source for Steele discredited anti-Trump dossier outed"*, Rowan Scarborough, July 26, 2020
"

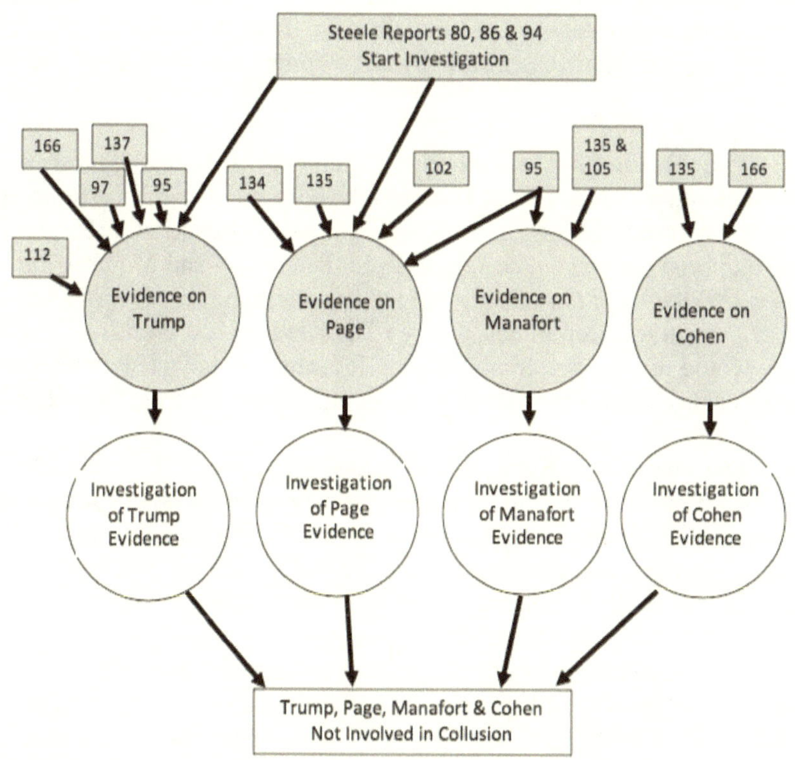

Figure 5-1 Connecting the Dots – Track 2 Investigation from Steele Supplied Evidence in His Numbered Reports to FBI's Conclusion that There Was No Evidence.

The evidence against Trump consisted of three basic allegations; (A) collusion, (B) conduct of blackmailable activities, and (C) suspicious financial activities.

The collusion-related charges (Charges "A") were; (1) Russians had been cultivating, supporting and assisting Trump for at least five years (Report 80), (2) there was a well-developed conspiracy of cooperation between Trump and Russian leadership (Reports 80 & 95), (3) the Trump campaign had a visceral dislike of Hillary Clinton and had the objective of swinging Bernie Sanders followers away from Hillary (Report 102), (4) Trump associates had established an intelligence exchange with the Kremlin for at least eight years, (Report 94 & 97), (5) Trump had delivered intelligence on the activities and business of leading Russian oligarchs and their families that Putin had asked Trump for (Report 94),

(6) Trump and his organization were using Alfa Bank servers in New York to communicate with Putin directly (Report 112) and (7) anti-Clinton hackers had been paid by the Trump team and the Kremlin (Report 166).

The blackmailable activities (Charges "B") that Trump was allegedly engaged in were, (1) he employed a number of prostitutes to perform a urination show in front of him in 2013 (Report 80), (2) Trump had explored the real estate sectors in St. Petersburg and Moscow *but in the end Trump had to settle for the use of extensive sexual services from local prostitutes* (Report 95), and (3) The Kremlin had promised Trump they would not use the compromising information collected as leverage given the high levels of voluntary co-operation from his team (Report 97).

The suspicious financial activities (Charges "C") included (1) Russian diplomatic staff in New York, Washington DC and Miami were engaged with Trump in a pension money laundering scheme (Report 95) and (2) Trump's previous business efforts had included exploring the real estate sector in St. Petersburg as well as Moscow (Report 95).

The three categories of allegations against Trump defined above completed the Steele planted evidence against Donald Trump within the FBI – As shown in Figure 5-2, this collection of evidence

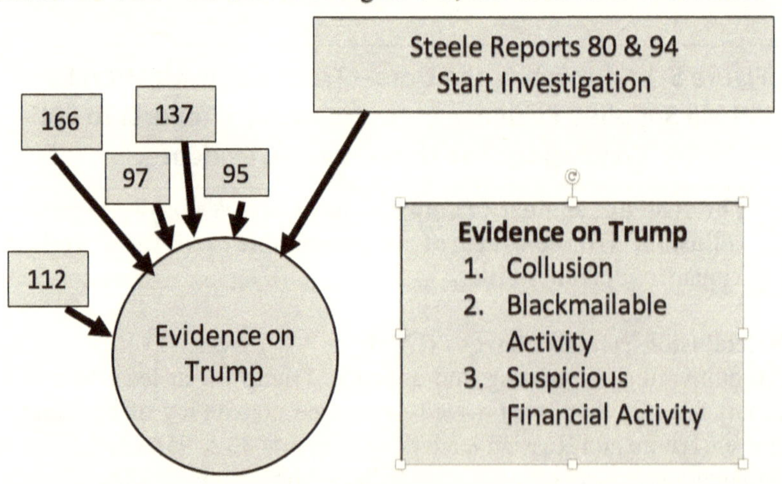

Figure 5-2 Evidence of Collusion, Blackmailable Activities & Suspicious Financial Activities Came Directly from Seven Reports in the Steele Dossier.

originated from seven of the seventeen Reports comprising the Steele dossier and completes the "dot" labeled "Evidence on Trump."

Investigation of the Evidence Against Trump Planted by Steele.

Much of this "evidence" is not even evidence at all, but idle gossip having no implications of illegality but is simply designed to make Trump "look bad." Most of it does not even meet the threshold of suggesting a "look-see" action, much less a formal investigation. This explains why despite having Reports 80, 94 and 96 in their possession when Crossfire Hurricane was started, the FBI didn't use them to predicate their investigation. It was irrelevant. Never-the-less, the FBI did later investigate the claims made in the Steele dossier reports.

(A) Validation of Evidence of Trump Collusion (Charges "A")-

(1) *The Russians had been cultivating, supporting and assisting Trump for at least five years* (Report 80); The only documentation of any specific FBI investigation into this assertion relates solely to a proposed Trump Tower – Moscow project in 2015 and early 2016. The Mueller report takes eleven pages to describe basically how a complex real estate deal progresses. The FBI assembled an extensive array of captured e-communications, letters, phone conversation between various Russian interest groups, American promoters, laws firms and Michael Cohen representing the Trump organization. Based on the Mueller Report, the FBI reached the same conclusion as any American would, the Russians and likely all foreign powers cultivate potential political players in other nations. The Trump situation is a little unique, though no more sinister, because Trump was a world-wide real estate developer before entering politics. As such, he had interest in developing property in Moscow and St. Petersburg. It is significant, that no deals were ever consummated between Trump and Russia. The Trump Tower-Moscow project received FBI scrutiny because the timing of the activity overlapped that of the Trump campaign. Had the project been consummated, Trump's only role in the whole project was to lend his name to the project in return for percentages of gross sales, condos sold, etc.[38] The deal never happened.

There is no record of the FBI probing much before the Trump Tower Moscow project for evidence of the Russians cultivating Trump. Steele

---

[38] Mueller Report, Op. Cit. Pages 67-78.

identifies this as a weakness in the FBI investigation.[39] What evidence exists is exculpatory against any charge that Trump positively responded to being cultivated or supported. Specifically, Donald Trump Jr. traveled to Russia a half-dozen times in an 18-month period looking for deals in the 2008-2009 time frame and concluded that the business environment there was dangerous and devoid of any trustworthy partners.[40] In 2015, Trump pulled out of a deal for a Trump Tower in Moscow which is consistent with the claim in the dossier that, Trump was offered but declined "various sweetener real estate business deals." ***INVESTIGATION FINDING: No cultivating of Trump was confirmed but even if there was any cultivating or assisting of Donald Trump by the Russians over the last five years it had no effect on promoting any collusion.***

There was a well-developed conspiracy of cooperation between Trump and Russian leadership (Reports 80 & 95) This was a claim relayed by Steele's "primary sub-source" from Steel's "Source E". What the FBI investigation determined was that the "primary sub-source was Igor Danchenko and Danchenko's "call-in" source for this "evidence" was non-other than Sergei Millian the premier unreliable source of disinformation in the whole Trump-Russia collusion investigation. Whereas, Steele represented his source as Source E, "an ethnic Russian close associate of Republican US presidential candidate Donald Trump" this was hardly true – Millian never worked in any capacity with the Trump organization![41] The FBI determined that Millian was an impeachable source of information and was likely being fed disinformation by the Russians. Millian was also the source of the "golden shower" sexual misconduct claim against Trump. Even Sergei latter disowned that claim. That said, Report 95 makes the strongest suggestion of coordination and collusion — a "conspiracy" — between the Russian government and the Trump campaign.[42] The memo claims an "agreed exchange of information in both directions" with "Trump's team using moles within the DNC and hackers in the US." The memo further states that Putin was "motivated by fear and hatred of Hillary Clinton." But that said, this "intelligence" came from an established liar and known unreliable FBI source.

---

[39] *Crime in Progress*", Glen Simpson and Peter Fritsch, Random House, November 26, 2019

[40] Annotated Dossier, annotateddossier.com

[41] ABC News, *"US-Russian Businessman Said to Be Source of Key Trump Dossier Claim".*, Brian Ross and Mathew Mosk, Jan 30, 2017.

[42] The Washington Post, *"What the Steele dossier said vs. what the Mueller report said."* Glen Kessler, April 24, 2019.

The Mueller investigation did not find any such level of coordination.[43] Instead, it suggested the Trump campaign was opportunistic about apparent assistance from Russia, but Mueller could not find evidence the conspiracy outlined in the memo existed. Instead, the report described Russian contacts that *"consisted of business connections, offers of assistance to the Campaign, invitations for candidate Trump and Putin to meet in person, invitations for Campaign officials and representatives of the Russian government to meet, and policy positions seeking improved U.S.-Russian relations."*

"Although the investigation established that the Russian government perceived it would benefit from a Trump presidency and worked to secure that outcome, and that the campaign expected it would benefit electorally from information stolen and released through Russian efforts, the investigation did not establish that members of the Trump Campaign conspired or coordinated with the Russian government in its election interference activities," Mueller concluded. ***INVESTIGATION FINDING: This statement of a well-developed conspiracy could not be substantiated by the FBI and the FBI determined it originated from a totally unreliable source, Millian.***

(3) the Trump campaign had a visceral dislike of Hillary Clinton and had the objective of swinging Bernie Sanders followers away from Hillary (Report 102). ***INVESTIGATION FINDING: The FBI didn't confirm or deny this assertion, but it is undoubtedly true but totally legal and commonly practiced in politics.***

(4) Trump associates had established and had intelligence exchanges with the Kremlin for at least eight years, (Report 94 & 97). This was another Sergei Millian sourced piece of "evidence." ***INVESTIGATION FINDING: This statement of 8 years of intelligence sharing between Trump and the Kremlin could not be substantiated by the FBI and the FBI determined it originated from a totally unreliable source, Millian.***

(5) ***Trump had delivered intelligence on the activities, business and otherwise of leading Russian oligarchs and their families that Putin had asked Trump for*** (Report 97). According to Steele's source, *"Putin's priority requirement had been for intelligence on the activities, business and otherwise, in the US of leading Russian oligarchs and their families.*

---

[43] Ibid.

Trump and his associates duly had obtained and supplied the Kremlin with this information." Unfortunately, when the FBI investigated, they learned that their favorite unreliable person, Sergei Millian was the source of this intelligence. ***INVESTIGATION FINDING: This statement of Trump sharing intelligence on Russian oligarchs could not be substantiated by the FBI and the FBI determined it originated from a totally unreliable source, Millian.***

(6) ***Trump and his organization were using Alfa Bank servers in New York to communicate with Putin directly*** (Report 112). This "evidence" was manufactured by two Perkins Coie lawyers, working for the Hillary Clinton campaign and DNC who had hired Fusion GPS to find the dirt on Trump. The very people who hired Fusion GPS and Christopher Steele were supplying them the evidence of collusion the FBI might not find by themselves. That is disturbing in itself, but even more troubling is that it was disinformation designed to bring down Trump using Steele not to FIND dirt on Trump, but to PLANT dirt on Trump in the FBI that Clinton's law firm had created. The two Clinton lawyers were Michael Sussmann and Marc Elias. Steele admitted that he was given information from Sussmann, about alleged "illicit ties" between the bank and Vladimir Putin, which acted as an "undercover messaging channel between the Kremlin and the Trump Organization."[44] It is interesting how the Washington Post tried to twist the findings of the Mueller Report into implying guilt when that was not the case at all.[45]

In actuality, the FBI investigated whether there were cyber links between the Trump Organization and Alfa Bank but had concluded by early February 2017 that there were no such links.[46]

---

[44] National Review, *"Steele Claims Clinton Lawyer Provided Tip about Trump Campaign Contacts with Russian Bank"*, Tobias Hoonhout, April 28, 2020

[45] The Washington Post in the April 24, 2019 article, "What the Steele dossier said vs what the Mueller report said", Glen Kessler says, *"This memo gets the essence of the relationship between Putin and Russia's largest commercial bank correct. "Aven told the Office that he is one of approximately 50 wealthy Russian businessmen who regularly meet with Putin in the Kremlin; these 50 men are often referred to as 'oligarchs,' whereas the Mueller report said, "Aven told the Office that he met on a quarterly basis with Putin, including in the fourth quarter (Q4) of 2016, shortly after the U.S. presidential election." The report recounts how, at Putin's direction, Aven sought to make contacts with the Trump transition team." This implies that the basic charge of the bank being a conduit for Russia-Trump collusion was confirmed but the details of who and how often bank executive Aven met with Russians differed a little. The actual facts are the FBI found that the bank was NOT used as a conduit for Trump – Russia collusion.*

[46] Horowitz Report, Op. Cit. footnote 259, page 119

Two principals at Alfa Bank, Aven and Fridman, sued Steele for falsely accusing him of being involved in Steele's Trump smearing scam. On July 8, 2020, Aven and Fridman were awarded $23,000 in damages in the High Court of England and Wales. The judge ruled several of the allegations in Steele's Memo 112 were "inaccurate or misleading as a matter of fact."[47]   Specifically the judge ruled that in Report 112: there were six factually inaccurate or unproven claims that Steele provided from Sussmann and Elias;

- Aven associate Fridman did not do favors for or receive favors from Putin as the memo claimed;
- Fridman and Aven did not provide informal foreign policy advice to the Russian leader as Steele alleged;
- Fridman did not meet with Putin in September 2016 as claimed by Steele's source;
- the businessman did not bribe Putin when he was Deputy Mayor of St Petersburg, and;
- Fridman and Aven did not do Putin's political bidding as the dossier alleged.

INVESTIGATION FINDING: Inspector General Michael Horowitz's report, released December 2019, detailed how the FBI, which finally received the Report 112 in November 2016, "concluded by early February 2017 that there were no such links" between Alfa Bank and the Trump campaign apparatus. The whole story was fabricated by political enemies.

(7) ***Anti-Clinton hackers had been paid by the Trump team and Kremlin*** (Report 166). Report 166 dated Dec. 13, 2016 stated that Cohen and three colleagues went to Prague. According to Report 166, one of their agenda items was to finalize a plan for processing "deniable" cash payments to operatives, including hackers, and contingency plans to cover up the operations. The report did not know the dates of that trip but placed it as being "around late August or early September of 2016. The FBI concluded that meeting never took place. There are no travel documents supporting that Cohen traveled to the Czech Republic during that time frame. The "three colleagues" have never been identified and Michael Cohen flatly denies he was there.

---

[47] Just the News, "*British court rules against Christopher Steele, orders damages paid to businessmen named in dossier,*" John Solomon, July 8, 2020.

The news source, McClatchy, supports Steele's claim in Report 166. **In early 2018** (Prior to the Mueller Report being released in March 2019) McClatchy reported that the alleged trip was a subject of focus for lawmakers on the House Intelligence Committee. According to McClatchy, the House Intel Committee interest in Cohen's whereabouts in 2016 was said to be fueled by what they considered to be weak documentation from Cohen. Unfortunately for McClatchy, Cohen provided documentation showing he was in New York and Los Angeles at the time of the alleged Prague visit. Even that was criticized so Cohen tweeted out a photo of his passport cover to prove that he didn't visit Prague in 2016. Cohen showed the inside of the document to BuzzFeed News. According to the publication, Cohen's passport did not contain a stamp for the Czech Republic.[48]

In December of 2018, McClatchy came up with more evidence that Cohen was in Prague in the August - September 2016 time frame. McClatchy reported that *"investigators had learned of a claim that a cell phone traced back to Cohen sent signals that ricocheted off cell towers in Prague late August or early September 2016."*[49] According to McClatchy news service, this was further evidence that Cohen was in Prague in that time period. The obvious question that an average American would ask is, "if a cellphone tower "ping" is detected from a phone, the exact date and time of that ping is known, so why was the report only able to isolate the "ping" to a two-month range of dates?"

As late as December 13, 2019, a year later, McClatchy news service maintained that Cohen was in Prague in the August 2016 time frame, citing the cellphone tower "ping" from Cohen's cellphone as evidence.[50] McClatchy noted that all the evidence that pointed to Cohen being in Prague in August 2016 was shared with Robert Mueller. Armed with all this "intelligence" Mueller concluded that Cohen was not in Prague in the August 2016 time frame. ***INVESTIGATION FINDING: The FBI found, and the Mueller report states, Cohen was not in Prague: "Cohen had never traveled to Prague and was not concerned about those allegations, which he believed were provably false," the report says on page 139. The allegation that Trump helped pay for hackers is based upon the discussions supposedly held in Prague between Cohen, his***

---

[48] Business Insider, *"One of the Steele dossier's biggest allegations about Russian hacking is back in the spotlight after a new Czech media report"*, Sonan Smith, Mar 21, 2019

[49] Ibid.

[50] The Washington Post, *"The story stands: McClatchy won't back off its Michael Cohen-Prague reporting"*, Ed Wimple, December 13, 2019

three cohorts and the Russians. That meeting could not have occurred because according to the FBI, Cohen wasn't in Prague. In footnotes to Inspector General Horowitz's report declassified on April 15, 2020, shows FBI knew Cohen didn't go to Prague nor that Russia had obtained kompromat on Trump during his visit to Moscow in 2013.[51] The report assessed "the Steele report was part of a Russian disinformation campaign to denigrate US foreign relations," according to the inspector general's footnote.

(B) **Investigation of Evidence of Trump's Blackmailable Activities (Charges "B") -**

(1) Trump employed a number of prostitutes to perform a urination show in front of him in 2013 (Report 80) - This was a claim relayed by Steele's "primary sub-source", Igor Danchenko. Danchenko got the "tip" from non-other than Sergei Millian the premier unreliable source of disinformation in the whole Trump-Russia collusion investigation. The Moscow Ritz Carlton episode involving TRUMP reported above from Sergei claimed several of the hotel staff were aware of it at the time. Sergei said he believed it had happened in 2013. Speaking separately in June 2016, Vyacheslav Trubnikav, former top-level Russian intelligence officer, asserted that TRUMP's unorthodox behavior in Russia over the years had provided the authorities there with enough embarrassing material on the now Republican presidential candidate to be able to blackmail him if they so wished. *INVESTIGATION FINDING: The Horowitz Report flatly states that "the February 2017 intelligence community report said that the allegations raised about Trump's activities in Moscow in 2013 were false, and the product of Russian intelligence "infiltrate(ing) a source into the network."[52]*

(2) Trump had explored the real estate sectors in St. Petersburg and Moscow but in the end Trump had to settle for the use of extensive sexual services from local prostitutes (Report 95) – Trump did explore the real estate sectors in St. Petersburg and Moscow in the normal course as a world-wide real estate executive. There is nothing nefarious about that. The Steele document added that *"...in the end, Trump had to settle for the use of sexual services from local prostitutes"* is simply trash that has never been confirmed. *INVESTIGATION FINDING: There is no documentation describing FBI investigation into this smear on Trump.*

---

[51] CNN, *"GOP seizes on newly declassified material to raise further questions about Steele dossier"*, Jeremy Herb and Evan Perez April 16, 2020

[52] CNN, *"GOP seizes on newly declassified material to raise further questions about Steele dossier"*, Jeremy Herb and Evan Perez April 16, 2020

It follows the same pattern as the smear on Trump concerning the golden shower performance by prostitutes in Moscow in 2013. It would appear that the FBI treated this as "more of the same" disinformation fed to Steele informants by Russian operatives to dirty-up Trump.

(3) The Kremlin had promised Trump they would not use the compromising information collected against him as leverage given the high levels of voluntary co-operation from his team (Report 97).- There is no documentation describing FBI investigation into this smear on Trump. *INVESTIGATION FINDING:* None.

(C) Validation of Evidence of Trumps suspicious financial activities (Charges "C")

(1) *Russian diplomatic staff in New York, Washington DC and Miami were engaged with Trump in a pension money laundering scheme (Report 95)* – This charge against Trump by Steele had more to do with charges of suspected collusion than with suspicious financial activities. The crux of the charge is that Trump sources were exchanging information about the lives and activities of rich Russian oligarchs and their families for information on Clinton and her campaign from Russian sources. Trump sources of information were largely Russians who had immigrated ("Russian emigres") to the U.S. and had contacts with the oligarchs, and knowledge of their activities.

The source of this item of "intelligence" was Sergei Millian. The activity was termed a "money laundering scheme" only because the alleged method of payment to the Russian emigres was through the Russian pension plan which paid emigres living in the U.S. The plan was administered by the U.S. Russian diplomatic staff.[53] This fee-for-service arrangement allegedly relied on "*Russian diplomatic staff in key cities such as New York, Washington, D.C. and Miami,*" who "were using the emigre pension distribution system as cover. *INVESTIGATION FINDING: The FBI found no evidence of this alleged activity. Besides the source had been discredited and there is no Russian diplomatic presence in Miami.*

(2) *Trump's previous business efforts had included exploring the real estate sector in St. Petersburg as well as Moscow* (Report 95). Trump

---

[53] According to Audit Report of Social Security Administration, Office of Inspector General, "*Supplemental Security Income Recipients Eligible For, or Receiving, Russian Pensions*", Report A-01-12-21238December 2012, Russian immigrants are eligible for Russian pensions when living in the U.S.______

did explore the real estate sectors in St. Petersburg and Moscow in the normal course as a world-wide real estate executive. There is nothing nefarious about that. ***INVESTIGATION FINDING: There is no documentation of the FBI investigating this claim since there is no meaningful charge being made.***

After investigating Steele's seven charges of collusion, two charges of committing blackmailable offenses and two charges of suspicious financial activity, the FBI dismissed them all as false, unverified, sourced from deliberate Russian planted disinformation and totally discredited sources. The FBI cleared Trump of any involvement in Russian collusion. Figure 5-3 connects the dots from the start of the investigation to the findings of the FBI.

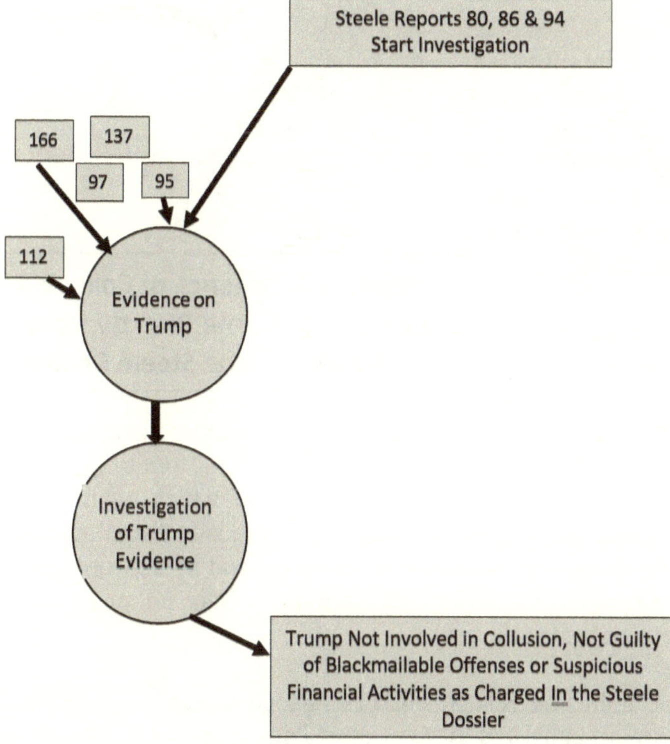

Figure 5-3 Connecting the Dots from Steele Dossier Charges of Collusion, Blackmailable Offences and Suspicious Financial Activity to FBI Determining That Trump Was Not Chargeable.

5.1.2 Validation of Steele evidence on Carter Page

As shown in Figure 5-4 Steele's evidence against Page was documented in Steele Reports 94, 95, 97, 102, and 134. These reports documented conversations that Steele's "Primary sub source", Igor Danchenko[54] had with others that implicated Carter Page. All of Carter Page's "misdeeds" documented by Mr. Steele involved charges of collusion or attempted collusion and identified "secret meetings" where this collusion took place. Although the evidence came from known unreliable sources infiltrated by Russians planting disinformation, it was used by the FBI to formally spy on Mr. Page using the authority granted by four separate FISA warrants granted serially by the FISA court. Warrants that upon review by the DOJ Inspector

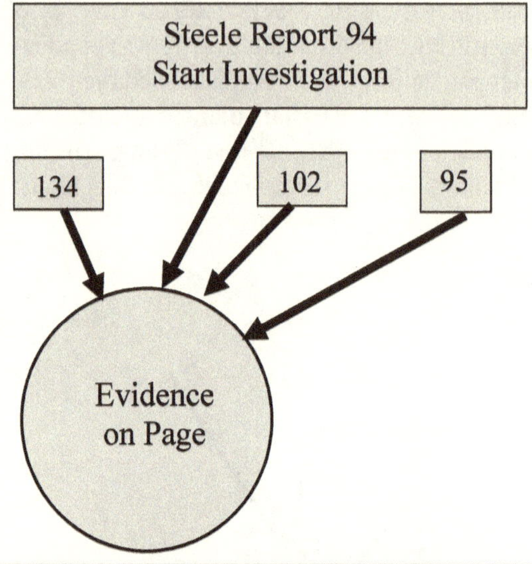

Figure 5-4 Evidence of Collusion, By Carter Page Came Directly from Four Reports in the Steele Dossier.

General, were clearly not justified and were contaminated by FBI tampering with a justification application, omitting exculpatory information and introducing "errors" all of which contributed to the inappropriate granting of the warrants. Instead of apologizing to Mr. Page, Jim Comey, blew the whole thing off and in his words said, *"Oh, I must have been misled."* This arrogance has no place in our law enforcement leadership ranks.

The collusion related charges against Carter Page named in the Steele Report consisted of; (1) Carter Page was told by Igor Divyekin a senior Kremlin Internal Affairs official, *"that the Russians had compromising information on Clinton and Trump, and allegedly added that Trump 'should bear this in mind"* (Report 94), (2) Carter Page met

---

[54] Washington Times, *"Source for Steele discredited anti-Trump dossier outed"*, Rowan Scarborough, July 26, 2020"

secretly with Igor Sechin, Chairman of Russian energy conglomerate, Rosneft to discuss future cooperation and the lifting of Ukraine-related sanctions against Russia (Report 94), (3) Carter Page had "*conceived and promoted*" the timing of the release of hacked emails by WikiLeaks for the purpose of swinging supporters of Bernie Sanders "*away from Hillary Clinton and across to Trump.*" (Reports 95 & 102), (4) Page was an intermediary between Russia and the Trump campaign's then manager (Manafort) in a "*well-developed conspiracy*" of cooperation, which led to Russia's disclosure of hacked DNC emails to Wikileaks in exchange for the Trump campaign's agreement to sideline Russian intervention in Ukraine as a campaign issue (Report 95), and (5) A close associate of Rosneft President Sechin confirmed a secret meeting with Carter Page in July; Sechin was keen to have sanctions on the company lifted and offered up to a 19 percent stake in return. (Report 134)

The five allegations itemized above define the Steele evidence against Carter Page planted right in the hands of the FBI. As shown in Figure 5-4 this collection of evidence originated from four of the seventeen Reports comprising the Steele dossier and completes the "dot" labeled "Evidence on Carter Page. The Mueller report concluded that Mr. Page did NOT coordinate with the Russians.[55]

Validation of the Evidence Against Carter Page Planted by Steele

Armed with what has been shown to be bogus FISA court authorizations to investigate Carter Page, the FBI interviewed Mr. Page many times to learn more about the charges leveled by Christopher Steele's reports. "302" reports documenting these interviews were created and reviewed by the FBI team working as part of the Mueller investigation. The FBI interviewed Carter Page five times in March 2017 prior to the formation of the Special Council.[56] Those 302 reports document the bulk of the investigation of Carter Page.

(1) Carter Page was told by Igor Divyekin a senior Kremlin Internal Affairs official, "that the Russians had compromising information on Clinton and Trump, and allegedly added that Trump 'should bear this in mind' (Report 94).* This exchange supposedly happened on July 7 or 8, 2016. In an October 2016 interview with an FBI CHS, Page denied even knowing who Divyekin was. Carter Page told the CHS during the

---

[55] Mueller Report, Op. Cit. Page 95
[56] Mueller Report page Op. Cit. 95, footnote 516.

meeting that the "core lie" against him in the media is that "[Page] *met with these sanctioned Russian officials, Sechin and a guy I had never even heard of (Divyekin)."* When asked about that person's name, Page said *"I can't even remember, it's just so outrageous."* This exculpatory information was conveniently omitted from the subsequent Page FISA application by the FBI filed in June 2017[57]. ***INVESTIGATION FINDING: There is no documentation of the FBI ever finding any evidence that Carter Page even knew Divyekin much less met with him to discuss any subject.***

(2) Carter Page met secretly with Igor Sechin, Chairman of Russian energy conglomerate, Rosneft to discuss future cooperation and the lifting of Ukraine-related sanctions against Russia (Report 94). In the interviews with Carter Page, Mr. Page said although he knew who Igor Sechin was and he had met and talked with him, he didn't talk to him about *"future cooperation and the lifting of sanctions against Russia."* ***INVESTIGATION FINDING: There is no documentation of the FBI ever finding any evidence that Mr. Page and Mr. Sechin ever met to discuss the subject of future cooperation.***

(3) Carter Page had "conceived and promoted" the timing of the release of hacked emails by WikiLeaks for the purpose of swinging supporters of Bernie Sanders" away from Hillary Clinton and across to Trump" (Reports 95 & 102*)*. This was discussed above in Paragraph 5.1.1 A (3) It was found to be an unactionable claim. ***INVESTIGATION FINDING: The FBI didn't confirm or deny this assertion, but it is undoubtedly true that Trump wanted Bernie Sanders votes swung to him rather than Hillary Clinton. There was no evidence of Carter Page conceiving and/or promoting the timing of WikiLeaks release of hacked emails.***

(4)Page was an intermediary between Russia and the Trump campaign's then manager (Manafort) in a "well-developed conspiracy" of cooperation, which led to Russia's disclosure of hacked DNC emails to Wikileaks in exchange for the Trump campaign's agreement to sideline Russian intervention in Ukraine as a campaign issue (Report 95*)*. Page says he was not involved in any conspiracy and has never met Manafort. The FBI could not find any evidence to dispute Carter Page's assertion. ***INVESTIGATION FINDING: The Mueller investigation did not find such a level of coordination. Instead it suggests the Trump campaign was opportunistic about apparent assistance from Russia, but***

Mueller could not find evidence of the conspiracy described in Steel's report 95.[58]

(5) A close associate of Rosneft President Sechin confirmed a secret meeting with Carter Page in July; Sechin was keen to have sanctions on the company lifted and offered up to a 19 percent stake in return. (Report 134) The Mueller report does not confirm a meeting between Page and Sechin. But Mueller did document a meeting between Page and a lower-level Rosneft official. The meeting included discussion of a possible sale of part of Rosneft, though apparently not in the context of a reward for lifting sanctions.

"Page said that, during his time in Moscow, he met with friends and associates he knew from when he lived in Russia, including Andrey Baranov, a former Gazprom employee who had become the head of investor relations at Rosneft, a Russian energy company," the Mueller report said. "*Page stated that he and Baranov talked about 'immaterial non-public' information.*" Page believed he and Baranov discussed Rosneft president Igor Sechin, and he thought Baranov might have mentioned the possibility of a sale of a stake in Rosneft in passing." *INVESTIGATION FINDING: The FBI didn't confirm the Page-Sechin meeting nor that there was any offer of trading 19% of Rosneft in return for lifting sanctions against Russia, something Carter Page would not have any power to deliver on. Furthermore. the Mueller report found that there was apparently no discussion of lifting sanctions.*[59]

The bottom line on Carter Page was summed up by Michael Horowitz, the Justice Department's inspector general, and his statement about the dossier and Page: "*We determined that prior to and during the pendency of the FISAs, the FBI was unable to corroborate **any** of the specific substantive allegations against Carter Page contained in the dossier.*" Figure 5-5 shows the connection of the "dots" from the planted Steele "evidence" to the FBI finding of no collusion.

---

[58] The Washington Post, "What the Steele dossier said vs. what the Mueller report said", Glen Kessler, April 24, 2019

[59] Ibid.

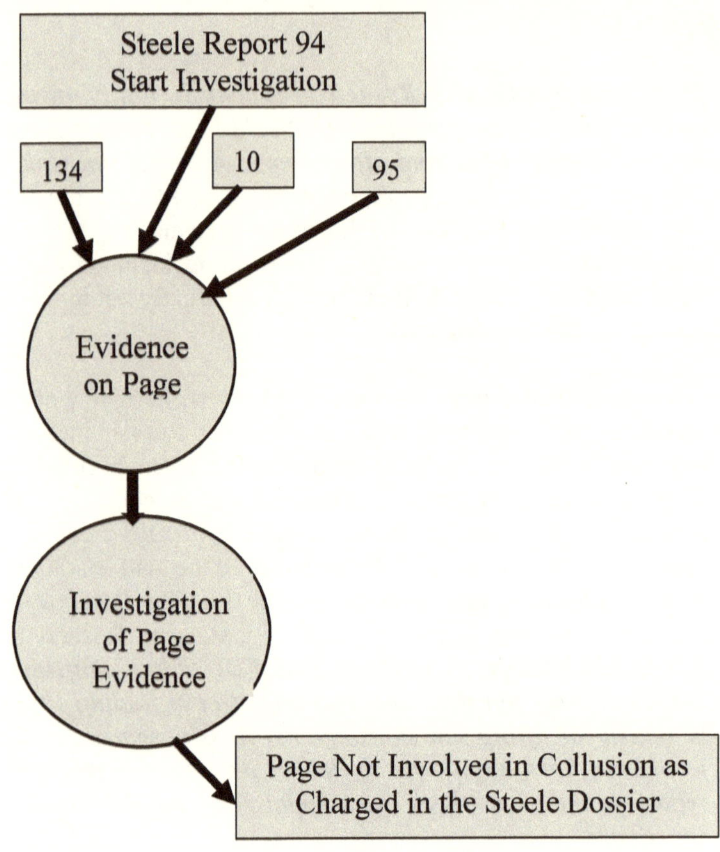

Figure 5-5 Connecting the Dots from Steele Dossier Charges of Collusion Against Carter Page and FBI Finding of No Involvement.

5.1.3 Validation of the Steele evidence on Manafort.

As shown in Figure 5-6, Steele's evidence against Manafort was documented in Steele Reports 95, 105 and 135. These reports documented bar room conversations that Steele's "Primary sub source", Igor Danchenko[60] had with his beer-drinking buddies that implicated Paul Manafort. All of Manafort's "misdeeds" documented by Mr. Steele involved charges of collusion or attempted collusion and identified "secret meetings" where this collusion took place.

---

[60] Washington Times, "*Source for Steele discredited anti-Trump dossier outed*", Rowan Scarborough, July 26, 2020"

1. **There was a well-developed conspiracy of co-operation between them and the Russian leadership. This was managed on the Trump side by the Republican candidate's campaign manager, Paul Manafort, who was using Carter Page as intermediaries.** (Report 95).- Sergei Millian was the source of this "information" and like all of his information requires confirmation. *INVESTIGATION FINDING: The FBI could not confirm any conspiracy between Russia and the Trump organization. Furthermore, the Mueller report did not find evidence that showed that Manafort* used Carter Page as an intermediary with Russia. In fact, Carter Page maintained he didn't even know Paul Manafort.

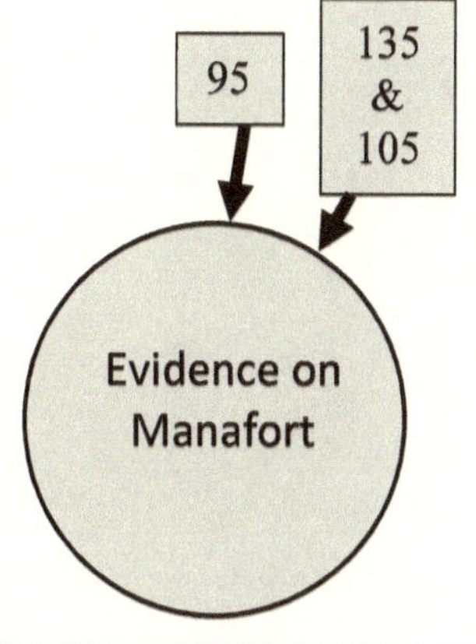

Figure 5-6 Steele Evidence on Manafort

(2) Manafort had a corrupt relationship with, the former pro-Russian Ex-Ukrainian President. Yanukovych (Report 105)
INVESTIGATION FINDING: The FBI confirmed this to be essentially true but was not tied to any collusion attempt by Manafort.

(3) Ex-Ukrainian President Yanukovych confided directly to Putin that he authorized kick-back payments to Manafort, as alleged in western media. Yanukovych however, assured the Russian President there was no documentary evidence/trail. (Report 105)
INVESTIGATION FINDING: The FBI confirmed this to be essentially true. The alleged payments had nothing to do with the Trump campaign.

The FBI pursued other evidence against Paul Manafort that was not sourced by Christopher Steele and did charge him with crimes identified from that evidence but did not find any credible evidence from the Steele planted evidence that implicated the Trump campaign, only Mr. Manafort personally. Figure 5-7 shows the connection of the "dots" from the planted Steele "evidence" to the FBI finding of no collusion on the part of Paul Manafort.

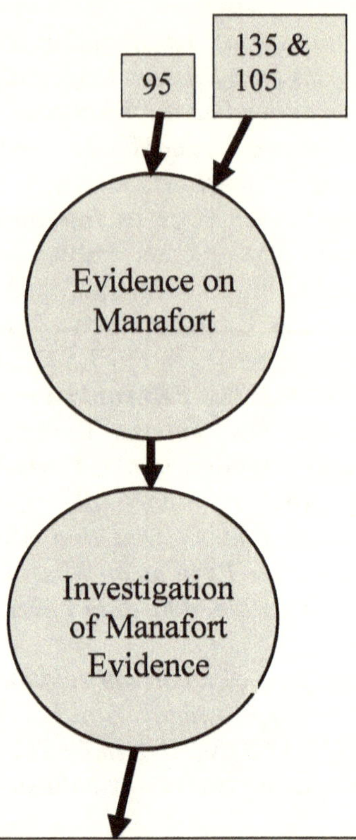

Figure 5-7 Connecting the Dots from Steele Dossier Reports 95, 105 & 135 Charges of Collusion Against Paul Manafort and FBI Finding of No Collusion.

The crimes Paul Manafort were convicted of that were unrelated to the Trump campaign were;

- On August 21, 2018, Manafort was convicted in the Eastern District of Virginia on eight tax, Foreign Bank Account Registration (FBAR), and bank fraud charges. These charges and convictions were for nefarious activities that predated any involvement with the Trump campaign and were unrelated to intelligence provided by Christopher Steele.
- On September 14, 2018, Manafort pleaded guilty in the District of Columbia to (1) conspiracy to defraud the United States and conspiracy to commit offenses against the United States (money laundering, tax fraud, FBAR, Foreign Agents Registration Act (FARA), and FARA false statements), and

(2) conspiracy to obstruct justice (witness tampering). Manafort also admitted criminal conduct with which he had been charged in the Eastern District of Virginia, but as to which the jury hung. The conduct at issue in both cases involved Manafort's work in Ukraine and the money he earned for that work, as well as crimes after the Ukraine work ended. This charge and conviction were unrelated to intelligence provided by Christopher Steele.

5.1.4 Validation of Steele evidence on Cohen

As shown in Figure 5-8, Steele's evidence against Michael Cohen was documented in Steele Reports 135, and 166.

(1) *Cohen engaged with the Russians in trying to cover up the scandal of Manafort and exposure of Page in secret liaison with Russian leadership in August of 2016* (Report 135). As documented above, Page didn't participate in "secret liaison" with Russian leadership that supposedly occurred in Prague in August 2016. That was just garbage delivered by the purveyor of Russian disinformation, Sergei Millian. There was no need to cover up anything because it didn't happen. *INVESTIGATION FINDING: The FBI determined that Cohen never went to Prague. They also determined that Page didn't participate in a secret liaison with Russian. There was no need to cover up a scandal that did not exist.*

Figure 5-8 Steele Evidence on Cohen

(2) *Anti-Clinton hackers had been paid by the Trump team and Kremlin* (Report 166). Report 166 dated Dec. 13, 2016 stated that Cohen and three colleagues went to Prague. According to Report 166, one of their agenda items was to finalize a plan for processing "deniable" cash payments to operatives, including hackers, and contingency plans to cover up the operations. The report did not know the dates of that trip but placed it as being "around late August or early September of 2016. The FBI concluded that meeting never took place. There are no travel documents supporting that Cohen traveled to the Czech Republic during that time frame. The "three colleagues" have never been identified and Michael Cohen flatly denies he was there.

The news source, McClatchy, supports Steele's claim in Report 166. **In early 2018** (Prior to the Mueller Report being released in March 2019) McClatchy reported that the alleged trip was a subject of focus for lawmakers on the House Intelligence Committee. According to McClatchy, the House Intel Committee interest in Cohen's whereabouts in 2016 was said to be fueled by what they considered to be weak documentation from Cohen. Unfortunately for McClatchy, Cohen provided documentation showing he was in New York and Los Angeles at the time of the alleged Prague visit. Even that was criticized so Cohen tweeted out a photo of his passport cover as proof that he didn't visit Prague in 2016, Cohen showed the inside of the document to BuzzFeed News. According to the publication, Cohen's passport did not contain a stamp for the Czech Republic.[61]

In December of 2018, McClatchy came up with more evidence that Cohen was in Prague in the August - September 2016 time frame. McClatchy reported that investigators had learned of a claim that a cell phone traced back to Cohen sent signals that ricocheted off cell towers in late August or early September 2016.[62] According to McClatchy news service, this was further evidence that Cohen was in Prague in that time period. The obvious question that an average American who ask is, "if a cellphone tower "ping" is detected from a phone, the exact date and time of that ping is known, so why was the report only able to isolate the "ping" to a two month range of dates?"

As late as December 13, 2019, a year later, McClatchy news service maintained that Cohen was in Prague in the August 2016 time frame, citing the cellphone tower "ping" from Cohen's cellphone as evidence.[63] McClatchy noted that all the evidence that pointed to Cohen being in Prague in August 2016 was shared with Robert Mueller. Armed with all this "intelligence" Mueller concluded that Cohen was not in Prague in the August 2016 time frame. ***INVESTIGATION FINDING: The FBI found, and the Mueller report states, Cohen was not in Prague: "Cohen had never traveled to Prague and was not concerned about those allegations, which he believed were provably false," the report says on page 139. The allegation that Trump helped pay for hackers is based***

---

[61] Business Insider, *"One of the Steele dossier's biggest allegations about Russian hacking is back in the spotlight after a new Czech media report"*, Sonan Smith, Mar 21, 2019

[62] Ibid.

[63] The Washington Post, *"The story stands: McClatchy won't back off its Michael Cohen-Prague reporting"*, Ed Wimple, <u>December</u> 13, 2019

The FBI pursued other evidence against Michael Cohen that was not sourced by Christopher Steele and did charge him with crimes identified

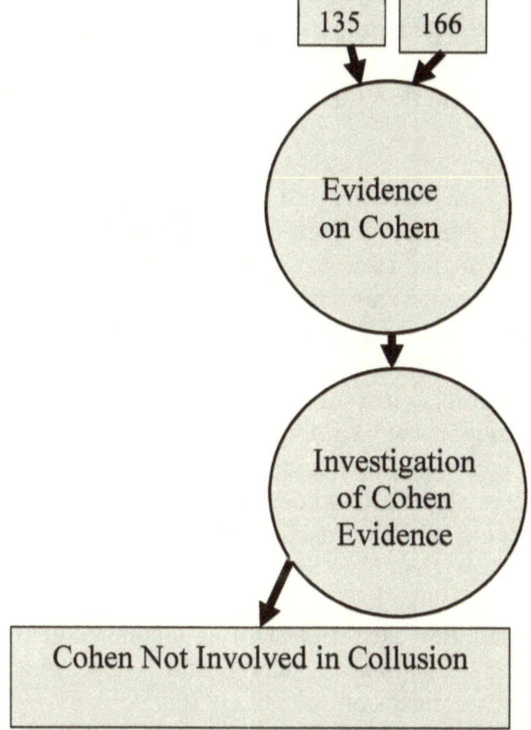

Figure 5-9 Connecting the Dots from Steele Dossier Reports 135 & 166 Charges of Collusion Against Michael Cohen and FBI Finding of No Collusion.

[64] CNN, "*GOP seizes on newly declassified material to raise further questions about Steele dossier*", Jeremy Herb and Evan Perez, April 16, 2020

from that evidence but did not find any credible evidence from the Steele planted evidence. Figure 5-9 shows the connection of the "dots" from the planted Steele "evidence" on Cohen to the FBI finding of no collusion on the part of Paul Manafort. Cohen was found guilty of other misdeeds, but not of any of the garbage that Christopher Steele found.

5.1.5 No Steele Collusion Evidence

To the average American, the damage done to the reputation of the intelligence community in general and to the FBI in particular from its unwarranted pursuit of the Trump-Russia collusion investigation based on the Steele dossier is disgraceful. What we had gleaned over time from the Mueller report, the Horowitz report and the subsequent removal of many initially redacted portions of the two reports plus results of multiple hearings on the subject sends two clear messages; (1) never cooperate with the FBI and (2) never believe anything our government or the press tells us.

What we Americans are told by politicians, the FBI and the media is based on an agenda, not on facts. The selected narrative drives what the "facts" are. Until this fiasco of an unwarranted investigation into Trump-Russia collusion, many of us believed the "deep state" was imaginary. We believed that the TV programs "24", "Designated Survivor" and "Homeland" were pure fiction involving "the deep state." Although the Trump-Russia collusion affair does not support a narrative of an evil deep state it does support the narrative of at least a deep state that allows and even encourages pursuit of investigations based on extreme and self-righteous biases. We have to make the choice of who to believe or spend much time doing what we used to rely on the press and FBI to do – conduct an independent investigation.

To illustrate how the "deep state" manipulated the American people and the illicit investigation, consider just the last two documents that were released to us Americans on July 17, 2020;[65]

- The first document is a 57-page summary of a three-day interview the FBI conducted with Christopher Steele's so-called "Primary Sub-source" (Igor Danchenko) in January of 2017, before the Mueller investigation was opened. This document not only demonstrates how unsubstantiated and unreliable the Steele dossier was, it shows that the FBI was

---

[65] Judiciary.senate.gov/FISA-investigation

on notice of the dossier's credibility problems and yet sought two more FISA application renewals based largely on this known false information. (This is what average Americans consider an act that a "deep state" would engage in.) Moreover, the recently released document demonstrates that the information that Steele's primary source provided him was second and third-hand information and rumor at best. This document shows that Igor disagreed with what Steele said he said. Igor didn't have any idea where much of Steele's reporting came from! Even Steele's primary sub-source said the report was fictitious.

- The second document contains Peter Strzok's type-written comments disagreeing with assertions made in a *New York Times* article about alleged Russian intelligence ties to the Trump campaign The document further shows that the FBI's assertion to the FISA court that *"the FBI believes that Russia's efforts to influence U.S. policy were likely being coordinated between the RIS [Russian Intelligence Services] and Page, and possibly others"* appears to be a misrepresentation. This is because, in his comments on the *Times* article, Strzok asserts that *"[we have not seen evidence of any individuals affiliated with the Trump team in contact with IOs [Intelligence Officials]. We are unaware of ANY Trump advisors engaging in conversations with Russian intelligence officials."*

- The document also indicates that the FBI may have been using foreign intelligence gathering techniques to impermissibly unmask and analyze existing and future intelligence collection regarding U.S. persons associated with the Trump campaign: *"Both the CIA and NSA are aware of our subjects and throughout the summer we provided them names and selectors for queries of their holdings as well as prospective collection."* The quote does not provide enough information to fully understand exactly what the FBI was doing but impermissible unmasking and analysis of existing and future incidental intelligence collection of U.S. persons would be troubling.[66]

---

[66] Committee on the Judiciary, *"Judiciary Committee Releases Declassified Documents that Substantially Undercut Steele Dossier"*, Page FISA Warrants, July 17, 2020

5.2 Salvage Something Out of Track 2 Investigation.

Misdeeds by the intelligence community leading to the planting of fake evidence of collusion are currently being investigated by John Durham. This book, in Chapters 2 & 3 connects those dots leading to the conclusion that John Brennan and the CIA were behind the attempt to incriminate Trump and his campaign by planting evidence of collusion. Chapter 4 connects the dots between the "evidence" planted by Joseph Mifsud using George Papadopoulos and finding it worthless in supporting any charge of collusion, but the FBI managed to salvage something out of the investigation by charging George with lying about when and how many times he had met with Joseph Mifsud.

Here in Chapter 5, the dots connecting "evidence" planted by Christopher Steele directly into the FBI and the finding of "no evidence of collusion" were well documented by the Mueller report and the Horowitz report and captured in the narrative above. Just as in the Papadopoulos case the FBI needed something for their exhaustive efforts and the time they spent on investigating a "dry hole" of Trump-Russia collusion. It almost seemed that the FBI wanted to make those associated with Trump and his campaign "pay" for hooking up with Trump. The pursuit of tax evasion, not registering as a foreign agent, and other possible infractions of federal law having nothing to do with Crossfire Hurricane was fair game.

Make Donald Trump pay – No charges of collusion or of any crime were made against Trump. But Trump needed to pay. Brennan didn't like him. Comey didn't like him. Comey took this assignment personally. He even admitted that he took notes of his meetings and conversations with Donald Trump to use them to trigger a Special Processor investigation of Trump – to "make him pay." Appendix E 1 provides the seven memos James Comey wrote documenting his communications with Trump. These memos were intended to "make Trump pay." They are almost laughable in their pettiness. It reminds us Americans of documented notes from an elementary school child who was going to "tell the teacher on you." James Comey succeeded. Comey made Trump pay for not only wasting the FBI's time on a meaningless investigation but for firing him. The FBI salvaged at least a strategic annoyance on President Trump.

Make Carter Page pay – No charges of collusion or of any crimes were made against Carter Page. But Page needed to pay. Carter Page paid by being subjected to countless interrogations by the FBI and multiple congressional hearings. Carter Page paid by having to have legal counsel to help him prepare for all the questioning he was subjected to. The FBI failed however to find anything they could charge him with. It was not for lack of trying. Mr. Page is the only suspect in the Crossfire Hurricane fiasco that was so suspicious that four FISA warrants were issued to investigate, wiretap and generally harass him. It has recently been determined that NONE of the warrants were justified. They were all based on inaccurate documentation in the warrant justification by the FBI. So yes, Carter Page paid for being a Trump associate but not for anything he did wrong. The FBI can take full credit for putting an innocent man through "hell" at a great personal cost. They can at least feel they accomplished something.

Make Paul Manafort pay – Paul Manafort came to the Trump campaign with a lot of legal, financial and political baggage. No charges of collusion were made against Paul Manafort for his activities associated with the Trump campaign. But Paul Manafort needed to pay for past misdeeds and he justifiably did as a result of this investigation. Specifically, Mr. Manafort was found guilty of eight tax, Foreign Bank Account Registration (FBAR), and bank fraud charges, conspiracy to defraud the US through money laundering, tax fraud, failure to register as a Foreign Agent and witness tampering. Congratulations to the FBI for these convictions. There is no evidence the FBI had any plans to investigate these crimes until Mr. Manafort joined the Trump team. This was simply a serendipitous result. This chance occurrence of detecting a crime causes the average American to wonder how many politicians and international businesspersons would be found guilty of similar crimes if the FBI would investigate them. Its unfortunate that it seems to have only happened once in our nation's history and that was to someone who had the audacity to join the Trump team. The FBI can at least feel they accomplished something.

Make Michael Cohen pay – Michael Cohen was Trump's personal lawyer with a lot of personal knowledge of Trump's business, legal and "other" affairs. Being named in the Steele dossier, gave the FBI a perfect reason to openly investigate Mr. Cohen. As Mr. Trump's lawyer, Cohen could be a treasure trove of "insider" knowledge of Trump collusion. The FBI didn't find any, but this was not an opportunity to be wasted. The more the FBI could "get" on Cohen, the more likely he would be to share dirt on Trump and if Michael Cohen didn't "sing", they would at least make him pay for being part of the Trump organization. That is exactly what happened. Cohen was convicted of tax fraud and lying. Michael Cohen paid; three years in prison, $500,000 in assets and $1.3 million in restitution to the IRS. Like Paul Manafort, Cohen was not under investigation for tax fraud or lying before the investigation into Trump-Russia collusion. It was just a serendipitous result. How could anyone have guessed that when investigating collusion with the Russians the FBI found tax fraud instead? Again, the FBI can at least feel they accomplished something.

5.3 What Others Are Saying About the Steele Dossier.

What Steele and Glen Simpson say about their dossier.

1. Steele said the dossier itself was *"not intended to be published and consisted largely of rumors and gossip."*[67]
    a. Mr. Steele is *"right-on"* about the dossier *"consisting largely of rumors and gossip."* So how does that translate to being *"so disturbing it was a matter of national security?"*
    b. *"Not intended to be published?"* Is that why he handed it to Michael Isikoff from Yahoo News on September 23, 2016? Was that done to achieve his goal of "not being published? Is that why on October 31, 2016 Steele gave nine of the reports to David Corn, a reporter for Mother Jones? Was that done to help ensure it never got published? Is that why he enlisted John McCain's aide, David Kramer to pass Report 166 to Ken Bensinger at Buzzfeed, Carl Bernstein at CNN, David Corn at Mother Jones, Tom Hamburger at The Washington Post, Bob Little at NPR, Peter Stone and Greg Gordon at McClatchy News Service, Brian Ross at ABC News and Alan Cullison at the Wall Street Journal? Was that orchestrated by Steele to achieve his intent of it not being published? There is something wrong with Christopher Steele. Its almost as if he was on the payroll of one of Trump's political opponents… Oh, that's right, he was!
2. *"The Dossier would explain why Trump liked Putin so much."*
    a. It doesn't explain **if** Trump liked Putin. Even if that premise is accepted it does not explain why Trump liked Putin.

---

[67] Washington Post, *"What the Steele dossier said vs. what the Mueller report said"* *Glen Kessler,* April 24, 2019.

3. *"The media failed to expose Trump. The media failed to write about Moscow potentially compromising Trump.*
    a. Are you kidding? The media printed everything Steele provided. To imply that the media was in Trump's pocket through all of this is perhaps the biggest whopper of the century! Christopher Steele has zero credibility with the average American.
    b. Other than the fact that there was no substantiated evidence that there was anything potentially compromising Trump, the media faithfully printed all that Steele provided.
    c. What is true is that the media failed to write anything about Moscow's potentially comprising information on Christopher Steele. Remember, according to Christopher Steele, it only has to be recorded in somebody's dossier to be *"potentially compromising."*
4. *"After three years of investigations, a fair assessment of the memos would conclude that many of the allegations in the dossier have been borne out."* (Steele's assessment in this book)
    a. Are you kidding? As detailed in Paragraph 5.1.1, exactly NONE of the Steele "evidence" against Trump has been borne out. The charges of blackmailable charges against Trump have been dismissed and even the person supplying the "intelligence", Sergei Millian disavows it; the charges of collusion have been dismissed, and the charges of suspicious financial activities have not only been dismissed, but Christopher Steele was charged and convicted of providing false information regarding the tie-in with Alfa Bank.
    b. Are you kidding? As detailed in Paragraph 5.1.2, NONE of the evidence against Carter Page have been borne out. Carter Page didn't even know Divyekin much less meet with him; Carter Page didn't have ANY "secret" meetings (maybe secret to Steele because Page didn't tell him about it?); etc. The IG report summed up Steele's memos involving Carter Page concluding that, *"the FBI was unable to corroborate **any** of the specific substantive allegations against Carter Page contained in the dossier."*
    c. Are you kidding? As detailed in paragraph 5.1.4, NONE of Steele's "evidence" against Michael Cohen has borne out. Steele's "evidence" of Cohen misdeeds stemmed entirely from Cohen's "secret meeting" with Russians in

Prague in or around September 2016. The FBI has determined that Cohen never went to Prague. They also determined that Page didn't participate in a secret liaison with Russia.

What the FBI, House Intelligence Committee and the IG report said about the Steele dossier that really upset Christopher Steele.

1. **On January 24, 2018** The Democrats in the House' Intelligence Committee released a ten-page memo from Adam Schiff stating that Christopher Steele's memos *"played no role in launching the counterintelligence investigation into Russian interference and links to the Trump campaign"*, and **on December 9, 2019** the US DOJ Office of Inspector General released the Review of four FISA Applications. Information provided by Christopher Steele was confirmed to have *"played no role"* in the investigation's opening.
    a. Everyone agrees Steeles reporting played no role in opening the Trump-Russia collusion investigation despite the fact that the FBI possessed three of the seventeen Steele Reports - reports so alarming that Steele deemed them a matter of national security.
    b. As documented by the House Intel Committee, the Inspector General and the FBI, information provided by Steele by July 31, 2016, didn't even make the screen as being relevant to opening an investigation. Steele's planted evidence of collusion activities got ignored while George Papadopoulos' bragging about his knowledge of a rumor of the Russians having dirt on Hillary Clinton, made the headlines and triggered an investigation. The embarrassment Steele must have felt being overshadowed in importance by a nobody with no real dirt!
    c. To add insult to injury, even his sponsors, the DNC and the Clinton campaign must have known that the report was garbage because they didn't give a darn about its national security implications and stopped funding Steele. The American people give the DNC enough credit for knowing it was garbage rather than accepting the alternative that they didn't give a s___ about national security. All this "dirt" on Trump and nobody cared. How embarrassing!___

Chapter 6: Questions the American People Want Answers To

The American people have paid for the Crossfire Hurricane investigation into Trump-Russia collusion, the Mueller investigation into Trump Russian collusion and obstruction of justice against Trump , the Horowitz investigation into the integrity of the investigation and investigators, the Durham investigation into the motivation of the investigators and the John Bash investigation into the huge unmasking activity in the Michael Flynn case.

To date, some of the information has been withheld from those of us who paid for it. Withholding of information has been justified on the basis of national security, on-going investigations, and revealing "sources and methods."

Some of this information has been unredacted or new reports made available so that it has become available to those of us who paid for it. That's good. What we have learned from the dribs and drabs of releases was that none of the new information ever had any basis for being withheld, it had little to do with on-going investigation, the "sources" had no basis for being withheld and the "methods" revealed were sophomoric at best.

What was apparent was that the recently revealed information was universally embarrassing to the FBI and the DOJ. That is most likely the reason it was redacted. The average American would like to read a report itemizing all redactions that have since been unredacted and the reasons for releasing the restrictions on the sharing of the redacted information We would also like to hear a defense of any revelation of "secret methods" that have been disclosed by the up-to-now protected information.

We, the American people want and deserve answers to the following questions:

1. Question about the original origin of suspicions of Trump-Russia collusion.
    a. What was the "troubling intelligence" that Robert Hannigan, then head of the UK's GCHQ, had in his possession that could only be shared directly in person with John Brennan in June of 2016? Was

this information given to him by Christopher Steele? Was it intercepted communications? What was it? Is the threat of what was intercepted something we should still be concerned about? If not, what the hell was that "troubling intelligence?" Nothing "troubling" has surfaced out of all the investigations so wouldn't one be still concerned about what was about to happen to the US because of Trump's misdeeds that Robert Hannigan could only share with one person in the US, John Brennan?

    b. Why did Hannigan need to share it with John Brennan and not Mike Rogers, his direct intelligence counterpart at the NSA? Okay, it was "supersensitive" but why did Hannigan choose an unconventional path to convey it?

2. Questions about Mifsud evidence planting track, Track I.

    a. Who was Joseph Mifsud? Who was Mifsud working for?

    b. What was Nagi Idris Director of LCILP, (Papadopoulos' employer)'s reason for arranging a meeting between Joseph Mifsud and George Papadopoulos? According to the reports Idris did it because he felt Mifsud could be "valuable" to Papadopoulos. Really? Idris, director of LCILP, would buy plane tickets and incur travel costs for three people in Rome to help a guy who was about to leave his job with LCILP just because he thought "Mifsud could be a valuable contact for Papadopoulos as a Trump campaign advisor? Did the FBI accept this as rational? Why? If Durham determines that Mifsud was working for the CIA or Western Intelligence, this IS the smoking gun! It is proof of entrapment by the CIA to ensure a Clinton victory.

    c. Why did Papadopoulos continue to draw a salary from LCILP for over a month when he wasn't doing any work for them, but instead serving as a member of Trump's advisory team and mostly meeting with Mifsud?

    d. Was Joseph Mifsud working for the CIA? Was he being paid to create evidence of collusion? (That is what he did, even if that wasn't his intent.) Who was paying him?

e. If Mifsud was trying to facilitate a Putin-Trump meeting, why didn't he take an active role in doing so instead of merely giving Papadopoulos names of people to contact? That seems like an obvious attempt to create a documentation trail implicating Papadopoulos of attempted collusion.

f. Did Brennan know Mifsud? Was Brennan part of the selection of Mifsud to plant evidence of collusion in the Trump campaign?

g. Was Alexander Downer selected by the CIA and/or British Intelligence to serve as an alternate path to Papadopoulos to plant the rumor of Russian possession of Clinton emails and dirt to the FBI and credit that rumor to Papadopoulos? (That is the role he played, knowingly or unknowingly. Papadopoulos failed to plant that evidence in the Trump campaign because to him it wasn't that important compared to arranging a Trump-Putin meeting.)

h. Was it actually Erika Thompson who was the Representative of a Friendly Foreign Government that Papadopoulos told of the Clinton email rumor? (Based on the date of the passing of that information in the Mueller report that is the only possibility. That was May 6, Downer and Papadopoulos met on May 10.)

i. Were Terrance Dudley and Gregory Baker actually tasked to check out Papadopoulos in preparation for George's meeting with Downer? Were they reporting to the CIA? The timing suggests that.

j. Why did Comey think Mifsud was a "Russian Agent?" Did someone from the CIA tell him that?

k. Why did it take the actual release of the Wikileaks emails to get the Australians to release the Clinton email rumors to "the US government?" Who in the US Government were they released to?

3. Questions about the Steele evidence planting track, Track 2.

a. Steele planted reports 80, 86 and 94 inside the FBI all prior to July 31, the opening date of Crossfire Hurricane. His reason for planting his evidence inside the FBI was that "it had such importance that it was a matter of National security. If he judged it to be so, why did the FBI totally ignore it when opening the investigation and instead used the Papadopoulos rumor of a rumor of Clinton emails to open the investigation? Either the FBI was ignorant of the significance to National security or they knew it was garbage from the get-go.

b. Why didn't the DNC or the Clinton campaign see the threat to national security uncovered by their investigator when they elected to cut off funding to Fusion GPS? Were they only interested in winning the election? Was national security not important to the democrats?

c. If Steele's role was to dig up dirt on Trump from Russian sources, why did he submit report 112 which was written by the lawyers for the DNC and Clinton campaign who were paying him? Was he merely being **paid to plant evidence of collusion** inside the FBI and not necessarily to discover it? That would explain why he needed a backup stooge to plant it, Bruce Ohr and a backup-to the backup, John McCain to deliver it directly to Jim Comey.

Appendix A Evidence Brennan Hated Trump

Motive is defined as *"a belief or emotion that impels a person to act in accordance with his state of mind."*

John Brennan had a strong emotion that impelled him to prevent Donald Trump from taking the office of the President of the United States, and if that failed to provide sufficient justification to have him removed from office through impeachment. That motive was intense hatred. John Brennan hated Donald Trump.

That hatred was so strong it led (i.e. "impelled") Brennan to participate in the planting of evidence of Trump-Russia collusion in the Trump campaign, encouraging the FBI to investigate it, and then leaking the evidence before it was properly vetted.

Timeline of Brennan statements providing evidence of Brennan's intense hatred of Donald Trump

December 1, 2016 – (Interview on BBC) John Brennan calls Trump's proposal to scrap the Iran deal *"disastrous,"*

May 23, 2017   (House Intelligence Committee Testimony) *"I encountered and am aware of information and intelligence that revealed contacts and interactions between Russian officials and U.S. persons involved in the Trump campaign that I was concerned about because of known Russian efforts to suborn such individuals,"* he told lawmakers. *"And it raised questions in my mind again whether or not the Russians were able to gain the cooperation of those individuals."*

July 23, 2018 – After Trump's press conference after his mini-summit with Vladimir Putin. Brennan called Trump's remarks *"nothing short of treasonous"* and said they exceeded *"the threshold of 'high crimes & misdemeanors.' "*

August 14, 2018 (Tweet to Trump) *"It's astounding how often you fail to live up to minimum standards of decency, civility, & probity. 'Seems like you will never understand what it means to be president, nor what it takes to be a good, decent, & honest person. – 'So disheartening, so dangerous for our Nation"*

August 16, 2018 "*Mr. Trump's claims of no collusion are, in a word, hogwash,*" Brennan wrote in a New York Times op-ed published the day after the White House announced revocation of his security clearance. (Turns out it wasn't hogwash as he admitted in the next item. It turns out it was Brennan who admittedly relied on "bad information.")

March 25, 2019 (Interview on MSNBC) Former head of the CIA John Brennan admitted on Monday that he may have relied on "bad information" for his relentless attacks on President Trump. Brennan who once warned that "*our Nation's future is at stake*" told MSNBC's "Morning Joe" that he may have been misled on the extent of connections to Russia.
"Well, I don't know if I received bad information, but I think I suspected there was more than there actually was," Brennan said. *"I am relieved that it's been determined there was not a criminal conspiracy with the Russian government over our election."*

April 26, 2019 (Interview on CNN) Commenting on Trumps assertion of an attempted 'coup' by the CIA to overthrow Trump: "*I don't think it's surprising at all that we hear these sociopathic ramblings from Mr. Trump claiming there was this effort to try to prevent him from being elected or to try to unseat him.*"

August 20, 2019 (MSN News), "Former CIA Director John Brennan warned President Trump that *the "protective cocoon" protecting him is "only temporary*" in an ominous tweet defending James Comey. (This is clearly a "warning" from an ex-member of "the deep state" – we will get you!)

September 28, 2019 (MSNBC INTERVIEW WITH Chris Hayes) Brennan, in an interview with MSNBC's Chris Hayes, said that he's been "very concerned" about Trump's behavior since "the very first day of Mr. Trump's presidency" but that the recent whistleblower complaint detailing Trump's request that Zelensky dig up information on former Vice President Joe Biden and his son Hunter go beyond the pale.

October 6, 2019 (Interview on CNN) "*I feel an obligation, as a former senior U.S. official, to call out Mr. Trump, when he lies to the American public, when he totally fabricates information just to advance his own political agenda. I am going to continue doing it."*

October 9, 2019 (Interview on NBC) *"I think it's no longer a democracy if an autocrat has it in his hands,"*

January 15, 2020 (MSNBC Hardball interview) *"Donald Trump is the most ignorant as well as incompetent individual who has ever held the office of the presidency. I worked for 6 presidents."*

February 21, 2020 (Interview on MSNBC) Former CIA Director John Brennan called the president's recent moves a *"virtual decapitation"* after the firings of the Director of National Intelligence and his deputy.

March 9, 2020 (Interview on CNN) He (BRENNAN) wondered whether President Trump was *"psychologically capable"* of putting *"the country's well-being first. ... we want to make sure there is truth and honesty coming out from our public officials. Certainly, from the White House and from someone who purports to be president of the United States."*

April 4, 2020 (Brenan Tweet) *One more example of Trump removing those who seek to stop his lawlessness.* (What is "lawless" about firing a disloyal employee?) *All Americans fed up with Trump's incompetence, venality, & narcissism have the opportunity to "fire" him in November—the most important election of our lifetime.* (On the firing of Michael Atkinson)

Appendix B Mifsud Ties to Western Intelligence

Joseph Mifsud had many ties with important people in the western intelligence community. It is hard to imagine that they all associated with a known (by James Comey) Russian agent. Here are some of Joseph's western intelligence friends and coworkers:

- **Claire Smith**, a career UK diplomat and former member of the UK Joint Intelligence Committee which oversees the UK's spying agencies. She completed an eight-year term as a member of the UK Security Vetting and Appeals Panel. (*Ms. Smith would not likely work closely with a known Russian Agent. As someone responsible for "vetting" security risks, she would likely know if Mifsud was a Russian Agent*)

  - o In October 2012 Ms. Smith taught a training program at Link Campus in Rome, organized by the London Academy of Diplomacy (LAD). *Tie to Mifsud*: Mifsud was Director of International Strategic Development at LAD and Director of International Relations at Link Campus University at the time.[68]
  - o In 2014, Ms. Smith was listed as a Visiting Professor at LAD in the School's brochure. *Tie to Mifsud*: Mifsud was listed in the Brochure as Director of LAD. (He actually was an "Honorary" Director of LAD.
  - o On November 29, 2017 Ms. Smith served as Guest Lecturer at University of Stirling. Her topic was, "Making Sense of Intelligence." .[69] *Tie to Mifsud*: In March of 2017, Mifsud was installed as a full-time "Professorial Teaching Fellow" at Stirling.[70] He was also listed as a Visiting Professor at Link Campus. (*This is AFTER all of Mifsud's meetings with Papadopoulos!*)

---

[68] Global Economic Forum Program, Sponsored by LAD & IBDE (International Business & Diplomatic Exchange), April 3, 2013

[69] Stir.ac.uk, University of Stirling Calendar of Events, "*Making Sense of Intelligence*" November 29, 2017

[70] The Columbian, "*London professor' in Trump case made many Russia trips*" Gregory Katz & Nataliya Vasilyeva (Associated Press) November 2, 2017.

- **Arvinder Sambei**, a UK prosecutor who worked on extradition cases with the FBI as well as counterterrorism, transnational crime, and war crimes cases with the US. Arvinder Sambei was also the former FBI British counsel working 9/11 cases for Robert Mueller when he was FBI director. (A simple call to Ms. Sambei from Robert Mueller to his old friend could have  established who Mifsud was working for!) Ms. Sambei is also connected to Australian intelligence. She was a consultant for the Global Center on Cooperative Security (GCCS), a counter-terrorism think tank which is sponsored by the Australia, Canada, UK and US governments. Alexander Downer's former Chief of Staff while at the Australian Department of Foreign Affairs and Trade now works for the Global Center. Mifsud was also due to meet with Australian private intelligence figures in Adelaide in March 2016.

  - On November 25, 2014, Ms. Sambei participated in a LAD, LCILP co-sponsored conference on "Counter-Terrorism: International Initiatives, Perspectives and Challenges". *Tie to Mifsud*: Joseph Mifsud participated in the same conference.[71]

  - Arvinder joined the London Center for International Law Practice (LCILP) in March 2015 as the Head of International Human Rights and Criminal Justice. *Tie to Mifsud*: Mifsud joined LCILP as "Board Advisor" in November of 2015. They knew each other at LCILP.[72]

- **Robert Whalley**, former director for counterterrorism and intelligence at the UK prime minister's department and the domestic security and immigration ministry. Robert was listed as "professional/guest speaker and International Security" at the London Academy of Diplomacy (LAD) 2011–2012 brochure.[73] *Tie to Mifsud*: Mifsud was the Honorary Director of LAD from 2010 to 2014.

---

[71] The Epoch Times, *"Mueller Overlooked Mifsud's Contacts in Western Counterterror Circles"*, *Peter Svab*, August 28, 2019. Updated: September 11, 2019

[72] Medium.com, *"The Trump-Russia affair and an odd company in London"*, Brian Whitaker, November 6, 2017

[73] The Epoch Times, *"Mueller Overlooked Mifsud's Contacts in Western Counterterror Circles"*, *Peter Svab*, August 28, 2019 Updated: September 11, 2019

- **Charles Crawford**, former British diplomat. *Tie to Mifsud*: Visiting Professor at LAD in 2015. Led a Workshop on, "Diplomatic Workshop for Junior Diplomats: 'Dealing with the Media'" on Saturday, May 16, 2015. Although Mifsud supposedly left LAD in 2014, he was listed on the program as, Director, LAD in 2015 when Charles Crawford spoke at the affair. Mifsud gave the keynote on *"Diplomatic Training and Education: Developments and Innovations"*
- **Ashton Carter**, 25th U.S. Secretary of Defense from February 2015 to January 2017 *Tie to Mifsud*: Both spoke at The Nature of Extremism and the Future of Terrorism conference in Riyadh, Saudi Arabia May 21, 2017[74]
- **Richard Barrett**, Former Head of Global Counter Terrorism Operations MI6, *Tie to Mifsud*: Both spoke at The Nature of Extremism and the Future of Terrorism conference in Riyadh, Saudi Arabia May 21, 2017[75]
- **Michael Hurley,** Career CIA officer, he led CIA personnel on the ground in Afghanistan immediately after the 9/11 attacks. He was also Senior Counsel and Team Leader on the 9/11 Commission; a co- author of The 9/11 Commission Report. *Tie to Mifsud:* Both spoke at The Nature of Extremism and the Future of Terrorism conference in Riyadh, Saudi Arabia May 21, 2017[76]

---

[74] Conference Brochure, May 21, 2017
[75] Conference Brochure, May 21, 2017
[76] Conference Brochure, May 21, 2017

Appendix C Joseph Mifsud?

The real Joseph Mifsud (1960 – 1995)

The real Joseph Mifsud is a wannabe important person. He uses his educational credentials as his entry to getting jobs, lecture assignments, and rubbing elbows with important people. He is totally capable of offering himself up as an inept spy for Russian or Western intelligence if it would further his ambition of being important and rubbing elbows with important people. To an average person he is a despicable, over-educated phony. Figure C1 tracks the 13-year evolution from being real to being mysterious. If one examines his connections with Russian intelligence vs Western intelligence it is more likely he is connected to Western intelligence.

Joseph Mifsud at Organization of American States in Washington November 12, 2014

The real Joseph Mifsud was born in 1960 in Malta. He received his BA in Education from the University of Malta in 1982. From 1982 to 1989 he bounced around the academic community, ending up with a PhD from Queens University of Belfast in 1995 at the age of 35.

Facts:

    Born in Malta in 1960
    Education:
    University of Malta 1982 (BA in Education)
    University of Padua, Italy 1989 (MA)
    Queens university of Belfast 1995 (PhD) (Age35)

Although one wonders why it took seven years to get a master's degree and another six years to get a PhD, the end of his pursuit of a formal education in 1995 is also the end of knowing who the "real" Joseph Mifsud is.

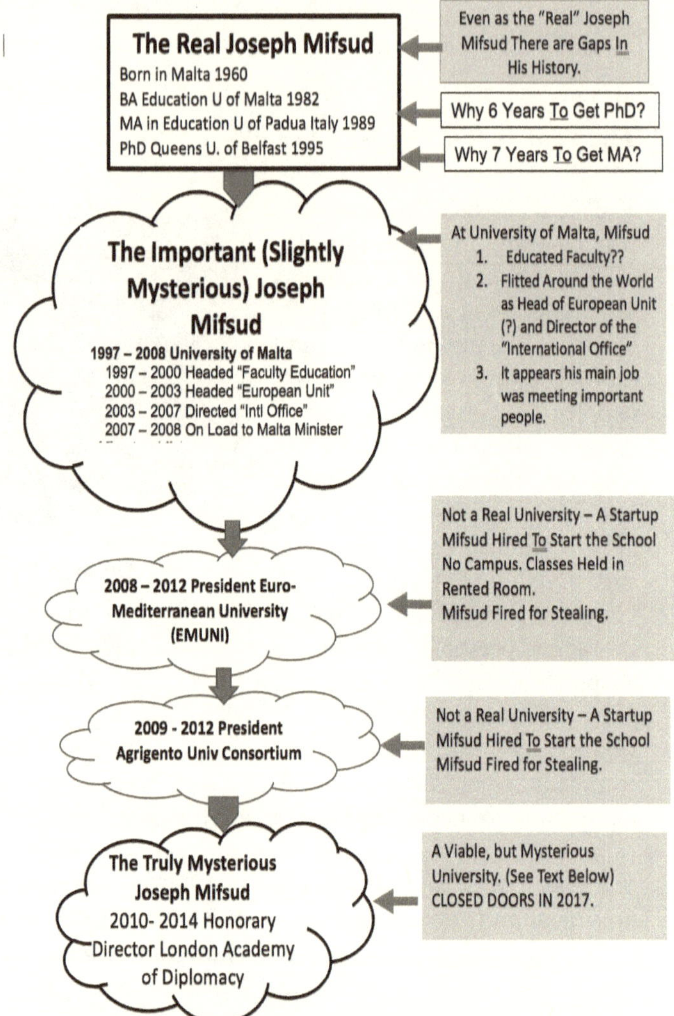

FIGURE C1 - BY 2012 MIFSUD HAD BECOME "MYSTERIOUS".

Transformation of Joseph Mifsud to the not-so real, "Mysterious Maltese Professor. (1995 – 2012)

1995–1997 – No Record of Joseph - Joseph Mifsud began his transformation to the "mysterious Maltese professor ", almost immediately after getting his PhD from the Queens University of Belfast in 1995. Where did Joseph Mifsud go for two years after getting his PhD? There appears to be no record of that.

1997–2007 – Back to Alma Mater, University of Malta - In 1997 Mifsud returned to his alma mater, the University of Malta. For the next eleven years he held different positions as somewhat of an educator. Although he titled himself as Head of Departments and General Manager, the university lists him as a "Senior Lecturer" when he left in 2007. He claims he served for three years as *Head of Department in "Faculty Education"* (he educated faculty?) and then in 2000 became *General Manager of Malta's European "Unit(?)* where his main job seemed to be schmoozing with "important people."

He continued with the University of Malta for the next six years as *"Director, International Office and Professor of International Relations"*[77] ?? where he bounced around Europe, the Mediterranean, the USA and Russia doing something important, no doubt.[78] In this role he had the opportunity to meet and rub elbows with important people from many countries. He obviously liked that and the political aspects of his role because he became a prominent figure in Malta's Accession Process to the European Union. In 2006 he was named *"Chef de cabinet of the Ministry of Foreign Affairs of Malta"*, on loan from the University of Malta, a position he held for a year.

When he left in 2007, he was listed by the University as "Senior Lecturer." Exactly what he did for the next year is unknown.

---

[77] The University of Malta disputes the title Mifsud gave himself. The University says "Dr. Mifsud was a Senior Lecturer when he resigned in December of 2007.

[78] In this role, he taught and researched extensively in Europe, the Mediterranean and in the USA and Russia. He was the Malta representative on the Board of the Bologna Follow up Group, on the Erasmus Mundus Committee and on the Tempus Committee. He also represented Malta on the Socrates Committee, on the Socrates Sub-Committee for Higher Education and on the Joint Research Centre (European Commission). He was also the Programme Committee Member for the 6th Framework Programme on Research & Infrastructure and Mobility. He was the University's representative on the Executive Board of the Compostela Group of Universities, Utrecht Network and Santander Group.

2008–2012 President of EMUNI

- In December 2008 he was unanimously elected as the President of Euro-Mediterranean University (EMUNI) in Slovenia. At the time, EMUNI was just getting started and had no students. It wasn't a university, but it wanted to be one and Joseph was thought to be the guy to make it happen. In a statement issued by the university: "The relationship and contact between the University and Mr. Mifsud has been completely severed since he resigned from his post as President of the University in July 2012.[79]

This didn't turn out well for Mifsud or EMUNI. EMUNI filed a lawsuit against him for misuse of funds (39,000 Euros). One of his few students, Leida Ruvina from Albania accused him and his program as being a fraud.[80] Although Mifsud was supposedly the President of EMUNI through 2012 it is really hard to tell. EMUNI declined to say whether their case had ever been sorted out.[81]

2009–2012 President of Consorzio Universitario di Agrigento -Almost totally overlapping his tenure as President of EMUNI apparently he also served as President of the Consortium of Agrigento from April 29, 2009 to 2012. Like EMUNI, Consortium of Agrigento didn't work out well either. The Consortium has filed a similar lawsuit for misuse of funds (49,000 Euros).

2009–2014 "Honorary Director" London Academy of Diplomacy. Also overlapping with serving as both the EMUNI and University Consortium of Agrigento was his appointment as Honorary Director of

---

[79] BuzzFeed, *"These Are The Contradictions Surrounding The Professor At The Center Of The Trump-Russia Probe"* November 4, 2017

[80] Associated Press, *"Malta academic in Trump probe has history of vanishing acts"* Raphael Satter, October 22, 2018. "it was her last day of class and Leida Ruvina was getting suspicious. The Albanian student had just finished the first module in what was purported to be a doctoral program co-administered by Slovenia's Euro-Mediterranean University, but the place didn't look like much of a university. It didn't have a campus; the room she was sitting in had been rented from a local tourism school in the Slovenian spa town of Portoroz. She didn't have a matriculation number, the code used by educational institutions to track students' progress. And the French translation of "Euro-Mediterranean" in the university's seal was misspelled. She raised her hand to ask Joseph Mifsud, the university's president what was going on. Mifsud assured Ruvina that everything was in order, complimented her on her English and offered to advise her on her dissertation. The Ph.D. program was bogus and Mifsud would soon be ousted in a scandal."

[81] BuzzFeed, Op. Cit.

the London Academy of Diplomacy.[82]   Whereas, EMUNI and the Consortium of Agrigento were "raw" start-ups with no students when Joseph Mifsud was named "President", the London Academy of Diplomacy was up and running. Professor Nabil Ayad, founder and Rector asked Mifsud to serve as Honorary Director. He did so until 2014 when the association between the University of East Anglia and the Corporate entity, INTO (cofounder of LAD), disassociated and INTO replaced University of East Anglia with a new association in 2014. This time with Stirling University.

In 2010 Mifsud was named Director of the London Academy of Diplomacy, a small graduate school catering to embassy officials living in the U.K. According to the Guardian[83], the London Academy resembled "just the type of front organization an espionage agency would establish." And when the academy shut down after the Russia scandal erupted in the United States, it was as if it were an intelligence asset whose cover had been blown."

By 2012 The Transformation of Joseph Mifsud to the "Mysterious Maltese Professor" was complete.

As shown in figure C-1, By 2012, Mifsud was certifiably mysterious as well as of questionable character. It was confirmed by the universities themselves that Mifsud simultaneously served as their president while he was the director of a third;

1. *EMUNI* says he served as President from December 2008 and resigned in July 2012.[84]
2. *University Consortium of Agrigento* says he served as President from 2009 to 2012.[85]
3. *London Academy of Diplomacy* says he was named "Honorary Director" in 2010.[86] (Mifsud was still Honorary Director when the London Academy of Diplomacy (LAD) affiliation with East Anglia University changed its affiliation to Scotland's University of Stirling in 2014.)

---

[82] See Appendix E4 for a description, history and significance of LAD.

[83] The Guardian, "Why has Britain given such a warm welcome to this shadowy professor?" Nick Cohen

[84] BuzzFeed, *"These Are Contradictions Surrounding The Professor At The Center Of The Trump-Russia Probe"*, November 4, 2017

[85] SicilyLab, *"University of Agrigento, Procura surveys on Mifsud's "crazy expenses""*, December 5, 2019

[86] BuzzFeed, OpCit.

So, according to the Universities themselves, Mifsud was simultaneously the president of two fledging universities and honorary director of a third. When Mifsud's tenure with the two universities ended in 2012, they both filed lawsuits against him for stealing funds. How can he do this?

With EMUNI, Slovenia wanted to have a legitimate University in 2008 and they thought Joseph Mifsud could make it happen. It turns out he couldn't, but the University has survived Mifsud's tenure and is still functioning successfully.

The University Consortium of Agrigento doesn't appear to have been as lucky. It didn't survive Mifsud. No trace of its existence can be found.

The London Academy of Diplomacy (LAD) folded in 2016. Mifsud was a minor player at LAD but its whole existence has its own intrigue as described in *Appendix E4, London Academy of Diplomacy.* Suffice it to say that INTO University Partnerships was the force behind its formation and fostered an "association" with University of East Anglia to start the Academy. East Anglia provided accreditation and teachers and granted degrees. INTO provided the marketing and recruitment of students and managed the business.

- INTO's association with East Anglia University lasted until July of 2014 when Scotland's University of Stirling took its place. When Stirling University closed the doors at LAD in the spring of 2016, Mifsud was appointed a part-time teaching professor at the University of Stirling, the degree-granting arm of LAD. In March 2017, Mifsud was installed as a full-time "Professional Teaching Fellow" at Stirling.
- After being hired full time, Mifsud did not make any appearance on the Stirling campus. He is not named on the university's list of experts and the university press office refused to say how often he is on campus, where a reporter on the student newspaper said *he does not maintain an office.*[87]
- "There is no evidence Professor Mifsud has even been to the university since joining the staff in May," said Craig Munro, a reporter at the campus newspaper, Brignews.[88]

---

[87] Brig Newspaper, "*Questions remain over Stirling's role in Diplomatic Academy run by Russia-probe professor.*" Warren Hardy, December 3, 2017

[88] Brig Newspaper, "*Trump-Russia academic resigns from Stirling University*" Craig Munro, November 30, 2017

- "He doesn't have an office here and is based in London. We haven't been able to find a single student who has met with Professor Mifsud or attended any lectures by him at Stirling."[89]
- He resigned his position on November 23, 2017.[90] He disappeared a year later on November 6, 2018.

Mr. Mifsud was granted 37,000 shares in INTO University Partnerships in 2014 when INTO shifted its "association" in the London Academy of Diplomacy from East Anglia to Stirling University.[91]

From 2012 until his disappearance on November 6, 2018 Joseph Mifsud's lived an even more mysterious life.

When Joseph Mifsud first became "affiliated" with the London Academy of Diplomacy in 2008, he was brought on board as "Honorary Director of LAD." That does not sound like a real job. Obviously, Mifsud felt the same way, so when LAD cosponsored the *Global Economic Forum* with the International Business & Diplomatic Exchange (IBDE) at the Link Campus University in Rome, his job magically became "Director of International Strategic Development of the London Academy of Diplomacy." Additionally, Mifsud identified himself as "Director of International Relations at the Link Campus University in Rome."

The Global Economic Forum Program
Sponsored by London Academy of Diplomacy and The International Business & Diplomatic Exchange
April 3, 2013

Professor Joseph Mifsud, Director of International Strategic Development, London Academy of Diplomacy, UEA Professor Mifsud is currently the Director of International Strategic Development of the London Academy of Diplomacy, University of East Anglia London Campus and the Director of International Relations at the Link Campus University in Rome. He has worked as an academic and as Director of the International Office at the University of Malta, and as Chef de Cabinet at the Ministry of Foreign Affairs for Malta. He has advised Governments on international education issues in many countries including Morocco, Syria, Russia. He is fluent in Maltese, French, Italian, Arabic, and English.[92]

---

[89] Ibid.

[90] Ibid.

[91] Ibid.

[92] Global Economic Forum Program, Sponsored by LAD & IBDE (International Business & Diplomatic Exchange), April 3, 2013

With Mifsud being such a key person in the Trump-Russia Collusion investigation it would seem relevant to know who was paying him during these years and for what?

Mifsud didn't seem to have a real job since 2012. As a professor, he had no students nor any record of publishing. He didn't have any known administrative responsibilities. In short, he didn't have a job. Mifsud didn't have any jobs with Russian Universities either. Instead, he had some "affiliations."

Persons involved in UK education also never heard of Joseph Mifsud. Prominent British academics say they have had little or no contact with Mifsud. I've never heard of him," said Robin Niblett, the veteran director of Chatham House, the prominent London think tank. Nor has Mr. Niblett heard of the now-defunct London Academy of Diplomacy, where Mr. Mifsud is said to have served as "honorary director" before it closed according to his biography. "He seems to be a classic case of someone floating around on the fringes of the academic world and the think-tanky world without landing anywhere," Mr. Niblett said. It would strike me that most of these positions are not paid, which raises questions."[93]

Friends, Coworkers, Bosses and Students Impressions of Mifsud

Very few people around Joseph Mifsud held him in high regard. His boss at Link Campus called him a loud-mouth know-nothing. His students called him a fraud. Two of his employers called him a "charlatan." Here are some specific assessments of Professor Mifsud.

Mr. Vincenzo Scotti, (Link Campus President) said, "Mr. Mifsud was a loudmouth know-nothing." [94] (This is from Mifsud's boss!) But despite this apparent distain for Joseph Mifsud;

- It was Scotti who was present when Mifsud sat at the table and was introduced to George Papadopoulos on March 14, 2016. It was also Scotti who then suggested to Mifsud that he should connect Papadopoulos with Mifsud's Russian contacts, according to Mifsud's lawyer, Stefan Roh.[95]

---

[93] Houzz Nov 2, 2017 *"WHO???? London Academy of Diplomacy, WHERE??"*

[94] New York Times, *"Rome University at Heart of Trump Inquiry Becomes a Vortex of Intrigue"* Jason Horowitz, October 15, 2019

[95] The Epoch Times, *"Mueller Overlooked Italian Ex-Minister Tied to Joseph Mifsud", Petr Svab, August 22, 2019,* ______

- Scotti is in a business relationship with Mifsud. "Link International" is owned 55% by Scotti's Link Campus, 35% by Joseph and 10% by Roberto Lippi, a Brazilian.[96] "Link International's" sole business purpose is to search for and recruit international students for Link Campus University. It is interesting that Link International has a reported payroll of 32 employees[97] but was only successful in recruiting 30 international students. (One could observe that productivity is low at Link International.) It is interesting that a woman named Vanna Fadini serves as President of GEM, the parent of Link Campus and Administrator of Link International, the subsidiary of Link Campus. Link International furnished Mifsud housing when he first went "underground" as a result of his name being linked to the Trump-Russia collusion fiasco. Link International has never filed a financial statement.
- Scotti is in a business relationship with Mifsud's lawyer, Stefan Roh. Mr. Roh owns 5% of Global Education Management (GEM), which in turn owns 100% of Link Campus University.[98] See Figure C2 for a picture of these convoluted relationships.

Pasquale Russo, (Link Campus director-general) refers to Mifsud as "Jo" and recalls him as extremely well-connected, fun, and a bon-viveur fond of restaurant dinners.

"This speculation that Jo was a spy for the Americans or the Russians, it's rubbish," Russo said at the university's elegant cafe, decorated with contemporary art. *"Jo was much too open and chatty to be a spy. I know – spies come to teach here. They're very discreet."* Staff said they are skeptical about the claim concerning Clinton's emails. *They say Mifsud sometimes stretched the truth, claiming to know people he didn't, or making promises he failed to fulfill when he worked there as an adviser on helping to attract foreign students.*[99]

Mr. Eugenio D'Orsi, President of Agrigento, Sicily from 2008 until 2013. (Mifsud was named president of the Agrigento university consortium in 2010 by D'Orsi, who later became disenchanted with

---

[96] PJ Media, *"Report: Mysterious Maltese Professor Mifsud Hid Out for Months in Rome, Helped by Shady University"*, Debra Heine, April 29, 2019

[97] Ibid.

[98] Ibid.

[99] Bloomberg, John Follain, Oct 4, 2019

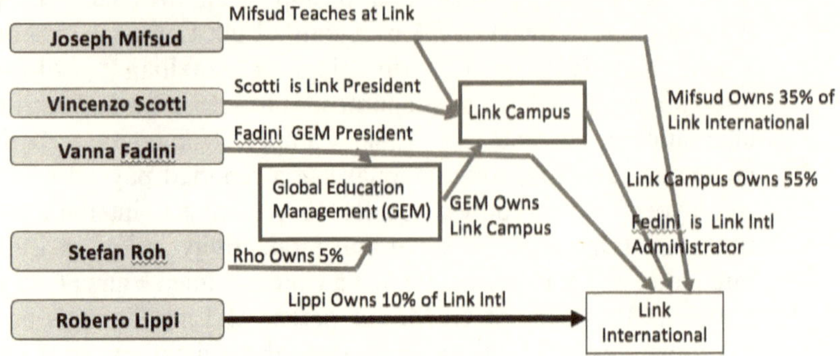

Figure C2 The Link Campus Mystery: No Russians Involved

Mifsud). According to D'Orsi, in December 2019[100], *"He was a brilliant person, with unlimited knowledge and we wanted to bring Sicily to the world. "The lecturer (Mifsud) put me in touch with Malta, and we were about to build the airport thanks to that. That was the best side of him"*.

Then, according to D'Orsi, something changed: *"In the second part of the experience with him he was, and I will say this bluntly, a charlatan"*. The same former President then confirmed that the decision to select Mifsud was at the time backed by all the shareholders of the consortium, in other words also by the city council of Agrigento, the Chamber of Commerce and the University di Palermo. But today, as mentioned above, there is a race to dump the Maltese professor first. The city council of Agrigento has, through the current mayor, Lillo Firetto, in the last few days announced that the body has entered a civil claim in the proceeding brought by the Public Prosecution Office of Agrigento in relation to the "crazy expenses" incurred by Mifsud during his presidency.

---

[100] Insider Dec 19, 2019, *"80% Sure That Mifsud is dead."* By Mauro Indelicato and Robert Vivaldelli.

Mr. Douglas Brodie, Dean of the University of Stirling (Scotland) Douglas Brodie, ex dean at the University of Stirling in Scotland, said, *"He (Mifsud) was incredibly well-connected with various people in embassies and that world in London. Mifsud appeared to be a genuine academic – though one with little interest in the administrative details of the school. He was far more interested in trying to bring in highflying guest speakers and much more interested in working the embassy drink circuit than the nuts and bolts stuff."*

Mr. Gianni Pittella, an Italian Senator (Ex. European Parliament's Socialists & Democrats group.

"Joseph is my dear friend," Pittella told the Italian press in November after news of Mifsud's alleged involvement in the Russiagate scandal spread. Pittella was a visiting lecturer when Mifsud was director of the London Academy of Diplomacy and is on the Link Campus Foundation's board.[101]

Matthew Caruana Galizia, a Mifsud student; the son of slain investigative journalist Daphne Caruana Galizia, was one of 15 participants at a 2006 university summer class taught in part by Mifsud. He said the academic floundered through his lecture and had "no idea what he was talking about."
"He spent the whole time trying to impress us and was coming off as a complete charlatan," Caruana Galizia said.

Joseph Grech, One of Mifsud's former deputies said Mifsud was a name-dropping networker focused on jockeying for funding and taking work trips abroad.
"He was hooked on travel," Grech said, who described working for Mifsud as the most stressful experience of his life. Grech called his ex-boss a *"hawwadi,"* a Maltese word roughly meaning "intriguer."

Leida Ruvina SWIEQI, Malta (AP) — It was her last day of class and Leida Ruvina was getting suspicious.The Albanian student had just finished the first module in what was purported to be a doctoral program co-administered by Slovenia's Euro-Mediterranean University, but the place didn't look like much of a university.

"It didn't have a campus; the room she was sitting in had been rented from a local tourism school in the Slovenian spa town of

---

[101] Real Clear Investigations. *"The Maltese Phantom of Russiagate"* May 30, 2018

Portoroz." She didn't have a matriculation number, the code used by educational institutions to track students' progress. And the French translation of "Euro-Mediterranean" in the university's seal was misspelled.

She raised her hand to ask the university's president what was going on. Joseph Mifsud, a paunchy middle-aged administrator with an easy manner and a graying widow's peak, assured Ruvina that everything was in order, complimented her on her English and offered to advise her on her dissertation.

"If you want, I can be your mentor," she recalled him telling her.

Mifsud, however, was in no position to be anyone's mentor. The Ph.D. program was bogus and Mifsud would soon be ousted in a scandal.

Russian Connections

The whole premise for Papadopoulos being investigated was his spontaneous association with Joseph Mifsud in March of 2016. Instead of investigating who Mifsud really was and who he may be working for, the FBI assumed he was a Russian agent and went about the task gathering evidence that he was. The FBI researched every possible tie with Russians and Russian intelligence. After what appeared to be a half-hearted attempt, the FBI demoted Mifsud from being a Russian Agent to being "a mysterious Maltese professor". In no case did Mueller or Horowitz allege that he did anything other than (1) teach with Russians, (2) attend the same functions as Russians, or (3) try to arrange a meeting with Russians. The FBI never found any damming emails, face book postings, covert meetings, wire taps or anything to hint Mifsud was a Russian agent. He didn't wear a trench coat or sunglasses.

The only Russian of consequence was Ivan Timofeev. Ivan was supposed to be able to assist Papadopoulos in setting up a Trump-Putin meeting. That meeting never happened and there is no evidence that Timofeev had the ability to make it happen. He was however instrumental in providing an email, skype and paper trail that could be used to support an investigation of George Papadopoulos and his supposed attempt to collude with the Russians. This apparently fake attempt to arrange a Trump-Putin meeting would have no apparent value to the Russian narrative, but it would help Brennan show that there was evidence of collusion. There is no other rational explanation for this fake attempt at setting up a Trump-Putin meeting.

Here's what was learned about Mifsud's Russian connections.

- Beginning in 2010 Mifsud started making numerous trips to Russia.
- He met with an unnamed former employee of Russia's Internet Research Agency,[102]
- He met with Russian Ambassador to the UK Alexander Yakovenko in May 2014,[103]
- He met with Ernest Chernukhin, embassy representative, July 2017,[104]
- He met with Alexey Klishin, department head and professor at Moscow State Institute of International Relations in early 2017.[105]
- He met with Yury Sayamov, a Russian professor, 2015.
- He met with Alexey Klishin who held a formal role as a professor and a department head at the Moscow State Institute of International Relations. He spoke at LAD at Mifsud's request January 2016. Aleksei Klishin, was a former Russian parliamentarian.
- Alex Klishin spoke at Rome's Link Campus University and Mifsud welcomed him December 2016. Mifsud welcomed a Kremlin-linked academic to speak at Rome's Link Campus University.
- Papadopoulos's court documents state that in April 2016, the professor introduced Papadopoulos via e-mail to an "individual in Moscow" identified as a "Russian national connected to the Russian Ministry of Foreign Affairs" and, alternately, as the "Russian MFA connection." While this individual's name is not provided, details of his interactions with Papadopoulos appear to indicate that the person is Ivan Timofeyev, director of programs at the Russian International Affairs Council (RIAC), a Russian government-backed think tank.
- Timofeyev is an associate professor at the Moscow State Institute for International Affairs (MGIMO), a well-known feeder school for the Russian foreign ministry and the

---

[102] Mueller Report, Op. Cit., page 91

[103] Mother Jones, *"Mystery Professor in Mueller Case Had Contacts with Russian Officials"*, Hannah Levintova and David Corn, October 30, 2017

[104] Ibid.

[105] Ibid.

Foreign Intelligence Service (SVR), where Timofeyev received his doctorate in 2006. Timofeyev is also program director for the Russian Council on International Affairs (RIAC), a thinktank whose board of trustees is headed by Russian Foreign Minister Sergei Lavrov.

- Unconvincingly, Lavrov denied in October 2017 that he was acquainted with Timofeyev after news broke of the FBI indictment of George Papadopoulos for lying under oath. Timofeev was discussed in the Papadopoulos' plea deal only as "a Russian national connected to the Russian Ministry of Foreign Affairs," but a ministry spokesperson said it learned this was Timofeev from its embassy in the Washington, and the Mueller Report cites his activities explicitly (his named transliterated as Timofeev). [106]

Here's what was learned about Mifsud's Russian connections from Mueller report directly:

- Mifsud maintained various Russian contacts while living in London, as described further below. Among his contacts was **IT** ,[415] a one-time employee of the IRA, the entity that carried out the Russian social media campaign (*see* Volume I, Section II, *supra*). In January and February 2016, Mifsud and **IT** discussed **IT** possibly meeting in Russia. The investigation did not identify evidence of them meeting. Later, in the spring of 2016, **IT** was also in contact **IT** that was linked to an employee of the Russian Ministry of Defense, and that account had overlapping contacts with a group of Russian military-controlled Facebook accounts that included accounts used to promote the DCLeaks releases in the course of the GRU's hack-and-release operations (*see* Volume I, Section III.B.1, *supra*). [107]

Western Intelligence Connections

The FBI only investigated Mifsud's connections with Russians. There is no evidence in the Mueller or Horowitz reports that there was any investigation of ties to western intelligence. This is an example where

---

[106] Daily Beast, *"Here's How Dumb Bill Barr's Great Mifsud Conspiracy Story Really Is",* Amy Knight, October 30, 2019"

[107] Mueller Report, Op. Cit. Page 83

bias of the FBI agents compromised the whole investigation. Jim Comey had declared Mifsud a Russian agent even before the FBI started their investigation. That assumption was driven by Director Comey's intense ego manifesting itself as "superior" knowledge. It affected the direction of the investigation. Had Mifsud's connections been investigated it might have been wrapped up in a week instead of 3 years! One particularly interesting tie is to John Brennan.

Here are just a few of the known connections of Joseph Mifsud's to western intelligence:

- **John Brennan** – Former Director of the CIA. *Tie to Mifsud* – This tie is through Nawaf Obaid, an ex Saudi intelligence analyst and Visiting Fellow for Intelligence and Defense Projects at Harvard Kennedy School's Belfer Center for Science and International Affairs. (Ashton Carter, ex Secretary of Defense also teaches there.) Mifsud introduced Obaid to Papadopoulos. Brennan and Obaid knew each other in Saudi Arabia when Brennan was Station Chief in Riyadh.[108]
- **Claire Smith** - a career UK diplomat and former member of the UK Joint Intelligence Committee which oversees the UK's spying agencies. She completed an eight-year term as a member of the UK Security Vetting and Appeals Panel.
  - In October 2012 Ms. Smith taught a training program at Link Campus in Rome, organized by the London Academy of Diplomacy (LAD). *Tie to Mifsud*: Mifsud was the Director of International Strategic Development at LAD and Director of International Relations at Link Campus University at the time.[109]
  - In 2014, Ms. Smith was listed as a Visiting Professor at LAD in the School's brochure. *Tie to Mifsud*: Mifsud was listed in the Brochure as Director of LAD. (He actually was an "Honorary" Director of LAD.)
  - On November 29, 2017 Ms. Smith served as Guest Lecturer at University of Stirling. Her topic was,

---

[108] *"The Looming Tower – Al-Qaeda and the road to 9/11"* Lawrence Wright Random House 2006 PP448.

[109] Global Economic Forum Program, Sponsored by LAD & IBDE (International Business & Diplomatic Exchange), April 3, 2013

"Making Sense of Intelligence." .[110] ***Tie to Mifsud***: In March of 2017, Mifsud was installed as a full-time "Professorial Teaching Fellow" at Stirling.[111]

- **Arvinder Sambei,** a UK prosecutor who worked on extradition cases with the FBI as well as counterterrorism, transnational crime, and war crimes cases with the US.
  - On November 25, 2014, Ms. Sambei participated in an LAD, LCILP so-sponsored conference on "Counter-Terrorism: International Initiatives, Perspectives and Challenges". ***Tie to Mifsud***: Joseph Mifsud participated in the same conference.[112]
  - Arvinder joined the London Center for International Law Practice (LCILP) in March 2015 as the Head of International Human Rights and Criminal Justice. ***Tie to Mifsud***: Mifsud joined LCILP as "Board Advisor" in November of 2015. They knew each other at LCILP.[113]
  -

- **Robert Whalley**, former director for counterterrorisim and intelligence at the UK prime minister's department and the domestic security and immigration ministry. Robert was listed as "professional/guest speaker and International Security" at the London Academy of Diplomacy (LAD) 2011–2012 brochure.[114] ***Tie to Mifsud***: Mifsud was the Honorary Director of LAD from 2010 to 2014.

- **Charles Crawford**, former British diplomat. Tie to Mifsud: Visiting Professor at LAD in 2015. 'Led a Workshop on, "Diplomatic Workshop for Junior Diplomats: 'Dealing with the Media'"on Saturday, May 16, 2015. ***Tie to Mifsud***: Although Mifsud supposedly left LAD in 2014, he was listed on the program as, Director, LAD in 2015 when Charles Crawford spoke at the affair. Mifsud gave the

---

[110] Stir.ac.uk, University of Stirling Calendar of Events, *"Making Sense of Intelligence"* November 29, 2017

[111] The Columbian, *"London professor' in Trump case made many Russia trips"* Gregory Katz & Nataliya Vasilyeva (Associated Press) November 2, 2017.

[112] The Epoch Times, *"Mueller Overlooked Mifsud's Contacts in Western Counterterror Circles"*, *Peter Svab*, August 28, 2019 Updated: September 11, 2019

[113] Medium.com, *"The Trump-Russia affair and an odd company in London"*, Brian Whitaker, November 6, 2017

[114] The Epoch Times, *"Mueller Overlooked Mifsud's Contacts in Western Counterterror Circles"*, *Peter Svab*, August 28, 2019 Updated: September 11, 2019

keynote on *"Diplomatic Training and Education: Developments and Innovations"*

- **Ashton Carter**, 25th U.S. Secretary of Defense from February 2015 to January 2017. *Tie to Mifsud:* Both spoke at The Nature of Extremism and the Future of Terrorism conference in Riyadh, Saudi Arabia May 21, 2017[115]
- Richard Barrett, Former Head of Global Counter Terrorism Operations MI6, *Tie to Mifsud:* Both spoke at The Nature of Extremism and the Future of Terrorism conference in Riyadh, Saudi Arabia May 21, 2017[116]
- **Michael Hurley,** Career CIA officer, he led CIA personnel on the ground in Afghanistan immediately after the 9/11 attacks. He was also Senior Counsel and Team Leader on the 9/11 Commission; a co- author of The 9/11 Commission Report. *Tie to Mifsud:* Both spoke at The Nature of Extremism and the Future of Terrorism conference in Riyadh, Saudi Arabia May 21, 2017[117]

It is difficult to believe that with all these connections Mifsud had with well-known western intelligence personnel that he was a Russian agent just pumping them for intelligence information. Either our intelligence community is extremely naïve or Mifsud really wasn't a Russian Agent. The later seems more likely.

Others have expressed their doubts that Joseph Mifsud is a Russian Agent;

- **Stephan Roh** (Mifsud's lawyer, among other things) said Mifsud was a *"Western intelligence element to be protected,"* saying that is why the professor felt the need to hide for the past two years.[118] He also claimed, without providing evidence, that Mifsud cooperated with Mueller in 2018 and was interviewed by "U.S. investigators".
- **Devin Nunes** (He was Chair of the House Intelligence Committee) has said, *"When you look into Mifsud closer, you realize he's connected with all kinds of intelligence agencies, including our own FBI If he is in fact a Russian*

---

[115] Conference Brochure, May 21, 2017

[116] Conference Brochure, May 21, 2017

[117] Conference Brochure, May 21, 2017

[118] Washington Post *"The enigma of the entire Mueller probe': Focus on origins of Russian investigation puts spotlight on Maltese professor."* June 30, 2019

agent, this would be one of the biggest intelligence scandals for the United States and our allies."

- **Rudy Giuliani** told The Post that *"Mifsud is a mystery to be explored,"* adding that the Papadopoulos episode *"looks like a rogue counterintelligence operation."*
- **Steve Hall,** who retired in 2015 after 30 years running and managing Russian operations for the CIA, said, *"in counterintelligence, you can almost never rule anything out completely."*

Mifsud, himself said in August 2017, *"My Russia contacts and interest [were] academic."* He said he was a visiting professor at Moscow State University but said it was *"an unpaid honorary position, similar to those I have with other institutions and think tanks globally."*

"I am an academic, I do not even speak Russian," he wrote. He told The Post then that he had *"absolutely no contact with the Russian Government."*

If Mifsud was a known Russian Agent (per Comey) UK Intel would know it also and it is unlikely he would be having a public meeting with Boris Johnson in October 2017. Letting Boris get physically right next to Joseph Mifsud knowing he was a Russian Agent is either highly embarrassing

Joseph Mifsud with Boris Johnson Kumar Singh October 2017

for the UK intelligence or Mifsud is known to be "one of them."

Mifsud is an embarrassment to the FBI.

According to the FBI themselves Joseph Mifsud triggered the whole Trump-Russia collusion investigation. At this point they still don't know who he is, who paid him to interface with Papadopoulos, how he made his money or where he is. To top it off, George Papadopoulos went to jail for making it harder for the FBI to question Mifsud. As American citizens we are all embarrassed for our FBI, for their bias, and for taking revenge on average citizens. If something is not done to curb this abuse of power and unacceptable investigative ability, we will be living in a police state.

Appendix D George Papadopoulos?

George Papadopoulos is pretty much just a regular ambitious young man. George's life is an open book with virtually no mystery involved. His major fault is exaggerating his accomplishments. He never was accused of knowing of or participating in any collusions with the Russians. Prior to joining the Trump campaign as an unpaid advisor, he had never known a Russian. His only crime was lying about the timing of the initial meeting he had with "mysterious Maltese professor", Joseph Mifsud and how many meetings he had with him. By all accounts, he lied because the whole Mifsud encounter was his doing and he didn't want to incriminate the campaign by his stupid liaison with the Maltese "professor." He wanted to be "important." He thought Mifsud could be useful to that goal. He was wrong.

George was born in Lincolnwood Illinois on August 19, 1987. He was not a "mover and shaker" in high school. His senior yearbook lists only one activity, the Hellenic Club.[119] George graduated in 2005 at the age of 18.

George followed the "low-key" profile set in high school into college at DePaul University. George graduated with a BA in political science on schedule in 2009 at the age of 22. Richard Farkas, a longtime political science professor at DePaul, said he had Papadopoulos in at least one, possibly two classes. Farkas said. *"He did not perform to the point of making himself known in my classes."*[120] *"As a student, I remember him to be nondescript,"* said Farkas.[121] In an interview with CBS, WBBM's Steven Miller, Farkas was even more negative, recalling George as "nondescript" and adding, *"I don't have any memory of George picking up on any of the complexities."* [122]

---

[119] Chicago Tribute, *"Week after bombshell, George Papadopoulos largely remains a mystery man,"* Jason Meisner and Patrick M. O'Connell, November 7, 2017.

[120] Ibid

[121] Chicago News, *"Chicagoan's path from Trump campaign to conviction to cooperation", Lynn Sweet,* Dan Mihalopoulos and Jon Seide, *October 30, 2017*

[122] CBS WBBM Chicago, *"Cooperating* Witness *in Russia Probe Was Unexceptional Scholar"* DePaul Professor Says" October 31, 2017

George has a slightly different view of his days at DePaul. In his mind, as he was finishing his degree, he had the world by the tail and knew exactly what he was going to do with his life. As he says in his book, "*I had my sights set on diplomacy and politics. So I enrolled at the University College London's School of Public Policy.*"[123] His teacher at DePaul described George as more aimless, with no passion for doing anything in particular. In George's mind, he was important. In the minds of others, he was not.

At least through age 22, George Papadopoulos was an ordinary guy, who stayed in the background.

George Papadopoulos's parents both came from Greece, but for the most part, did not live in the same city. Both parents were successful.

His mother, Katy (Kiki) Papadopoulos, worked in real estate property management, home remodeling, jewelry designing, and was a part time actress. She lived most of her life and had her career in Boston,

George's father, Antonios Papadopoulos, originally from northern Greece, graduated from medical school in Belgium and is a nephrologist in Addison, Illinois and affiliated with multiple hospitals in the area. He has been in practice for more than 20 years.

Antonios has also served as an executive vice president of the United Hellenic Voters of America, according to an online biography on the group's website.[124] He's 61 and lives in Addison, Illinois. Papadopoulos lived for years in a large house on the corner of a tree-lined street in Lincolnwood, just across the border from Chicago. Neighbors in the quiet neighborhood south of Pratt Avenue — a mix of ranches, expansive two-story homes and a few pillar-adorned mansions — either said they interacted with Papadopoulos only from afar or had moved in after his family returned to the city.

George's Life After Graduation from DePaul in 2009 until his first "job" in March 2011.

---

[123] *Deep State Target*, George Papadopoulos, Diversion Books, March 2019

[124] Chicago Tribute, "*Week after bombshell, George Papadopoulos largely remains a mystery man,*" Jason Meisner and Patrick M. O'Connell, November 7, 2017.

It would appear that George's life up through 2009 was uneventful. He had two very strong parents who were not close. This would possibly explain why he lived "under the radar" through those years – no record of little league, no high school sports, band, drama or anything. No outside affiliations at DePaul. It is not hard to imagine that he had pent up ambitions to make a mark in the world, once he "left the nest." His parents before him certainly had.

George, His Brother and His Mother "KiKi" in Chicago

Graduate Studies at University College London - That need to make a mark began to show itself when he elected to go to graduate school in London. "Spreading his wings" a little. He pursued an MS in Security Studies degree at University College London. To his credit, he graduated one year later 2010.

Why does one pursue a degree in "Security Studies?" According to the brochure from University College London, this MSc prepares one to work as a practitioner and researcher in counterterrorism, intelligence, law enforcement, risk assessment and security technology.[125]

According to his online resume, Papadopoulos wrote his thesis in November 2010 on the "deleterious effects of low governance and state capacity levels in the Middle East." To a layman, a thesis on explaining

---

[125] *UCL Graduate Degrees*, Update on 17 March 2020.

how bad things happen ("deleterious effects") to a country if they don't have strong people in charge ("low governance") and the inability to get anything done ("state capacity level") has very little to do with counter-terrorism, intelligence, law enforcement, risk assessment or security technology! It has more to do with public policy the career path he had originally selected at College of London and switched to security studies soon after he started his Masters program.

George clearly did not have a focus. Additionally, he had a different evaluation of the contribution of his thesis. He explained that his paper was about the "The rise and fall of Islamist governments." He said, "his paper was well received."[126] (In the business world those words translate to "nobody cared."

He had trouble finding a job after finishing his thesis and graduating. In his defense, 2010 was not a good time to be looking for a job in any field.

First Job – Hudson Institute (2011 – 2015) - George ended up accepting an offer from Richard Weitz,[127] a researcher at Hudson Institute to work from home and help him write some papers on public policy. The position was an internship with no pay.

Papadopoulos quickly learned how the business of contract research works. The "company", in this case, the Hudson Institute, is like a "holding tank" for researchers. It gives the researchers a "home" from which they solicit contracts or grants from clients using the Institute's name as a corporate cover. If the job requires additional research, writing or administrative skills, the researcher can tap into unpaid interns or hire outside help from a "body shop" subcontractor. If, after collaborating with a real researcher, the intern or body-shopped contract employee can start soliciting business directly as an Institute employee.

George started working at home as an unpaid intern. He decided to move to Washington DC where the Hudson Institute was located to better position himself for a real job. Somewhere along the line, he was hired as a "body-shop" subcontract employee and started getting paid, while working on an angle to get his own contract or grant. He was eventually successful and at the beginning of 2013, he got a client to pay the Institute $100,000 for a study resulting in a paper, hosting a conference, and promoting the concept. Basically, when Hudson Institute's overhead,

---

[126] *Deep State Target*, George Papadopoulos, Diversion Books, 2019
[127] Ibid.

G&A and other direct costs including the conference cost are subtracted, George got about $50,000 salary for a years' worth of work. The conference was held in October 2013. He was still a subcontractor at Hudson Institute and having difficulty getting the next client. After the contract was over, it is unlikely that he continued to get paid. If he did, it would have to be on Hudson Institute overhead. Overhead dollars are very precious so it is unlikely he was paid much after the $100,000 contract was completed. Hudson Institute claims he was only paid in 2013 & 2014, so when George left the Institute in mid 2015 he still wasn't on the payroll. He still doesn't have any money.

Surviving in this business requires cultivating potential clients who want research performed in an area that the researcher works. Becoming successful requires developing a "name.". That takes time and a string of successes. The bottom line is that George Papadopoulos was not cut-out to be a contract researcher. He left the Hudson Institute in the summer of 2015 – still without a real job.

Second job – Energy Stream September 2015 – December 2015

George took a job with a friend, Anthony Livanios. Anthony had a two-person London-based company that organized energy conferences. Livanios had a conference scheduled for October 26, so Papadopoulos agreed to help out. Besides, it gave George a chance to get back to London, and he liked that. The conference was over and in December 2015, George was looking for another job.

Summary – George's life before politics

To sum it up, George Papadopoulos started his Masters program at University College London in public policy. He changed majors to Security Studies because he was "more interested in security."[128] Then he wrote his thesis on public policy not security. He worked four years in a subservient capacity at Hudson Institute for a real researcher as an intern and briefly as a sub-contract employee. Then he switched companies to help set up an energy conference. George really wanted to be important, but he wasn't. He wanted to make a contribution, but he had made little. He wanted to be recognized, but he wasn't. He was no different than many graduates, five years out of school. He was still not making a mark.

---

[128] Ibid.

Nobody on the record, praised him. His teachers and professors basically said, *"George attended school here but didn't shine."* No clients have spoken up about his contributions. His employer confirms he was an unpaid intern for a while and worked as a sub-contract employee from a body shop contractor for a while and left. They barely remember him even though he was there for four years. This was very similar to the reaction of his teachers during his high school and college years. George has not offered any performance appraisals or documentation of his achievements. He paints a different picture of himself in his book.[129] He claims having "big ideas" and being admired for his work while at Hudson Institute.

Third Job – Ben Carson Campaign – November 2015 – February 2016 - Like his previous jobs, there is nothing that appears to stand out about his tenure with the Carson campaign. He joined the campaign because he wanted to become involved with politics and the power associated with it. He wanted to be important, a "somebody." Politics is an obvious starting point.

Carson's campaign manager, Barry Bennett, told The Hill that he hired Papadopoulos in a moment of desperation: Carson needed to fix his foreign policy shortcomings and all of the "foreign policy A-listers" were employed by Bush and Rubio.[130] "Here's this 28-year-old kid who is not terribly sophisticated, but he solved my problem of needing to put a bunch of names on a list," Bennett said. "I'm sure he wrote some things for us, but I don't know that we used any of it.[131] According to Bennett, *"As it turns out, Papadopoulos was exaggerating even the meager experience listed on his resume."[132]*

The mark he made on the Carson campaign followed the same pattern that started with high school, through college and his first five years in the job market – unremarkable. Observations regarding his tenure on the Carson campaign included:
- Armstrong Williams, who served in various roles in Carson's campaign, told TIME that Papadopoulos was paid $8,500 for his work in December 2015 and January 2016,

---

[129] Ibid.

[130] The Hill, *"How young Trump aide became key player in Russia probe"*, Morgan Chalfant & Johnathan Easley November 1, 2017.

[131] Newsweek *"George Papadopoulos Lied On His Resume To Get Trump Campaign Foreign Policy Job, Former Employer Says"* November 1, 2017

[132] The Hill, Op.Cit

and then received only a partial salary, $2,125, in February, when he left the campaign.[133]

- No one in the Carson campaign remembers much about Papadopoulos. Bennett said. *"If there was any work output, I never saw it,"* he told TIME. *"It never ended up on my desk."*[134]
- *"I don't remember the guy,"* Shermichael Singleton, Carson's communications director told TIME. *"I remember his name in emails, but I can't remember meeting him. I don't want to lie — maybe we did meet once or twice — but I don't remember it."*[135]

So once again, another job but nothing to show for it. Still no money in his pocket. But George had "cut his teeth" on the pollical scene. He started to gain a little swagger after he started working on the Carson campaign. He started dating a gal – a "never-Trumper."

The girlfriend said she first met Papadopoulos when he was still working for the Carson campaign. Though he talked a lot about his role as a foreign policy adviser, he offered few specifics. She got the impression he was not as big a fish as he claimed to be, she said, but he was also not the "low-level volunteer" as described by Trump after Papadopoulos' charges were unveiled.

She also said Papadopoulos was one to "avoid conflict as much as possible," a possible explanation for why he seemed so easygoing about her anti-Trump views. This conflict avoidance seems to be a throw-back to his high school and college days of "not getting involved."

The job with the Carson campaign ended by early February 2016 and George started looking for his next mountain to climb.

Between Jobs

When George went to London for a couple of months to help out his friend arrange an energy conference, Mr. Papadopoulos wrote in his book[136] that while still in London, *"I am approached by a man named*

---

[133] Time, *"The Short, Happy Political Career of George Papadopoulos."* Haley Sweetland Edwards, October 2017

[134] Ibid

[135] Ibid.

[136] *"Deep State Target"*, Op. Cit. _________

Nagi Khalid Idris who offers me a position at The London Center of International Law Practice (LCILP)."

REALLY?! It doesn't work that way! Think about that. Even if you are Albert Einstein or Henry Kissinger, you don't get approached by a man who offers you a position out of the blue. It is doubly unlikely if you don't have any proven track record or haven't achieved anything. It is triply unlikely if they don't even have a job for you!

> *HYPOTHETICAL: So what <u>really</u> happened? In December 2015 George wanted to connect to a presidential campaign in some capacity. He was overheard talking in public about his interest. He mentioned he has approached the Carson and Trump campaigns.*

> *Someone with an interest in having a "stable" of potential campaign insiders heard of George's political interest. That person was Nagi Idris or someone who knows Idris. Nagi may have clients who approach him from time-to-time for such individuals to be placed as unknowing "plants" in organizations. He sized George up as a wannabe important person who could possibly be used as an unsuspecting campaign insider – just the kind of person his usual clients may want. Idris said, "Keep in touch." Within a week, Papadopoulos had landed an advisor role with the Ben Carson campaign. He went to Washington to work with the campaign.*

So, to recap, as George is leaving London and Energy Stream, to return to Washington to work on the Carson campaign in early November 2015, Nagi Idris told George that he would like to hire him at LCILP. George then went to Washington and stayed with the Carson campaign for two months.

According to Papadopoulos, *"I moved back to London and checked in with the LCILP. They seemed happy to have me back. As far as Nagi was concerned, my experience working with a US presidential campaign was a feather in the LCILP's cap."*[137]

---

[137] Ibid, page 33

Wait a minute, it sounds like George was returning to his old job at LCILP after two months absence to work for the Carson campaign and they are happy to have him back.

That's not exactly how it happened, according to the Mueller Report. From discovery materiel from the Mueller investigation, Papadopoulos applied for a job on February 4, 2016. He didn't just bop into the Idris's office, say hi and pick up where he left off as he implies in his book. George sent an email to Idris on February 4, 2016 asking if Idris was interested in hiring him. The next day, Idris emailed Papadopoulos an offer. Later, in early February, George accepted the offer to join LCILP and traveled to London to start work. His actual start date and salary is not known.

At exactly the same time Papadopoulos is applying for and accepting a job at LCILP, he is aggressively pursuing a job with the Trump campaign. In fact, on the same day George asked Idris for a job, (February 4, 2016) he contacted Corey Lewandowski by Linkedin message and Michael Glassner (Glassner is putting together a foreign policy team for Trump) by email, asking to join the Trump campaign. Certainly, he has to disclose this alternate job pursuit with his new employer. Afterall, Papadopoulos may be leaving in a week or two. It is the only fair thing to do.

Fourth Job - London Centre of International Law Practice LCILP[138] February 2016 –April 2, 2016[139]

George's first month on the job was disappointing - In early February 2016, Papadopoulos started working at LCILP as Director of the Center for International Energy and Natural Resources Law & Security. After almost exactly one month, on March 6, 2016, George figured out he didn't have a real job. He figured out that nobody had a real job at LCILP. Not only wasn't he doing anything productive, but he noticed neither was anyone else. He asked himself, *"Honestly, I'm not entirely sure how or why LCLIP exists"*?[140] Eventually he discovered he was not the only one with questions about the organization.

---

[138] See Appendix D *"Description of London Centre of International Law Practice'*
[139] Most reports say Papadopoulos worked at LCILP from February 6 , 2016 to until April or May, but he attended the American Jewish Committee meeting in DC on July 20, 2016 listed as representing LCILP.
[140] *Deep State Target*, Op. Cit., page 33

By March 2, 2016, things are looking good for joining the Trump team and on March 6, Papadopoulos accepted Clovis' offer to join the Trump campaign as a foreign policy advisor-an unpaid position.

So, in the real world, if you took a new job and three weeks later you announced you were leaving to take a different job, your employer would be justifiably pissed-off. If the guy you hired was for a Director-level job to start a new consulting service in International Energy and Natural Resources Law & Security, your boss would really be pissed. The whole initiative would have to be scrapped. But Nagi Idris, LCILP President apparently was delighted. Not only will LCILP pay George to do nothing for the company, they will buy him a plane ticket to Rome to introduce him to Joseph Mifsud who can introduce him to some people who could really help him in George's endeavor to make a positive contribution to the Trump campaign. To hell with starting a new consulting business we'll pay George Papadopoulos just to do nothing for us so he can work for the Trump campaign for free. How is this laissez faire attitude even remotely rational?

HYPOTHETICAL: One of the "product offerings" of LCILP is to source "plants" for clients who want an unsuspecting insider to extract or plant information into a targeted organization. Clients could be companies, competing political campaigns, or government intelligent agencies – anyone who wants to plant or find dirt.

So in Papadopoulos's case, Nagi Idris, President of LCILP had a client who would pay LCILP to source and place a stooge inside the Trump campaign. It was either a Russian sponsor, a party that wanted to incriminate the campaign, or an industry executive who wanted inside access for financial gain.

Looking back, now that the role Papadopoulos actually played is known, it could only be a party that wanted to plant evidence of Trump-Russia collusion. Russia had nothing to gain to fake a potential meeting with Putin or feed George garbage on having dirt on Hillary. If they had actually set the meeting or delivered dirt, a different conclusion could be drawn. But they didn't.

Nothing that transpired with regard to George's relationship with LCILP was designed to help any commercial interest.

That leaves only one logical conclusion – someone who wanted evidence of collusion between Trump and Russia planted. That someone is well documented as a Trump hater – John Brennan. British intelligence was highly motivated to help John. They didn't like Trump either.

Bottom line – George was hired by LCILP at the direction of Brennan's CIA to plant evidence of Trump-Russia collusion. It is well documented that that is what Papadopoulos did. It is well documented that Mifsud provided the paper/email trail that comprised the evidence. It is well documented that Brennan had the motive and access to the resources to make it happen. There is no other rational explanation.

LCILP didn't have a job for George Papadopoulos. George had done nothing to lead a potential employer to think they could build a business around George's expertise. They knew he would potentially be going to the Trump campaign and they had a client willing to pay LCILP to recruit, vet and place a stooge in the Trump campaign. Unfortunately for George this role would not be a good career path but he was not aware what path he was being led down.

So, George's only experience in his first month on the job was learning that he didn't have a real job.

George's second month of the job takes a weird turn - On March 6, 2016, exactly one month after accepting the job at LCILP, Papadopoulos told Indris, *"I'm taking an unpaid job with the Trump campaign, see ya!"* Indris apparently said something to the effect, *"That's great. You should do that. I'll still pay you, but I don't need you to do anything here. I want you to meet someone who can really do you some good with the Trump campaign, but we'll have to go to Rome to meet him. His name is Joseph Mifsud. No trouble I'll pay all the expenses."*

Papadopoulos stayed on LCILP's payroll through the end of March. He did nothing that would even remotely be considered "working for LCILP" through March 31. Instead George was introduced to Joseph Mifsud who started directing George's activities. By the end of March, Joseph Mifsud had vetted George, set the hook and made sure George was part of the Trump team.

MIFSUDS ASIGNMENT – VET PAPADOPOULOS , CREATE A PAPER TRAIL OF TRUMP-RUSSIA COLLUSION, AND GET GEORGE TO PLANT IT

March 2016 is the month where Papadopoulos is being paid by LCILP but working for the Trump campaign for free.

On March 12, George Papadopoulos, Nagi Idris and another LCILP associate, Rebecca Peters traveled to Rome where Idris introduced Papadopoulos to Mifsud. Mifsud was very interested in helping Papadopoulos make Russian connections for the Trump campaign once he found that Papadopoulos was really joining the Trump campaign. Mifsud vetted George enough to know that he had found the "patsy" to plant Joseph's collusion evidence. Mifsud told George that, *"I'm going to be your middleman around the world. I have contacts everywhere. I'm going to set up a meeting between Trump and Putin."* Papadopoulos returned to London on March 17, 2017.

Mifsud arranged to meet with Papadopoulos in London on March 24, 2016. Mifsud brought "Putin's niece", Olga Polonskaya to the meeting. (Olga turns out not to be Putin's niece, but a wine store manager from Moscow.) As was the plan, George emailed the details of his meeting with Mifsud and Polonskaya and that a plan for setting up a Putin-Trump meeting had been initiated. The first piece of evidence of Trump-Russia collusion had been planted into the Trump campaign by Papadopoulos.

At the end of March, George Papadopoulos had been vetted by Joseph Mifsud. He was formally imbedded in the Trump campaign and George was to be the one to plant evidence of Trump-Russia collusion. Mifsud successfully tested Papadopoulos's ability to take a piece of collusion evidence and plant it right in the middle of the Trump campaign. Introducing Putin's "niece" to George was a nice touch. She was enough of a distraction for George to keep him from pestering Mifsud too much. Mifsud handlers must have been pleased.

George was still on the LCILP payroll. Although Papadopoulos accepted the job of advisor with the Trump campaign on March 6, 2016 the only thing he did for the campaign in March was to attend a meeting in Washington with national security advisors on March 31, 2016 where he reported he might be able to set up a meeting between Putin and Trump. He got a ho-hum response.

On April 2, 2016 George flew to Israel to speak at an energy policy conference. He was finally doing something on behalf of the Trump campaign. Papadopoulos returned to London on April 5. He signed out of LCILP. No more expense account.

Fifth Job Trump Campaign -April 1, 2016 – October 6, 2016

On April 18, Mifsud introduced Papadopoulos by email to Ivan Timofeev, who was program director at the Russian International Affairs Council. Timofeev suggested a meeting in Moscow or London.[1] Papadopoulos notified the Trump campaign. Over the next several weeks, Papadopoulos and Timofeev had multiple conversations over Skype and email about setting "the groundwork" for a "potential" meeting between the Campaign and Russian government officials.

On May 4, 2016, Papadopoulos forwarded to Lewandowski an email from Timofeev raising the possibility of a meeting in Moscow, asking Lewandowski whether that was "something we want to move forward with." The next day, Papadopoulos forwarded the same Timofeev email to Sam Clovis, adding to the top of the email "Russia update." He included the same email in a May 21, 2016 message to senior Campaign official Paul Manafort, under the subject line "Request from Russia to meet Mr. Trump," stating that "Russia has been eager to meet Mr. Trump for quite some time and have been reaching out to me to discuss.[141]

---

[141] The Mueller Report, Op. Cit. page 91

The second paper trail of evidence of Trump – Russia collusion had been planted. There is now real evidence that Papadopoulos is talking to a real Russian about a Trump-Putin meeting. No meeting ever occurred. Timofeev is the only Russian, other than "Putin's niece" that George ever met.

For the next six months starting in mid-April 2016 George's time is spent (1) getting more bogus "incriminating information" from Mifsud and planting it inside the Trump campaign, (2) getting maneuvered into spilling this "incriminating evidence of collusion" to "a representative of a foreign government"[142] in an effort to speed up the entry of the FBI into investigating Trump-Russia collusion, and (3) getting secretly interrogated by an FBI "Confidential Human Resource" (CHR), Stefan Halper and his female companion, Azra Turk.

The Mifsud disinformation – An effort to further incriminate the Trump Campaign using Papadopoulos

After the email introduction to Ivan Timofeev on April 18, 2016, Mifsud returned from Russia. He and George met for breakfast at the Andez Hotel in London on April 26, 2016. George expected Joseph had an update on arrangements for the Trump-Putting meeting. This was George's goal.   Instead, Joseph Mifsud passed the "bombshell" information that **"THE RUSSIANS HAD DIRT ON HILLARY CLINTON AND THOUSANDS OF EMAILS."**

The problem was, George wasn't that interested. What if George's lack of interest translated to not even mentioning the existence of this dirt to the campaign? To Mifsud, knowledge of Russian possession of dirt on Hillary AND thousands of her emails was just the kind of thing that investigations into collusion are made of. This was the ultimate plant of incriminating information passed from Mifsud to Papadopoulos. If a paper trail of this knowledge was found in possession of the Trump campaign, it would be hard evidence that Trump and Russia were really colluding.

The "Downer encounter" – Ensuring that Papadopoulos Clinton "dirt" rumor makes it to the FBI.

---

[142] The *Representative of a foreign government* is either Alexander Downer, Australian Ambassador to the UK or Erika Thompson, an Australian intelligence agent assigned to the embassy.

Mifsud got concerned that Papadopoulos did not plant that perfectly good evidence of collusion into the Trump campaign. The Mueller Report confirmed that Papadopoulos did NOT share the story about Clinton dirt with the campaign staff.[143] Mifsud came up with "Plan B."

*HYPOTHETICAL- Mifsud, his sponsor and handler were concerned that perfectly good evidence of collusion would not see the light of day. Mifsud et.al. had a problem. If George was not going to tell anyone in the campaign about access to dirt on Hillary, the "evidence" would never be discovered. Mifsud had to stage a "George encounter" with a "trusted person" who could draw this rumor out of George and then relay it to the FBI. Alternately, if George was so disinterested in the rumor that he didn't mention it, at least the trusted person could just tell others that George **had** told him of the dirt rumor. This would be good enough to provide the evidence the FBI needed.*

The "trusted person" had to have several attributes;

- *He/she had to have legitimate access to the FBI,*
- *He/she could not be "suspicious" to George,*
- *He/she had to be "trusted" by Mifsud's employer,*
- *He/she had to be "legitimate" and unconnected to any investigation if the scheme was uncovered.*

Mifsud, his employer and his handler came up with the ideal person, Alexander Downer. He lived in London. He had established access to the FBI. He was trusted by Mifsud's sponsor (CIA), and he had no prior connection to the investigation.

Downer wasn't that thrilled with his proposed "volunteer assignment." Downer didn't know Papadopoulos. How would the introduction occur? What if Papadopoulos got suspicious? Was Papadopoulos more savvy than he was being portrayed? Downer had to protect himself from getting played. He

---

The stage is set. The history of what transpired is a matter of record.

The Downer-Papadopoulos-Thompson meeting got set up without raising any suspicions - On May 3, 2016 George got a call from his Buddy at the Israeli embassy saying he wanted to introduce George to his girlfriend, Erika Thompson. The three of them met for dinner that evening.

Later Erica set up a date for her, George and her boss at the Australian embassy, Alexander Downer to get together for a drink. That "get together" was scheduled for March 10, 2016. That date is well established. It has been confirmed by both George and Alexander and their calendars.

The date is further evidenced by the fact that Papadopoulos noted in his book that it was raining hard the night they met at the Kensington Wine Rooms, a ten minute walk from his apartment.[144] (A check on the weather record for London on May 10, 2016 confirms it was raining that evening. It also confirms that it wasn't raining on May 6, 2016, the day

---

[144] *"Deep State Target"*, Op. Cit. page 73

that the Mueller Report said the information about dirt was transmitted to "a representative of a foreign government".)

The reason the date is significant is the Mueller report[145] says, "*One week later, on May 6, 2016, Papadopoulos suggested to a representative of a foreign government the Trump Campaign had received indications from the Russian government that it could assist the Campaign through the anonymous release of information that would be damaging to candidate Clinton.*"

May 6 is NOT May 10. Either Mueller got the date wrong or the "*representative of a foreign government*" was Erika Thompson not Alexander Downer. It is likely that George told Erika when she called on May 6, 2016 to set the date for their meeting with Downer that, " *he (Papadopoulos) had received indications from the Russian government that it could assist the Campaign through the anonymous release of information that would be damaging to candidate Clinton*". This is the most logical interpretation since (1) the Mueller document was never amended to "correct the error", (2) both Papadopoulos and Downer denied that the subject came up at their meeting on May 10, 2016, and (3) both Downer and Papadopoulos say their meeting occurred on May 10, 2016.

Alexander Downer   **Erika Thompson**

Papadopoulos was vetted and OK'd for Downer to meet with him - May 9, 2016 - Papadopoulos met with Terrence Dudley, a defense attache at the U.S. Embassy in London and his colleague Greg Baker. According

---

[145] "Mueller Report" Op. Cit. page 81

to Papadopoulos, Dudley called him "out of the blue". This was one day after Erika Thompson, *an Australian who was a political counsellor at Australia's London High Commission* talked to Papadopoulos about meeting up with Downer for drinks. Dudley and Baker met with Papadopoulos 3 more times. (As developed in "HYPOTHETICAL" above, Dudley and Baker were "checking out" Papadopoulos and vetting him prior to Downer's scheduled meeting with George the next day.)

The rumor that the Russians had emails and dirt on Hillary Clinton got communicated – According to the Mueller Report[146], *Papadopoulos suggested to a representative of a foreign government that the Trump Campaign had received indications from the Russian government that it could assist the Campaign through the anonymous release of information that would be damaging to candidate Clinton.*

Regardless of whether the HYPOTHETICAL scenario above is correct or not, the record of what actually occurred reflects exactly what is surmised in the HYPOTHETICAL.

Downer (or Thompson) passed on the information about dirt on Clinton to Australian Intel by cable. Australian Intel sat on it until just after the DNC emails were published by WikiLeaks on July 22, 2016. (Australian Intel thought there might be a connection between Papadopoulos's apparent knowledge of "dirt" on Clinton being held by the Russians and WikiLeaks publishing it.) Based on this possible connection, Australian Intel notified their US counterparts on July 26, 2016.

Mifsud had achieved his goal. Evidence that Papadopoulos had colluded with the Russians and was "in on" the Russian hacking had been planted and had now been "discovered" by the FBI. If Mifsud was on incentive compensation pay with the CIA, he should have received the maximum.

"Halper and the Halper helper" – Starting the FBI investigation into Papadopoulos's role in Trump-Russia collusion.

George is about to enter the second phase of his tenure with the Trump campaign – the "being investigated phase." The first phase of his tenure was to serve as a CIA patsy to plant evidence of collusion. That phase was over.

---

[146] Mueller Report, Ibid., page 81

The FBI was now taking over for the second phase. It was the FBI's job to find and verify the evidence that had been planted in the first phase. They kicked off the investigation into Papadopoulos's role in the Trump-Russia collusion using Confidential Human Sources (CHS's) to gain Papadopoulos's confidence and extract information from him. The hope was Papadopoulos would incriminate himself and the campaign.

The CHS's were Stefan Halper and his "helper", Azra Turk, a very

Stefan Halper

Azra Turk

sexy blonde who made advances to Papadopoulos in an effort to get close to him to get incriminating evidence on the campaign collusion. Halper was a long-term CHS. He was already working for the FBI to get collusion evidence on Carter Page.

After only two meetings with Papadopoulos on September 2, 2016 and September 15, 2016 Halper and Turk concluded that Papadopoulos could not help their collusion case. The second meeting was recorded by Halper.   The Muller investigation found that the recording was exculpatory rather than incriminating. Mr. Horowitz rapped the FBI for not including them in four sworn affidavits agents presented to federal judges to authorize Foreign Intelligence Surveillance Act (FISA) electronic and physical spying on Mr. Page.

The FBI did NOT obtain a FISA warrant to investigate George Papadopoulos. Halper's and Turk's finding of no collusion was not helpful to the FBI's case. There was no evidence to leak to the press at this time.

Entrapment Attempt 1 - Sergei Millian - October 6, 2016 to January 26, 2017

The only thing George managed to do for Trump during this six months was work on a foreign policy speech for Trump for a May 1, 2016 delivery.

In the middle of the six months, Papadopoulos moved back from London to his mom's house in Chicago. He had no money and no income at this point and needed a place to live. He moved back to Chicago in June 2016.

It is now October 6, 2016 and at this point in his life, George is broke, has achieved nothing and has a pretty empty resume of accomplishments. To his credit, he has moved in some important circles and rubbed elbows with some pretty important people.

George hoped to get a Job in Trump Administration. Just after being dropped from the campaign, George started lobbying for some kind of position in the Trump administration.

The FBI was frustrated. Halper didn't help their collusion case and they don't think they have enough on Papadopoulos to accuse him of anything. They need to dirty him up and at least make him regret working for Trump and who knows, if they make things tough enough, he may be coerced into giving up a little dirt on Trump-Russia collusion.

At this point, the FBI turns from a CHS strategy to extract evidence of collusion to Part 1 of a 2-part entrapment strategy. They can at least make Papadopoulos sorry he hooked up with Trump.

Part 1 of the entrapment strategy started on November 9, 2016, after Halper and Turk failed to extract evidence of collusion from Papadopoulos. George was unable to help Brennan prevent Trump from winning, but he could still be useful in assisting in an impeachment process. Besides, Papadopoulos needed to pay for being part of the Trump campaign.

On October 7, 2016, Papadopoulos got a call from a guy named Sergei Millian. Millian is an American citizen, but a native of Belarus, He was the president of the NY-based Russian American Chamber of Commerce. Millian tells Papadopoulos that he wants to discuss a business deal with him.[147] (Millian had first contacted George on July 15, 2016 by email. Sergei claims he can help make connections for George with Russians.[148])

On November 9, 2016, shortly after the election, Papadopoulos arranged to meet Millian in Chicago to discuss business opportunities, including potential work with Russian "billionaires who are not under sanctions." The meeting took place on November 14, 2016, at the Trump Hotel and Tower in Chicago. This sounded like entrapping Papadopoulos into running afoul with the Foreign Agents Registration Act (FARA), the same trap that caught General Michael Flynn got caught in.

According to Papadopoulos, the two men discussed partnering on business deals, but Papadopoulos perceived that Millian's attitude toward him changed when Papadopoulos stated that he was only pursuing private-sector opportunities and was not interested in a job in the Administration.[149]

Two months later, on January 21, 2017, Sergei arranges to get together with George in DC right after the inauguration. Sergeio brings a friend who jokingly tells Papadopoulos that Sergei is FBI.[150]

The job prospect seemed to be a dead issue. George didn't bite and his value is diminished because George had yet to land a job in the Trump Administration. But George tried. George scheduled phone interviews with person's charged with staffing the new administration. Nothing worked out. This entrapment scheme failed.

FBI Investigation Part 1 – January 27, 2017 – February 16, 2017

---

[147] Mueller Report, Ibid. page 94
[148] *Deep State Target*, Op. Cit. page 89
[149] Mueller Report, ibid., Page 95
[150] "Deep State Target", Op. Cit. page 127

Switching from Job Search to doing interviews with the FBI – Less than a week after the Millian entrapment scheme failed, on January 27, 2017, the FBI starts dogging George, asking him questions. In the first interview, agents Curtis Heide and Michael McSwain question George about his lifestyle, a little about Millian, a little about Russians, a little about Israelis and then about Russian hacking of Clinton emails.

The second interview was with just Curtis Heide on January 31, 2017. He asks George to wear a wire and meet with Mifsud. Papadopoulos refuses.

The third interview was on February 16, 2017. This interview was with a full contingent of FBI'ers including Heide and McSwain and also including Kevin Clinesmith. (Clinesmith is the same FBI lawyer who altered the FISA warrant application to say Carter Page was NOT a CIA operative, when the real application said he WAS a CIA operative.)

This is the end of contact with the FBI for a while. But in the weeks ahead, George hears from friends that the FBI has been questioning them.

The Next Step – Courting Simona February 19, 2017 to July 27, 2017

The next segment of George Papadopoulos's life makes little sense. He doesn't have a job, he has no money, and he's living with his mom. In late 2016, he noticed on the LCILP Linkedin site that a woman named Simona Manigiante had started working at the LCILP. He was smitten. He introduced himself by email and they started e-communicating

Simona Manigiante

In April 2017, Simona had the opportunity to travel to the US to visit her aunt. He arranged to meet her in New York and picked her up at JFK. They had a couple of days together and really hit it off. George was very interested in pursuing the relationship further and so was she.

In mid-May, George flew to Europe to spend some time with Simona. He returned to the US 2 ½ months later on July 27, 2017. George bopped around Europe with Simona. He landed in Athens. He spent some time there with friends, then went to the isle of Mykonos, about 90 miles from Athens to meet up with Simona who is at the film festival in Cannes

France about 1400 miles away. The Cannes festival was over on May 28. 2017. They got together for a week. They party and spend time at the beach.

The party is interrupted when Charles Tawil calls George and wants to get together and talk about a business proposition. On June 8, George leaves Simona goes to Tel Aviv, then on to Cyprus with Tawil. It is unclear why Tawil and Papadopoulos have to meet in three different countries to discuss one business arrangement. Then George flies to Thessaloniki, Greece on June 14 for a two-day energy summit.

Then back home to family in Greece. George and Simona had 1 ½ months left before George was scheduled to return home. They spent time with her family in Naples. They partied on the Isle of Capri. They then go back to Athens to meet George's family. He flew home on July 27, 2017

What doesn't make sense at this point is where did Papadopoulos get the money to spend 2 ½ months partying in Greece with Simona? He doesn't have that kind of money. In the long run, the partying paid off for George. Seven months later he and Simona got married. Although this relationship could be what it appears, true love, or a Simona attempt to use George as her route to the US and a career in Hollywood, or a long-term international conspiracy plot, or ??? This question is never answered in this book. One thing is highly likely. It is NOT a scheme hatched by George. His whole life to this point would indicate he is not an effective plotter and schemer.

Charles Tawil, Entrapment 2 or Legitimate Attempt To Buy Influence in Trump Administration? - June, 2017 to July 27, 2017

Just like the question raised above about Simona's motivation to get involved with George, the question about Charles Tawil's motivation to get involved with George is not answered in this book.

Unlike Joseph Mifsud and Sergei Millian, Charles Tawil has legitimate business reasons to cultivate George Papadopoulos. He actually is a business facilitator. One of his clients is Shai Arbel a legitimate businessman who runs Terrogence, a company that has very good facial recognition software. Shai could use an "in" with the Trump administration if George actually ended up there. The US intelligence community uses his software.

Although the events leading up to the meeting in Tel Aviv, are a little suspicious as are the events following the meeting with Arbel, there is no clear way to connect the dots.

On June 7, 2017, Charles called George while he was partying with Simona isle of Mykonos. Charles said he wanted to meet with George. George agrees, probably thinking it would impress Simona as to how important he was. Besides, George needs a job!

Charles flew to Mykonos on June 8, 2017 and convinced George to go to Tel Aviv, Israel to talk business with Charles Tawil. Shai Arbel, in addition to being CEO of Terrogence is an ex-Israeli intelligence officer. The meeting seemed to have gone okay. Charles Tawil and George go to their hotel and they meet in Charles' room.

What happened next is significant, but Charles and George differ on what actually went down. George said that Charles threw $10,000 cash down on the bed and told him to take it as a "down payment" for services.[151] Charles said George asked him for a $10,000 loan and he gave it to him. Charles said George was "desperate" to keep working with him.

Knowing that George didn't have any money before he traveled to Greece and he had been spending a lot wining and dining Simona, it is not hard to believe that George asked for a loan. That is unknown, however. Neither party disagrees that $10,000 was transferred from Charles Tawil to George Papadopoulos. Also no one disagrees that Papadopoulos did not have the $10,000 on him when he arrived back in the US on July 27, 2017.

What happened next is unexplainable also. Tawil and Papadopoulos flew together to Cyprus the next day, June 9, 2017. No reason for that trip is available.

George then went on to Thessaloniki, a Greek port city to attend an "energy summit" on June 14 —15 2017.[152] George said he dropped the $10,000 cash off with a lawyer acquaintance he had there in Thessaloniki. According to George he was suspicious that they were "marked bills" and could be traced as coming from a foreign entity and that could get him in trouble. George said he got a receipt. George never produced a receipt.

---

[151] "Deep State Target", Ibid. page 162
[152] Ibid, page 163.

He said after the fact that he would retrieve the bills from the lawyer and have the FBI check to see if they were marked. He never followed through on that retrieval.

Charles Tawil has denied this account. *"The guy is a pathetic liar"* Mr. Tawil said of Mr. Papadopoulos. *"I met him when he was out of a job and offered him a job and gave him, on his demand, a loan, cash as he requested because he did not have an account in Europe."* Mr. Tawil continued, *"I have copies of emails and WhatsApp communication with George that can prove that he is a liar. Instead of thanking me, he is trying to drag me in his mud."* He finished his denial by stating, *"He is coward and a liar and probably other things too."*

Papadopoulos could easily put this controversy to rest. He could show the receipt and/or the "marked" bills. It is looking more likely that he has neither.

As described above, George finished off his European vacation with Simona more smitten than ever. He got on a plane in Athens, headed for Munich then on to Dulles and then to Chicago. He got stopped in Dulles and was arrested by the FBI.

Arrest, Charges & Two Nights in Jail – July 27, 2017 – July 29, 2017

There were five FBI agents to greet George Papadopoulos when he got off the plane in Dulles including Agents Heide and McSwain. This time Heide and McSwain are working for the Mueller investigation, not the FBI. Obviously, the Mueller team thinks that George is valuable to their investigation. They searched his stuff and he spent the night in jail.

The next day he was charged with lying to an FBI agent and obstruction of justice. The FBI agent was Curtis Heide. The lie was that he told Heide that he didn't have contact with Mifsud in April when actually he had one email with him in April. The obstruction of justice charge was that George had deleted his Facebook account. George is held overnight again. The next day he was released. No explanation. He flew back home to Chicago.

Court Hearing & Plea Bargain, Sentencing and Prison, July 30, 2017 – December 7, 2017

On August 7, 2017 George met in Chicago with prosecutors for the first time. George agreed to cooperate with the investigation and is offered a plea deal. The plea deal was filed on October 5, 2017. George's plea deal was unsealed on October 31, 2017. Simona moved to Chicago and they spent the winter of 2017-2018 living with George's mom, Kiki.

On August 17, 2018 the sentencing memorandum is filed by Mueller. George's sentencing hearing was held a year later on Friday, September 7, 2018 at E. Barrett Prettyman Courthouse in Washington DC– Simona, and George's parents are there. His sentence was handed down; 14 days in jail, 200 hours of community service, 112 months of supervised release and a fine of $9,500.

The next thing we know is that George and Simona are in Los Angeles. After the sentencing hearing, George and Simona left for California. They came back to Chicago in time to drive up to Oxford Wisconsin to report to prison on November 26, 2018.

George spent twelve days in Oxford Prison, a medium security prison in central Wisconsin, about 200 miles northwest of Chicago. He felt he was treated well by both the inmates and the prison staff. His now, wife Simona drove up with him when he checked in and was there to pick him up when he was released on Friday. December 7, 2016 at around 10:00 AM.

The Continuing Simona Saga July 27, 2017 to April 2020

After learning of George's arrest on July 27, 2017, Simona flew to Chicago in early August to be with George.[153] She was immediately interviewed by the FBI. In November 2017, she left Chicago to go back to London to close things down for good including her work and her apartment. She returned to Chicago 10 days later. She and George spent the winter of 2017 – 2018 with George's mom in Chicago. George's mom KiKi, did NOT like Simona. Neither did George's father.

George and Simona moved out of mom's house into a small apartment. They decide to get married on March 2, 2017. Then it was the hearing, the plea bargaining and the sentencing for George. Following the sentencing hearing on September 7, 2018, Simona and George go

---

[153] Business Insider, *"George Papadopoulos' fiancée opens up about her FBI interview, that mysterious London professor, and her wedding plans,* Natasha Bertrnd, Jnuary 6, 2018.

back to Chicago and then move out to Los Angeles where they remain until George is to report to prison on November 26, 2018.

This move is likely Simona's idea. George is in the spotlight because of his sentencing news. Simona is interested in an acting career. The place you get an acting role is Hollywood. With George's instant name recognition, Simona Papadopoulos will likely be "visible."

Sure enough. George and Simona got to LA in mid-September and on September 30, 2018, none other than Tom Arnold post a picture on Instagram of himself, George and Simona. They spend some time together until George leaves to do his time. On November 23, 2018, Simona posts an Instagram with a picture of the three of them together before they leave for Chicago. Simona describes Tom Arnold as "my rock!"

After prison, the Papadopoulos's move back to Beachwood Canyon in L.A. George and Simona have a contract to do a docu-reality series about their life. He finally has an income!

Papadopoulos announces he is running for Katie Hill's seat, California's 25th congressional district. He makes the filing date of December 6, 2019 and by the end of the year he has raised $100,000.

The primary was held on March 3, 2020. George didn't do so well. He got 2500 votes. The two winners got 58,000 and 41,000 votes. George managed to underachieve once again.

Life with Simona still doesn't make any sense, except for the fact that they both like to be in the spotlight. If Simona had not entered George's life, he would probably be back in Chicago selling real estate like the rest of his family.

The marriage has not been without problems. In early March 2020, Simona announced to the world that she is going to divorce George. The wife of George Papadopoulos, Simona Manigiante Papadopoulos announced she is divorcing him after he allegedly disrespected her on a Monday episode of his podcast.

———

"Officially divorcing [Papadopoulos] after the months of abuses and ultimately the huge disrespect he showed this morning in his podcast. I am tired of him and playing his wife," Simona wrote Monday evening on Twitter. "He is a monster." She also called her husband "an opportunist" who used her for his public benefit. "you know what George? As much as I thought you were an honest man deserving respect, I realize you are a grifter with no integrity, and I don't like you," she wrote.

The Papadopoulos' podcast with Tom Arnold and Austen Fletcher is not available, but Arnold said: "This too shall pass." Mangiante later deleted her tweet announcing the divorce and appeared to briefly deactivate her account. Whether the tiff is behind them remains a question.

The Relationship with the Mangiante and Papadopoulos families.

George had met Simona's family when he was on his 2 ½ month visit to Europe during their early courtship, but in January of 2020 the couple went to Italy to be with Simona's father when he was ill. He got to spend time with her family and bonded. He liked it.

The same cannot be said about Simona bonding with the Papadopoulos family. To put it bluntly, they hate each other. George's mom truly believes Simona is a Russian spy. Kiki is suspicious of Simona's clothes and her motivation. Her assessment of Simona is highlighted in the box on the following page.

The bottom line.

George Papadopoulos is an average guy. He is driven by wanting to be important. Up to now he has failed, but that may be changing – but likely that is temporary.

He is important now, though. He has a beautiful, dynamic wife. He is famous. He has developed confidence to match his aspirations.

What he doesn't have is a record of success. Whether he can leverage his current fame into something lasting is doubtful. So far he has been the victim, the stooge used by others to achieve their purpose.

He is clearly innocent of colluding with the Russians.

George's Mom's Assessment of Simone

From The Daily Beast, *"George Papadopoulos' Wife Says She's Divorcing Him After 'Months of Abuses"*, Julia Arcig, March 9, 2020 -
We reached out to Kiki Papadopoulos to get her side of the story, and she flat out denied the allegations regarding abuse on her part, which led to a miscarriage.

Simona is a liar! - *"Everything she has said thus far is completely incorrect. She is mentally off. I don't know why she is lying. She has lied from the very beginning," Kiki told us. "If true, the first thing she would have done is taken a test.*

Simona did so many things - *I could have her arrested for what she has done. I can say so much about her, but we are very private, decent people. We live a pretty simple life but a happy life. My son was excelling and I was there for him. I was a single parent, and I was pretty strict," she said.*

Advice to George – When The Daily Beast asked Kiki if she had anything to say to her son and Simona, her reply sounded heartfelt and fearful: *"Run George, the further away from her, the happier you will be. And Simona, I don't want to see her again in my lifetime. She is nothing but a negative, fighter, name calling abuser. I have never ever in my life had such a dark, dark person, a deceitful con artist in my life. Really, I am afraid of her.*

Moms feelings about Simona - *She is mentally off. You don't know 90% of what she has done. If this is bad, there is a lot worse. What she's done to my poor son. It's been a horror. I am scared for my son. She's a really lowlife sick person. That's all I can say."*
As for the whole issue with her age, it does appear that Simona lied several times about how old she was.

More suspicions about Simona: - *"Simona u have 3 large suitcases u left in my apt and said those suitcases are over 300,000 all my money inside were unworn boots shoes and purses top of the line name brand Prada and so on ...who gave those we will use our imagination.*

Appendix E FBI Players

The FBI was handed the foundation of the evidence of Trump-Russia collusion by two individuals, Joseph Mifsud and Christopher Steele. After three years, the FBI concluded there was no evidence of Trump-Russia collusion.

The logical question is, "Why would two individuals want to mislead the FBI? Obviously their "evidence" was not real. They had to be motivated to want to do damage to the Trump campaign and then to his presidency.

The FBI didn't investigate why or how that happened. Why did the FBI show such little interest in investigating the origin of the disinformation? It appears it was because of their bias and ego. Contrary to the justifications advanced in the books written by James Comey, "*A Higher Loyalty*" and William McCabe, "*The Threat*", it wasn't because they were answering to a higher power of loyalty or wanting to protect us Americans from the threat of Donald Trump. If, for example they wondered if maybe Mifsud was a CIA operative instead of a Russian agent, they may have discovered that the CIA was responsible for planting disinformation, in addition to the Russians. They didn't investigate the origin of the disinformation, because as their own inspector general discovered, they were perpetrating it knowing it was disinformation. Their own Inspector General discovered that Comey, McCabe and Strzok were conducted themselves consistent with being active players in a "deep state." Because of their egos and biases they didn't see it then and even now.

The tragedy is Comey and McCabe were the leaders of the FBI and their egos and biases bled down to others in the organization and tarnished the image of what was a great organization.

The other tragedy is that Jim Comey and Andy McCabe are basically "good guys." Unlike John Brennan, ex director of the CIA, they are not evil people. They are smart, personable people. They were good at what they did. The FBI will be hurt by their loss. Unfortunately, their egos and biases were their downfall and rightfully so

This appendix describes all the key FBI players. It describes their roles on Crossfire Hurricane and their individual contributions. It also identifies their missteps mainly resulting from their egos, biases and the reward system in an FBI under James Comey.

The FBI organization and key people – Figure E 1 shows the key people comprising the FBI personnel primarily involved in Crossfire Hurricane. Table E 1 lists the key people and their roles.

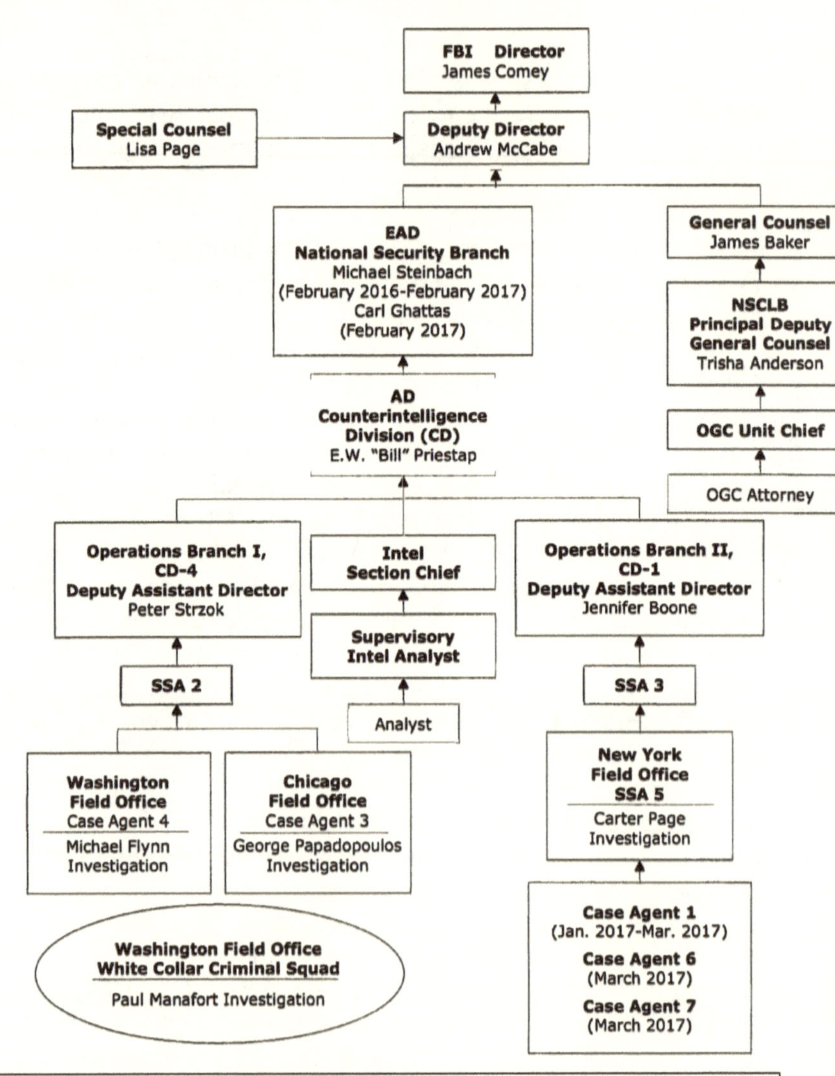

Figure E 1 - FBI Crossfire Hurricane Organization

Table E 1 Key FBI Crossfire Hurricane Players

First	Last Name	Organization	Description
David	Archey	FBI	FBI Agent Replaced Strozk
James	Baker	FBI	FBI General Council
William	Barnett	FBI	FBI Agent Investigating Flynn
John	Carlin	FBI	Mueller Team
Kevin	Clinesmith	FBI	FBI Attorney, AKA FBI Atty 2
James	Comey	FBI	FBI Director
Michael	Gaeta	FBI	FBI Agent - Steele Handling Agent 1
Curtis	Heide	FBI	FBI Investigative Agent - Papadopoulos
Andrew	McCabe	FBI	FBI Deputy Director
Michael	McSwain	FBI	FBI Investigative Agent - Papadopoulos
Johnathan	Moffa	FBI	FBI Agent
Lisa	Page	FBI	FBI Asst. General Council
Joe	Pietka	FBI	FBI SSA1 (Flynn)
Bill	Priestap	FBI	AssistantDirector FBI Counterintelligence
Stephen	Somma	FBI	Case Agent 1 (Many errors & omissions)
	SSA 1	FBI	Ohr contact post-Steele
	SSA2	FBI	
	SSA3	FBI	Ohr contact post-Steele Replaced SSA1
	SSA4	FBI	
Peter	Strozk	FBI	

E1 FBI –James Comey

FBI Director: September 4, 2013 to May 9, 2017

Contribution to investigation:

Negative – Set a tone of "We need to nail these guys. They are guilty of colluding with the Russians." He encouraged misconduct by rubber stamping FISA warrants without even reading them. His ego demanded that Trump live up to Comey's standards, but that would never happen, so he immediately began building a file to nail his boss.

Author's assessment: His ego got him fired. He deserved it.

Facts:

Born: December 14, 1960 In Yonkers NY

High School: Northern Highlands Regional HS in Allendale, NJ. 1978.

College: College of William & Mary, 1982. Major: Chemistry and Religion

Law School: Juris Doctor (J.D.) from the University of Chicago Law in 1985.

Career:

1985 – 1993 – Law clerk for US District Judge John M. Walker Jr. in Manhattan; Associate for Gibson, Dunn & Crutcher in NY; US Atty. Southern District of NY Deputy Chief of Criminal Div.
1996 – 2001 – Asst US Atty in charge of Richmond Division
2002 - 2005 – US Atty for Southern District of NY
2005 – 2010 – Sr. VP & General Counsel for Lockheed Martin
2011 – 2013 – Sr Management at Bridgewater
2013 – 2017 – Director of FBI

By all accounts, James Comey is a decent guy. With regard to the Trump-Russia collusion investigation, he had two failings; (1) his ego and (2) his ego.

Prior to serving under President Trump, Comey got in trouble with the democrats because he was a man of his word. On July 5, 2016, FBI Director James Comey announced that the bureau would recommend that charges not be filed in the probe into Clinton's use of a private email system while heading the State Department.[155] In testifying before congress on September 28, 2016 Director Comey was asked both specifically in the Clinton email case and generally, "if new evidence became available, would the FBI reopen the case?" His answer was essentially, "yes if the evidence was material."[156]

New information did come to light. On Sept. 26, 2016, the FBI executed a search warrant on former Rep. Anthony Weiner's iPhone, iPad and laptop computer, and discovered 141,000 emails on the laptop that were potentially relevant to the FBI's closed investigation of Clinton.[157] Anthony Weiner was Huma Abedin, Clinton Aide's husband. Legally the FBI could not investigate those emails because they did not relate to the on-going Weiner investigation. They related to the Clinton investigation. The Clinton investigation was reopened so the FBI could examine the emails. Comey had represented to congress that he would notify them when and if a Clinton email investigation was reopened. A month later, on Oct. 28, 2016, Comey notified lawmakers by letter that the FBI had "learned of the existence of emails that appear to be pertinent to the investigation" and that investigators would "review these emails to determine whether they contained classified material."[158] This was unfortunate, but Jim Comey should not be faulted for notifying congress. He had made a commitment and he was simply following through on it. Clearly if Comey either had NOT reopened the investigation, or NOT notified congress that the investigation had been reopened, he would be in much deeper trouble. He did what he had to do. He reopened the investigation and he told congress that he had.

The FBI found no incriminating material. On November 6, 2016, Comey told Congress in a follow-up memo that the FBI had *"reviewed*

---

[155] FBI Press Release, July 5, 2016

[156] Comey Testimony to House Judiciary Committee, *"Asked if he would reopen the Clinton case if he found new information, Comey said: "It's hard for me to answer in the abstract. We would certainly look at any new and substantial information."* September 28, 2016

[157] CNS News. *"Nunes: 'Good FBI Agents' Told Us About Weiner Laptop At the Time, 'But We Couldn't Do Anything"*, Susan Jones, June 15, 2018

[158] October 28, 2016 memo to Congress saying, *"In connection with an unrelated case, the FBI has learned of the existence of emails that appear to be pertinent to the investigation"*

all of the communications that were to or from Hillary Clinton while she was Secretary of State" and that officials *"have not changed our conclusions."*[159]

Comey's two faults, (1) his ego and (2) his ego.

Although he was morally and ethically justified and really, **required** to take this series of actions, he "learned" how powerful he and his position were. Most likely, to this day, he doesn't understand what happened to him and his ego in late 2016. Already a victim of an inflated ego, it just got a significant boost. One individual with one action was able to materially "shake" a whole nation. Jim Comey, defender of all that is good for the American people, could bring powerful people to their knees through his "higher loyalty." He rattled the great Hillary Clinton. Within a week he rattled the great Donald Trump. Independent of whether he was justified in what he did, he "learned" he could bring presidents to their knees.

To an objective person up to this point, however, Director Comey's judgement and actions could be justified despite the fact that the Inspector General Michael Horowitz said Comey clearly departed from FBI norms.

But, even before his big ego boost in September- October 2016, Jim Comey's already big ego got in the way of being a good FBI director. Here are a few examples;

- Comey's ego made his FBI infallible. According to Director Comey, his FBI didn't submit any FISA request that left out exculpatory evidence. The FBI under James Comey would not alter a FISA application to prevent it from being disapproved. By admitting signing FISA applications without challenging them he was attesting that he didn't need to question his agent's honesty and integrity. His FBI was infallible.
- That's what a big ego will do to a person. It will not allow the person to critically review what he/she does. It was Comey's ego that led to FISA applications against an innocent person to get approved. The Inspector General's (IG) report stated that is exactly what happened. Comey's

---

[159] November 6, 2016 memo to Congress saying, *"Based on our review, we have not changed our conclusions that we expressed in July."*

deadpan response; "I must have been misled."[160]   This "great leader" wasn't so great after all. He just had a blind spot when he trusted his people. In fact, the IG looked at all the FISA requests made under Comey's watch at the FBI and found;[161]

> o The IG's office "could not review original Woods Files for 4 of the 29 selected FISA applications because the FBI has not been able to locate them and, in 3 of these instances, did not know if they ever existed." Of the 25 files they were able to review, there were "errors or inadequately supported facts *in all of the 25 applications*" (emphasis added).[162]
>
> o Those errors included "facts stated in the FISA application that were: (a) not supported by any documentation in the Woods File, (b) not clearly corroborated by the supporting documentation in the Woods File, or (c) inconsistent with the supporting documentation in the Woods File." While Horowitz noted the review was ongoing, his team had already "identified on average of about 20 issues per application," with one application actually having 65 issues.[163] This is not the record of a "great leader", which is what Comey had been christened by James Comey. Comey signed the first three Carter Page FISA warrant applications testifying to their accuracy and completeness.[164] He lied. The fourth Carter Page FISA warrant application was signed by Andy McCabe[165] who replaced the fired Comey. Following in the

---

[160] AXIOS, *"Comey defends FBI but admits FISA failures: "I was wrong"*, December 15, 2019

[161] The Federalist, *"Latest Inspector General Report Slams Comey's FBI for Massive Failures to Document FISA Claims"*, Margo Cleveland , April 2, 2020

[162] Office of the Inspector General, US Department of Justice, *"Management Advisory Memorandum for the Director of the Federal Bureau of Investigation Regarding the Execution of Woods Procedures for Applications Filed with the Foreign Intelligence Surveillance Court Relating to U.S. Persons."* Michael Horowitz, March 30, 2020, Page 3.

[163] Ibid. , page 7

[164] Heritage Foundation, *"Warrants to Spy on Trump Campaign Lacked Probable Cause, DOJ Admits"* Charles "Cully" Stimson, January 30, 2020

[165] Ibid.

footsteps of his mentor, he also lied when he testified to its accuracy and completeness. He had followed the example of his mentor, Jim Comey. Neither of them had any idea if the applications were accurate or complete. It was the Comey FBI "way." They lied. Jim Comey called it "being careless." "Comey did not take responsibility for his actions as Director of the FBI. As the IG stated in his critique, *"Former Director Comey failed to live up to this responsibility," the report said. "By not safeguarding sensitive information obtained during the course of his FBI employment, and by using it to create public pressure for official action, Comey set a dangerous example for the over 35,000 current FBI employees."[166]*

- o The IG Management Advisory Memorandum also noted that about half of the files reviewed contained facts attributed to Confidential Human Sources, or CHSs, but many of those files, in violation of the Woods Procedures, failed to include a statement from the handling agent regarding the CHS's reliability and background and the accuracy of the information derived from the CHS. The FBI likewise violated the Woods Procedures' mandate that case agents re-verify the facts contained in renewal applications. That was not consistently done, and in some instances the case agents stated they "only verified newly added statements of facts."[167] The FBI was, as Donald Trump stated, "out of control" under Comey's leadership.

- Comey's ego made him an easy mark for John Brennan – Brennan scammed Comey into converting a legitimate investigation into Russian interference into a bogus investigation into Trump-Russia collusion. Even after the FBI had enormous amounts of exculpatory evidence on

---

[166] Office of the Inspector General, US Department of Justice, *"Report of Investigation of Former Federal Bureau of Investigation Director James Comey's Disclosure of Sensitive Investigative Information and Handling of Certain Memoranda"* August 2019

[167] Office of the Inspector General, US Department of Justice, *"Management Advisory Memorandum for the Director of the Federal Bureau of Investigation Regarding the Execution of Woods Procedures for Applications Filed with the Foreign Intelligence Surveillance Court Relating to U.S. Persons."* Michael Horowitz, March 30, 2020

both the Mifsud track and the Steele track, Comey's ego and growing dislike for Trump, prevented him from acknowledging it.

- Comey's ego made him an easy mark for Christopher Steele – Even after the FBI had overwhelming evidence that the Steele dossier was an outlet for Russian disinformation, Comey's ego and growing dislike for Trump, prevented him from acknowledging it. "The FBI got played — the Steele Dossier was Russian disinformation."[168] The very thing Comey was warning us stupid Americans about- not getting duped by Russian disinformation, the great leader of the FBI fell for. If he is that great leader than he writes about, he is one of the dumbest "great leaders", based on how easily he is duped.

- Comey's ego wouldn't allow for him to accept that Joseph Mifsud was anything other than a Russian agent. Even Mueller changed Mifsud's status from being a "Russian agent" to just being a "mysterious Maltese Professor." Comey never admitted that the FBI never found any evidence of Mifsud acting as a Russian agent. His ego prevented the FBI to even look at the possibility Mifsud was a CIA operative. His ego compromised an investigation.

- Comey's ego led him to believe he couldn't be fired - *"I thought there's no way ... I'm not going to get fired, because I'm in charge of the Russia investigation. The president is not going to fire the FBI director who's handling the Russia investigation."*[169]

- Comey's ego got him fired – In his June 8, 2017 testimony before a joint session of congress, James Comey testified, *"I served at pleasure of president. I could be fired for any reason."* If he believed that in his heart, he would never have documented every meeting he had with the President. Afterall, he would never have to use it. Trump wouldn't fire him! Jim Comey documented those meetings so he would have evidence that he had the high ground if Trump ever attempted to fire him. He could use that as one of the arrows to get the President impeached for "obstruction of

---

[168] The Washington Examiner, *"Declassified notes in FISA report have GOP investigators asking about James Comey and Robert Mueller"*, Daniel Chaitin, April 11, 2020.

[169] USA Today, *"In his own words: 8 key quotes from James Comey on Donald Trump and what's next."* Susan Page and Kevin Johnson, April 16, 2018

justice." He could bring a sitting president down. That's why he documented and published memos of those meetings. Think about the absurdity of Comey's thought process in light of the fact that it has now been determined that General Flynn was set up and he <u>was</u> a good guy as Trump said, and that Trump was justified in asking Comey to announce the truth that Trump was not under investigation. Mr. Comey's ego would not allow him to consider that Trump was right, Michael Flynn WAS a good guy. He had done nothing wrong. He apparently was set up by Comey's FBI. Comey leaked those memos to GET Trump. That is the mark of a weak leader, not a great leader. (General MacArthur didn't cry when Truman fired him.) To Comey's credit, he freely admitted that he did it to get even. He admitted he did it so a Special prosecutor would be named to investigate Trump. Comey must have felt awfully bad about having to put the nation through all that turmoil when he was wrong all along. That is NOT honorable. At this point it was known that there was nothing to the Papadopoulos and Steele rumors of collusion. It was revenge. Comey's ego would not allow him to accept that he was fired, even though, in his own words, it was the President's prerogative. It had to be Trump's fault. He had to be able to prove that it was Trump's fault. He could use his memos to ensure that a Special Prosecutor was named to investigate Trump for obstruction of justice.

- Comey's ego discredited the FBI – In an April 13, article in the Washington Examiner, by James Gagliano, ex FBI agent, he expressed a position held by many FBIers, *"James Comey, stop embarrassing retired FBI agents like me."*

  - And yet as late as April 13, 2020, days after freshly declassified footnotes from the inspector general report revealed that Comey's team had been repeatedly alerted to the fact that portions of the Steele dossier were connected to a concerted "Russian disinformation campaign to denigrate U.S. foreign relations," the self-aware former FBI Director wrote a column on "crisis leadership." This just enhanced the image of Comey's lack of understanding that he was an awful leader. He had gotten duped. He couldn't admit it.

Comey's ego led him to believe that HIS FBI could do no wrong. This attitude from their leader allowed certain agents in his chain of command to interpret his support as "we can get away with anything as long as it supports the greater good "(as WE determine it to be.) They were emulating their boss. Unfortunately, their boss was an egomaniac, and in many ways, an awful leader. Emulating Comey was NOT good for someone who wanted to be a career FBI agent. The IG report documents Comey's lack of moral leadership.

Unfortunately, the American people, Michael Flynn and Carter Page were dragged through hell because of Comey's ego. Not only <u>could</u> FISA applications be submitted that were false, misleading and altered, they <u>actually were</u> in Carter page's case. Comey's explanation, "I must have been misled." Comey personally approved these applications swearing they were accurate. Was he being evil? Probably not. He was serving a "higher loyalty", his ego. Unfortunately, Comey was ruining innocent people's lives in the process. It doesn't appear he "gets it."

Comey's explanation for misleading the FISA court, congress and the American people was – "the procedures were wrong."

In Director Comey's own words, "He's (IG Horowitz) *right, I was wrong (*about the 17 errors and omissions by the FBI in Carter Page's FISA warrant applications). *I was overconfident in the procedures that the FBI and Justice had built over 20 years. I thought they were robust enough. It's incredibly hard to get a FISA. I was overconfident in those because he's right, there was real sloppiness. Seventeen things that either should have been in the applications or at least discussed and characterized differently. It was not acceptable, so he's right, I was wrong."*

For Comey, who the inspector general said "clearly departed from FBI norms" to suddenly blame "procedures" for his misdeeds is bizarre and not credible. Trying to hide behind "procedures" is not the mark of even a mediocre leader, much less a great one.

Jim Comey's representation that Its **"incredibly hard"** to get a FISA application is a huge lie. Even given all the documented misrepresentations the IG found in the applications filed under Comey's leadership (in other words the applications were far from "pristine" and many should have been disapproved) the FISC approved 98.75% of the applications (5801/5874)![170]

The data demonstrates that It is **"incredibly easy"** to get a FISA application. The data shows in practice almost all misrepresentations are missed by the FISA court.

To Comey when the FBI lies, it is "sloppiness." When Trump lies, it is a "lie". In the Nixon era, a lie was defined as, "a statement that is no longer operable." In the Clinton era, "the occurrence of a lie depends on what your definition of "is" is. The bottom line- they are all lies. Comey is one of the least capable persons to define a "lie." According to Comey, an FBI agent lying is just "sloppiness".

The "awful" things Comey accused Trump of, Comey was guilty of.

Mr. Comey has testified that, *"Millions of people believe what the President says. Today, there are millions of Americans walking around thinking that the FBI is corrupt and out to get the President of the United States, the Justice Department is corrupt and out to get the President of the United States.*

The Horowitz report documents and confirms that Trump was correct and rightfully critical of the FBI. Under Comey's leadership, *the FBI was corrupt and arguably out to get the President of the United States.* Under Comey's leadership, the FBI lied on FISA applications with the implied objective to "get" the President of the United States (all errors and omissions tended to make Trump's team look worse than they were). Other "awful' things that Director Comey accused Trump of that the Inspector General officially found Comey guilty of;

- Inspector General Michael Horowitz said that at key moments Comey clearly departed from FBI norms and his (COMEY's) decisions negatively impacted the public's trust in the Justice Department and FBI. Unlike Comey's <u>opinion</u> of the impact of Trumps actions, the IG <u>investigated</u> Comey's actions and found they smeared the FBI. So far Comey has refrained from calling Horowitz "a liar" but has

---

[170] Electronic Privacy Information Center (EPIC), *"Foreign Intelligence Surveillance Act Court Orders 1979-2017)"*

not apologized to Trump for accusing him of what the IG said Comey was guilty of. It is that ego and bias thing.

- Horowitz warned there's potentially more trouble ahead for Comey. He confirmed he's conducting another investigation into Comey's handling of his classified memos on his private meetings with President Trump.
- Aside from the 500-page report that already found Comey insubordinate, Horowitz dinged Comey for keeping his own job security in mind when handling the Clinton case, especially since he believed Clinton would win and one day become his boss. He was concerned about his survivability," Horowitz said. (Not answering to a higher authority as James Comey would say). So far, Comey has not called Horowitz a liar.
- IG Horowitz found that Comey violated agency policies when he retained a set of memos documenting meetings with President Donald Trump early in 2017 and caused one of them to be leaked to the press. The report states that *Comey set a "dangerous example" for FBI em*ployees in an attempt to "achieve a personally desired outcome." (In other words, it is Comey, not Trump who was damaging the reputation of the FBI.) Unlike calling Trump a liar, so far Comey has not called Horowitz a liar for stating that Comey was a bad leader by *setting a dangerous example* for the FBI rank and file.
- Comey has said, "The President of the United States has convinced millions of people that they (the FBI) are corrupt, when that's a lie." Based on the IG report, the FBI WAS corrupt under Comey (lied to and misled the FISA court, telling Flynn he didn't need a lawyer, falsely calling Mifsud a Russian agent, etc.). President Trump should be thanked for exposing the corruptness of the FBI. This is not to say that Comey wanted the FBI to be corrupt, it is saying that his leadership led to the corruption and his ego prevented him from seeing it.)

The pettiness of the seven memos written after Comey's contacts with Trump document why Trump was justified to ask for some loyalty from Comey and when he didn't get, to fire him.

A boss who does not have some loyalty has disloyalty. Disloyalty HAS to be dealt with. As a leader, Comey should have known that. Instead he decided to undermine his boss instead of quitting as he should have. To stay he had to either believe he could be on the same team with Trump or win the power struggle. Obviously, Comey felt he could win. It is that ego thing.

Memo #1 January 7, 2017 Written and sent to Andrew McCabe, James Baker and James Rybicki *(This was NOT as Comey represented, a personal diary entry. It was officially sent to FBI personnel.)* Comey told Trump about Russian claims that they had evidence of Trump being with prostitutes in Russian hotel in 2013. Comey recorded two Trump responses he thought would look bad if leaked, (1) "there were no prostitutes, there were never any prostitutes. And (2) "then he started talking about all the women who had falsely accused him of grabbing or touching them and gave me the sense that he was defending himself to me." **Interpretation** – Comey wanted to leave the impression that Trump was guilty by even commenting on the allegations. This is equivalent to witnesses who have no facts, testifying that they "felt the defendant had evil thoughts" – a common legal maneuver to imply guilt without having any facts. **Investigation result** – Comey and FBI fell for Russian disinformation. The FBI could not confirm the allegation. Comey just wanted to document Trumps reaction because, to Comey it implied guilt.

Memo #2 – February 28, 2017 Dinner with Trump. "I felt uncomfortable throughout. Trump asked for loyalty twice. **Interpretation** – Comey implied that Trump expected Comey to "cover for him." Comey could not allow himself to imply that Trump wanted loyalty as opposed to "disloyalty." **Investigation Result** – Trump did not demand anything. Comey did not respond to "implied" pressure. The old legal maneuver if you have no facts, just say, I "felt" he was pressuring me!

Memo #3 – February 8, 2017 Oval Office meeting with Trump and Reince Priebus - Comey first documented a private conversation with Reince Priebus at the White House. Priebus asked, "Do you have a FISA order on Mike Flynn?"

Comey's Response: *"I then explained about the normal channel was from DOJ leadership to the WH counsel about such things. I would normally make sure the AG and DAG were aware and they would likely inform the WH Counsel and he could decide whether to inform the COS. I explained that it was important that communication about any particular case go through that channel to protect us and to protect the WH from any accusations of improper influence."*

Authors Observation: This is the same FBI Director who told MSNBC'S Nicole Wallace during a December 2019 conversation that he directed his agents, in violation of standard protocol of working through White House counsel and having discussions and approvals, to just go over his head and interview Michael Flynn. According to Comey his agents did that just because he "sent them." He admitted that it was "something we, I probably wouldn't have done or gotten away with in a more organized investigation -- a more organized administration." In this case, Comey didn't give a shit about "channels" to protect the FBI from accusations of improper influence in one of their investigations. Jim Comey, the FBI Boy Scout, was proud that HE violated protocol, but shame on Priebus for even suggesting it! He discredited the FBI by his arrogance of wrongdoing and "getting away with it." Jim Comey is blinded by his ego.

Back to the memo: The remaining part of the memo documented Comey's conversation with Trump and Priebus in the Oval office. "The President brought up the "Golden Showers thing" and said it really bothered him if his wife had any doubt about it. He then added that he hadn't stayed overnight in Russia during the Miss Universe trip." **Interpretation**: Comey wanted to leave the impression that Trump was guilty by just commenting on the allegations. **Investigation Result:** Golden shower incident was part of Russian disinformation. It had no basis in fact. The Russians had a gullible disinformation target, FBI Director, James Comey.

Memo #4 – February 19, 2017 Oval Office homeland threat briefing. After the briefing, President Trump wanted to meet with Jim Comey alone. According to Comey's memo, *"He (Trump) began by saying he wanted to "talk about Mike Flynn." He then said that although Flynn "hadn't done anything wrong" in his call with the Russians, he had to let him go because he misled the Vice President, whom he described as a "good guy." He explained that he just couldn't have Flynn misleading* *the Vice President and, in any event, he had other concerns about Flynn, and had a great guy coming in, so he had to let Flynn go.* **Interpretation:** The purpose of documenting this is unclear. **Investigation Results:** The FBI set up Michael Flynn. He was just as Trump said, "a good guy."

Memo #5 – March 1, 2017 Telecon. Comey's memo just says Trump called to see how he (Comey) was doing. **No interpretation. Nothing to investigate.**

Memo #6 – March 30, 2017 Telecon - Comey wrote that Trump "asked what he could do to lift the cloud," Comey answered, "I explained that we were running it down as quickly as possible and that there would be great benefit, if we didn't find anything, to our Good Housekeeping seal of approval, but we had to do our work." Comey also wrote that he reiterated that the FBI wasn't investigating Trump. "He said it would be great if that could get out and several times asked me to find a way to get that out." Trump closed the call, Comey wrote, by reiterating how "the cloud was hurting him" and how he "hoped I could find a way to get out that he wasn't being investigated." That call, Comey noted, led to a follow-up call later that morning to then-acting deputy attorney general Dana Boente, who was overseeing the Russia investigation due to Sessions' recusal. Comey wrote that he informed him of the substance of Trump's call "and said I was telling him so he could decide what guidance to give me, if any." **Interpretation:** Comey wanted to document that Trump asked him to tell the public that Trump wasn't under investigation. He wanted to document that Trump was "pressuring" him. **Investigation Results**: Trump was NOT under investigation. Comey had no trouble telling the public when Hillary Clinton was not under investigation. But then again, that wasn't an investigation, it was a "matter." (The record shows that Comey was **not** the Director of the Federal Bureau of "Matters".)

Memo #7 – April 11, 2017 Telecon - Comey wrote that he was returning a call from Trump. "He (Trump) said he was following up to see if I did what he had asked last time — getting out that he personally is not under investigation," Comey wrote of Trump. "I replied that I had passed the request to [Dana Boente] and had not heard back from him." **Interpretation:** Comey wanted a record of Trump asking him again to tell the public what he had told Trump, that Trump was not under investigation." **Investigation Results**: Trump was NOT under investigation.

These memos had nothing to do with advancing the investigation of Trump-Russia collusion. It is a pretty small person who would document interchanges with his boss in hopes that the recorded notes of meetings could be used to help depose his boss. The fact that Comey thought Trump saying (1) "Flynn was a good guy", (2) "I didn't visit a prostitute in Moscow, and (3) you told me I wasn't under investigation, please tell the American people also, would rise to the level of impeachable gossip reflects badly on Comey's judgement and a smallness that is reflective of a very weak non-leader. Comey no doubt has a rationalization for this behavior, but it is beyond comprehension what that rationalization would be.

A partial answer came when Senator Warner asked Comey in Comey's June 8, 2017 testimony before Congress why he documented his meeting with Trump, Comey's answer was, "I was alone. The subject matter and then the nature of the person."

Similar to Comey taking notes of this meetings with Trump, Comey's people took notes with their meetings with Comey

Bill Priestap, FBI head of counterintelligence took notes of meeting he attended with Director Comey and Deputy Director Andrew McCabe (Priestap's boss) shortly after the 2016 election. In the meeting they were discussing the investigation of Michael Flynn. His handwritten note questioned the ethical nature of the FBI investigation. His note stated, *"What is our goal? Truth and admission; or to get him (Flynn) to lie, so we can prosecute him or get him fired?"* Presumably, Priestap, relatively new to his position, was sensing that Comey and McCabe were up to no good and framing General Flynn. Apparently, now that the facts have come out, that is exactly what Comey was doing.[171]

But there are always two sides to every story.

Comey argues, *"The central conspiracy that President Trump and his allies have pushed about the Russia investigation — that it was a "treasonous" attempt by the FBI to overthrow the president — was "nonsense." Horowitz concluded that there was no evidence of political bias in the FBI's opening of the investigation.*
Barr counters that argument - Attorney General Bill Barr, whom Comey criticized for suggesting that the FBI's errors were "intentional" and politically motivated.

---

[171] Newsmax, *"Newly Revealed Texts Show Strzok, Page Altered Flynn Interview Notes"* David Patten, April 30, 2020. ________

To which Comey counters - *"He does not have a factual basis as the attorney general of the United States to be speculating that agents acted in bad faith. That doesn't make it any less consequential, any less important, but that's an irresponsible statement."*

The question is, how would Comey know what Barr had found out?

All of Comey's actions were designed to elevate his importance, try to intimidate his boss and he got caught. To his credit, he made a lot of people pay for questioning his patriotism. Apparently, that is all the satisfaction he required.

E2 –Andrew McCabe

E2 Andrew McCabe – FBI Deputy Director
February 2016 – January 2018; Acting Director
of FBI. May 9, 2017 to March 16, 2018 after
Jim Comey was fired.

Contribution to investigation: Huge.
Andy McCabe, even as an FBI executive, was
one of the top four contributors to Crossfire
Hurricane. He was more "hands-on" than his
direct reports Michael Steinbach or even
Michael's direct report, Bill Priestap. In fact, Peter Strzok, the lead FBI
Agent, kept Andy more informed of day-to-day happenings on the case
than he did with either his boss, Bill Priestap or Michael Steinbach.
Several factors that contributed to this uncharacteristic high level of
involvement in the case were; (1) Justifiably Andy did not like Trump.
Andy's wife was running for office as a Democrat at the same time as the
presidential election was ongoing and had been attacked by Trump for the
financial help she was getting from the Clinton machine and by inference,
that Andy's investigations were biased because of it; Nothing would
make McCabe happier than to find that Trump was guilty of something.
(2) Lisa Page worked directly for Andy. She promoted strong Strzok-
McCabe interactions.

Author's assessment: Andrew McCabe was made in the image of
Jim Comey. Andy's ego was not quite as big as Jim's, but his bias was
stronger.

>Born March 18, 1968
>Boles HS, Jacksonville FL 1986
>BA Political Science, Duke University, 1990
>JD Washington University, St. Louis 1993
>Joined FBI in 1996 after 3 years in private practice in

Philadelphia

Andrew McCabe was fired on March 16, 2018 by then Attorney
General, Jeff Sessions. Andy's firing came after the Inspector General
(IG) and the Office of Professional Responsibility (OPR) found McCabe
had "lacked candor," including under oath, on multiple occasions in his
statements to IG investigators conducting a leak investigation and had

made unauthorized disclosures to the news media.[172] Andrew McCabe admitted to misleading them about his involvement in a media leak and subsequently apologized for the lie, according to newly released transcripts of McCabe's interviews with investigators. McCabe spun a false narrative that he was not responsible for leaking the information cited in a October 2016 *Wall Street Journal article* that detailed a new probe into Hillary Clinton's email use.[173] Initially, the former deputy director told bureau investigators in May 2017 that he was "disappointed" the story "was appearing in the publication," and was not sure how it leaked to the press.

McCabe also denied that he had authorized the article, which included a conversation between himself and a top Obama DOJ official, and presented himself as a "victim" to the agent interviewing him, who at the time "wasn't surprised by his response." In its February 2018 report, the OIG detailed how McCabe had told former FBI special counsel Lisa Page to speak to the *Journal*, stating that McCabe's intent was "an attempt to make himself look good" after a previous article detailed how McCabe's wife had received nearly $500,000 from a Clinton ally to run for office in Virginia.

DOJ did not pursue a case against McCabe for lying.

In August 2019, Andy filed a wrongful termination lawsuit against the DOJ. As of this writing the case has not been litigated.

Andy McCabe's ego and bias and its effect on tarnishing the FBI is very disturbing to average Americans. Just as Comey did, McCabe wrote a book praising himself for simply saving the American people from Trump and for correcting the FBI's reputation that Trump had tarnished. To understand why this is so disturbing consider what McCabe personally has done to destroy the rule of law and tarnish the reputation of the FBI:

- McCabe lied to the FBI IG under oath.
  - Papadopoulos was sent to jail for that. McCabe was not prosecuted. That's not equal justice as demanded by the rule of law.

---

[172] Citizens for Responsibility and Ethics in Washington (CREW) , "*FBI Documents Offer New Details About Dismissal Of Andrew Mccabe*", Eli Lee, October 14, 2019

[173] National Review, "*FBI Investigators Say McCabe Apologized for Lying about Clinton-Probe Leak*".Tobias Hoonhout, January 2, 2020

- o In Andy's eyes he was justified in lying because it was for the "greater good."
- McCabe stated as one of the reasons he wrote his book "The Threat", *"I wanted more citizens to be aware of: the FBI's investigative techniques; the way it gathers and presents intelligence; and the set of ironclad authorities on which FBI investigative techniques are based."*
  - o Andy's ego didn't allow him to see what a IG review of his "ironclad authorities" uncovered – an almost total disregard for those "ironclad authorities" - The Inspector General found that FISA Applications produced under Andy's watch included errors in facts that were: (a) not supported by any documentation in the Woods File, (b) not clearly corroborated by the supporting documentation in the Woods File, or (c) inconsistent with the supporting documentation in the Woods File." While Horowitz noted the review was ongoing, his team had already "identified on average about 20 issues per application," with one application actually having 65 issues.[174] This blindness to violations of "ironclad authorities" under Andy's watch are extremely damaging to the FBI. Trump had every reason to challenge the motives of the FBI.
- McCabe lied when he signed the Carter Page FISA Warrant. When you sign a FISA warrant, you approve the accuracy and completeness of the content. Andy signed the warrant. The IG found many errors and omissions. Andy lied. To Andy it was a detail, an oversight. To Carter Page it was hell. Andy wants his job back? What does Andy owe Carter Page?
- McCabe stated in his book that, "FBI is being undermined by the current President. He and his partisan supporters have become corrosive to the organization." That may be a biased opinion. The official position by the FBI's watchdog, Michael Horowitz, the Inspector General is that Andrew McCabe and James Comey and their supporters had become corrosive to the organization. On the other hand, three years of investigation has revealed that Trump was justified in calling out the FBI. McCabe has yet to blame Horowitz and

---

[174] Ibid., page 7

his supporters of being "corrosive to the organization." Could Andy possibly be displaying bias against Trump?

- McCabe said, "President Trump's treatment of the bureau and its probe of Russian interference in the 2016 presidential campaign was so profoundly disturbing during the spring of 2017 that Justice Department officials discussed contacting Cabinet members to initiate Trump's removal from office under the 25th Amendment."
- This sounds like t "deep state" fighting back from being "outed." Horowitz confirmed every one of Trump's allegations. Is the FBI planning to initiate Horowitz's removal from office?
  - Based on the evidence of the practice of entrapment and blackmailing innocent people, changing the wording of FISA warrant applications, 17 errors and omissions that would have prevented unlawfully targeting US citizens, the FBI's treatment of the duly elected president of the United states is profoundly disturbing to the average American.

E3 –Michael Steinbach

E3. Michael Steinbach – FBI Executive Assistant Director National Security Branch

Contribution to investigation: Little, if any. Michael was just in the management chain between Strzok and McCabe, but apparently never got materially involved. He was involved in the Clinton email investigation and essentially blamed Clinton for creating the whole mess by insisting on using private email servers.[175] The FBI was just doing its job to ensure that National Security was not compromised.

Author's assessment: Straight shooter. Too bad he wasn't more involved in Crossfire Hurricane

Born March 18, 1968
BS Aerospace Engineering USNA, 1988
Naval Aviator 1988 – 1995.
Joined FBI in 1995 in Chicago Field Office.
Served as head of FBI operations in Guantanamo Bay,
Deputy commander of FBI operations in Afghanistan and
Head of Jacksonville and Miami field offices.

Michael was up to speed on the Clinton email investigation. He dismissed both the pro- and anti-Clinton laptop conspiracy theories. Rather, he says "the roughly three weeks that elapsed between the seizing of Weiner's laptop and Comey's decision to reopen the investigation were consumed by ordinary law-enforcement bureaucracy. The Weiner investigation was opened up based on Weiner's inappropriate contacts," Steinbach says. "In the course of that investigation, New York got a warrant and searched the laptop. As soon as they identified some evidence, the head of the New York office, **Bill Sweeney,** called down and spoke to the deputy director and a few others. I wasn't at that

---

[175] Propublica, *"The Problems With the FBI's Email Investigation Went Well Beyond Comey"*, Peter Elkind, May 11, 2017

meeting, but he called me later that day and said, 'Hey, we've got something.'"[176]

Steinbach was very critical of how Clinton and her supporters blamed the FBI for Trump's election. "I don't find it credible," Steinbach said. "It's a mess she helped create from start to finish, with start being when she elected to use a private server. Even if you were to assume the investigation influenced the election, her actions created the environment. You can second-guess how it played out. But our guiding principle was to protect the American people and the Constitution of the United States."

---

[176] Vanity Fair, *"It Wasn't Conspiracy: A Former F.B.I. Official Reveals What Really Happened With Andrew McCabe"*, Chris Smith, January 21, 2018,

E4
–William Priestap

E4. Bill Priestap Assistant director of FBI - Counterintelligence Division from January 16, 2016 – December 2018.

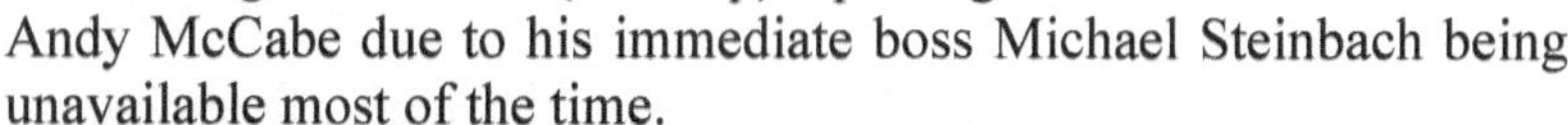

Contribution to investigation:
Neutral – Little involvement despite Strzok, Page & Pientka reported to him during the investigation and he (Priestap) reporting to Andy McCabe due to his immediate boss Michael Steinbach being unavailable most of the time.

Positive – Priestap raised the question of; *"what is the FBI trying to do, get General Flynn to admit he violated the Logan Act, or trick him into lying about it?*

Author's assessment: Retired in place.

Born April 5, 1969
BS Hillsdale College 1991
MA Educational Administration, Norwich University
JD University of Detroit-Mercy
MBA University of Detro1t-Mercey
April 2019 Retired

Priestap is a typical government bureaucrat who happened to be named Assistant Director of FBI Counterintelligence Division as his last job before retirement. It was a very responsible position. Bill didn't do it justice. Priestap reported to Mr. Steinbach, Executive Assistant Director, but Steinbach was hardly ever in his office. On paper, Steinbach in turn reported to Andy McCabe.

Bill Priestap wasn't really "allowed" to be important in his last year before retirement because; (1) He didn't want to be important and (2) the Crossfire Hurricane team didn't want him to be important. This was clear when he stated under sworn testimony to the Senate Intelligence Committee June 21, 2017 that the FBI *"didn't want to stand behind inclusion of unverified information from ex-British spy Christopher Steele."* Hey. Good old Bill didn't think much of the Steele dossier, but what could he do? He was just the head of the FBI Counterintelligence Division.

It was also made very clear on January 24, 2017, when Bill. doodled on a note pad at an FBI meeting concerning General Flynn's "lies," writing; *"What's our goal? Truth/Admission or to get him to lie, so we can prosecute him or get him fired? If we get him to admit to breaking the Logan Act, give facts to DOJ & have them decide. Or, if he initially lies, then we present him [redacted] & he admits it, document for DOJ, & let them decide how to address it."[177]* (The question he was asking himself was why is the FBI doing this? The FBI can just hand over the evidence of violation of the Logan Act to the DOJ and they can decide if DOJ wants to prosecute or not. Otherwise we have to set him up to lie about talking to Russian Ambassador Sergey Kislyak, then turn that over to the DOJ and they can decide if DOJ wants to prosecute the lie crime.

Bill had it right. The FBI's job is to investigate wrongdoing. If they thought that Flynn's calls to Russian Ambassador Sergey Kislyak during the presidential transition period was a "wrongdoing," they should have confronted him and referred the matter to DOJ for a decision to prosecute for a violation of the Logan Act or not.   The FBI didn't need to investigate. They had recorded the call. But, as Bill Priestap suggested in his doodle, the FBI (Peter Strzok) wanted to create a crime. They knew DOJ would probably not prosecute Flynn for a Logan Act violation, but if they innocently asked Flynn if he had any conversation with Kislyak and Flynn said no, they could nail him for lying to the FBI because they knew the answer – they were listening.

In contrast to Midterm Exam (Clinton email scam) Bill was on the outside looking in on Crossfire Hurricane (Trump-Russia collusion scam) Those teams were both headed by Peter Strzok and according to Priestap's testimony at the Judiciary Committee House of Representatives June 5, 2018 [178] Peter pretty much kept Bill out of the loop on Crossfire Hurricane, reporting two levels up directly to Andy McCabe on the important stuff.

One would think that if Bill Priestap wasn't plugged in to the important stuff, he would be right on top of signing travel requests and approving expense accounts and other mundane administrative activities of the counterintelligence staff. Again, according to his testimony at the Judiciary Committee House of Representatives June 5, 2018 he couldn't remember if he had signed any travel requests for Peter Strzok or any of

---

[177] VOX , *"The new Michael Flynn documents aren't the bombshell Trump is making them out to be"*, Aaron Rupar. April 30, 2020

his staff or where they might have traveled to or when. He couldn't even remember when or where he personally had traveled or who he talked to or what they talked about despite the fact he had "only taken two or three trips." In fact, Bill had made two trips to London and Strzok at least three trips to London.

Bill started his job with Counterintelligence when he took over from Randy Coleman. In 2016 Dana Corsi, Robert Jones and Gordon Johnson reported to Priestap. Peter Strzok and Johnathon Moffa did not report to Bill in the chain of command but did in context of the Clinton and Trump investigations. Priestap testified to Congress twice:

- Senate Intelligence Committee June 21, 2017 – Priestap testified that the FBI "didn't want to stand behind inclusion of unverified information from ex-British spy Christopher Steele" in an Intelligence Community Assessment supplied in a Memorandum for the President in December 2016.[179]"
- Judiciary Committee House of Representatives June 5, 2018-
    - Priestap identified the core management of Counterintelligence as: Peter Strzok (the lead); Jonathan Moffa (FBI Agent), Sally Moyer (Legal) & Rick Mains also reported to Strzok. They reported to Priestap about 3 times a week.
    - Priestap went overseas 2 or 3 times. (He couldn't remember when or where he went. That is not credible!)
    - Either Sally Moyer or Johnathon Moffa reported on Page-Strzok affair to Bill Priestap. Priestap confronted Strzok and Page.

Judging from the transcripts of his testimony Bill Priestap was not "plugged in" to the investigation despite it being his responsibility. It was his last job at the FBI before his retirement.

---

[179] Washington Post, *"Senate committee unanimously endorses spy agencies' finding that Russia interfered in 2016 presidential race in bid to help Trump"* Ellen Nakashima, April 21, 2020.

E5 –Peter Strzok

E 5 Peter Strzok Head of Counterespionage Section
(Reported to Bill Priestap)

Contribution to investigation:
Extremely Negative – Extreme bias. His
bias was documented in email exchanges with
Lisa Page. His bias was the most influencing
factor in entrapping General Flynn even after
knowing Flynn was not guilty of any
wrongdoing. Strzok's bias subconsciously
perhaps, prevented him from discovering that
Joseph Mifsud was potentially working for the
CIA and that he was not a Russian Agent.

Positive – Capable guy. He was a victim of his bias and ego.

Strzok's lawsuit against the FBI and DOJ for wrongfully firing him
was and still is ill advised.

Born March 7, 1970 in Sault Ste Marie, Michigan (Father Career
Military - US Army)
St. Johns Prep School, Minnesota, 1987
BA Georgetown Univ, 1991
1991 – 1996 US Army (Officer)
1996 – 2018 (August) FBI (Fired)
MA Georgetown Univ, 2013
Joined FBI in 1996 after 5 years in Army

Peter suffered greatly from having an office affair, the affair being
outed and then released to the public. Perhaps his biggest contribution to
Crossfire Hurricane was the email trail with Lisa Page that he left behind.
The good news is there wasn't any "romantic nonsense" involved. It was
all "work related insider strategy and intrigue exchanges." We, the
American people learned a lot about the functioning of the FBI behind
the scenes from Peter Strzok and Lisa Page. We have an unedited e-
communication trail of damning evidence of collusion to "get Trump."
(Collusion evidence was something Peter was unable to uncover in the
Trump campaign investigation.)

We also have an unedited record of the extreme bias and the tremendous superiority Peter enjoyed over all the smelly Trump supporters. Peter would have had a heyday investigating misconduct and collusion if he was let-loose on investigating the misdeeds of his FBI in this case. He likely would have had so much more damning evidence to weave an unchallengeable case against him, Lisa and his coworkers.

Things that Peter Strzok did that were unethical –

- Peter argued to keep the investigation of Michael Flynn open even though there was no evidence of collusion. When he was successful in keeping it open, he succeeded in planting evidence of Flynn lying to him – just as his boss, Bill Priestap had anticipated was Strzok's goal.

- Peter was part of the Comey, McCabe, Priestap, Lisa Page, Strzok meeting that decided to open Crossfire Hurricane based on the flimsy hearsay evidence that Papadopoulos bragged about his knowledge of the Russians having dirt on Hillary Clinton. Knowing this was just gossip doesn't take 20/20 hindsight. Deciding to go forward with a full investigation into Trump Russian collusion with that information was laughable even in real time. That was clearly a decision based on a bias that was anti-Trump. That was one of the subtle ways bias sneaks into investigations. Strzok was guilty of it. Had it been a rumor that someone in the Clinton campaign bragged about having knowledge of the Russians having dirt on Donald Trump, there probably would not have been an investigation started on Clinton-Russian collusion. (Wait! That is exactly what happened! Glen Simpson hired by the Clinton campaign, bragged directly to the FBI about his knowledge of the Russians having dirt on Donald Trump. No investigation of Clinton - Russian collusion was started!)

Things that illustrate Peter Strzok's ego and ability to single-handedly save America from Donald Trump:

- Lisa Page forwarded a news article to Peter Strzok and texted, "And maybe you're meant to stay where you are because you're meant to protect the country from that menace." Strzok responded, "Thanks. It's absolutely true that we're both very fortunate. And of course, I'll try and approach it that way. I just know it will be tough at times. *I can protect our country at many levels, not sure if that helps."*[180] **This is the definition of a big ego.**

- On August 8, 2016, Lisa Page texted Strzok, "[Trump's] not ever going to become president, right? Right?!" Strzok replied, "No. No, he's not. We'll stop it.[181]" *When asked about this text message, Strzok stated that he did not specifically recall sending it, but that he believed that it was intended to reassure Page that Trump would not be elected, not to suggest that he would do something to impact the investigation.*[182] **How important must one be to be able to keep a Presidential candidate from ever becoming president? This is the definition of a big ego.**

- On August 15, 2016: In a text message exchange Strzok told Page, "I want to believe the path you threw out for consideration in Andy's office—that there's no way he gets elected—but I'm afraid we can't take that risk. It's like an insurance policy in the unlikely event you die before you're 40..." From Referenced Report[183] - *In substance, Strzok told us that he did not remember the specific conversation, but that it likely was part of a discussion about how to handle a variety of allegations of "collusion between members of the Trump campaign and the government of Russia." As part of this discussion, the team debated how aggressive to be and whether to use overt investigative methods. Given that Clinton was the "prohibitive favorite" to win, Strzok said that they discussed whether it made sense to compromise sensitive sources and methods to "bring things to some sort of precipitative conclusion and understanding." Strzok said the reference in his text message to an "insurance policy" reflected his conclusion that the FBI should investigate the allegations thoroughly right away, as if Trump were going to win. Strzok stated that Clinton's position in the polls did not ultimately impact the investigative decisions that were made in the Russia matter.* **It is unlikely that mentioning an "insurance policy" in case Trump gets elected, would not be remembered. That representation is not credible.**

---

[180] Horowitz Report, Op. Cit., page 67

[181] Ibid

[182] Report: A Review of Various Actions by the Federal Bureau of Investigation and Department of Justice in Advance of the 2016 Election June 2018

[183] Ibid

Appendix F London Academy of Diplomacy

Joseph Mifsud and London Academy of Diplomacy – A Perfect Match.

The term, "affiliated with" occurs frequently in the histories of both Joseph Mifsud and the London Academy of Diplomacy (LAD). It is a way of "fogging up" a relationship.

In Joseph Mifsud's case, referring to his associations with institutions as "affiliations" is one of the reasons it is impossible to tell who he actually worked for and when. So many of his relationships with organizations were "affiliations." The same is true with the London Academy of Diplomacy.

Significance of London Academy of Diplomacy to Trump-Russia Collusion Narrative

LAD ties UK Intelligence to Joseph Mifsud - Claire Smith, former member of the UK Joint Intelligence Committee which oversees the UK's spying agencies, interacted with Joseph Mifsud at LAD in 2012 and with University of Sterling in 2017.

In October 2012 when Mifsud was Director at LAD and Ms. Smith taught a training program at Link Campus in Rome, organized by the London Academy of Diplomacy (LAD). At the time, Mifsud was supposedly Director of LAD and simultaneously, Director of International Relations at Link Campus University[184]. (*Ms. Smith would not likely work closely with a known Russian Agent. As someone responsible for "vetting" security risks, she would likely know if Mifsud was a Russian Agent*)

On November 29, 2017 Ms. Smith served as Guest Lecturer at University of Stirling. Her topic was, "Making Sense of Intelligence."[185] At the time, Mifsud was a full-time "Professorial Teaching Fellow" at Stirling.[186] He was also listed as a Visiting Professor at Link Campus. (*This is AFTER all of Mifsud's meetings with Papadopoulos and being*

---

[184] Global Economic Forum Program, Sponsored by LAD & IBDE (International Business & Diplomatic Exchange), April 3, 2013

[185] Stir.ac.uk, University of Stirling Calendar of Events, "*Making Sense of Intelligence*" November 29, 2017

[186] The Columbian, "*London professor' in Trump case made many Russia trips*" Gregory Katz & Nataliya Vasilyeva (Associated Press) November 2, 2017.

outed by the FBI! Ms. Smith would not likely work closely with a known Russian Agent.)

LAD history;

- **Founded 2006 "Affiliated" with East Anglia University** - LAD was started in 2006 by INTO in "affiliation" with East Anglia University. This "affiliation" lasted until 2014. It appears this "affiliation" was for the purpose of adding legitimacy to a commercially owned "University" owned by a company named INTO University Partnerships (INTO), headed by Andrew Collin.[187] East Anglia provided staff and granted degrees for LAD. INTO recruited students and provided financial management.
- **"Affiliation" With East Anglia University Terminated 2014** - The LAD affiliation with East Anglia terminated in 2014.
- **"Affiliation" With University of Stirling started in2014** - The LAD's "affiliation" transferred to Scotland's University of Stirling at the same time when the "affiliation with East Anglia University terminated. This "affiliation lasted just until 2016 when Stirling closed the doors. Apparently, the same arrangement for staffing and granting of degrees that was part of the INTO/East Anglia University "affiliation" was transitioned to Stirling.
- **University of Stirling Closed LAD in 2016** – LAD was quietly shut down in 2016, in circumstances which have yet to be explained.

The funding of LAD resulted from an innovative joint venture model that emerged from a collaboration in 2005 between then-Vice Chancellor Sir David Eastwood of the University of East Anglia and INTO's co-founder Andrew Colin.

Sir David's ambitious plans for internationalization depended on first developing a globally diverse student body, but he recognized that a significant increase in international students was beyond the university's ability to accomplish alone

By the same token, he was unwilling to outsource such a critical university goal, so deeply rooted in academic programs, to a commercial entity over which the university had no direct control.

Ultimately, Sir David and Andrew Colin set about designing an affiliation in which the university could access private sector investment

---

[187] Wikipedia, *INTO University Partnerships*

while retaining critical control over the university's brand and its academic programs.

The result was the world's first public-private partnership in higher education predicated on a joint venture model of shared mission, shared investment, shared risk, shared governance, and shared reward.

LAD's "affiliation" with Mifsud

Mifsud was asked by then Founder and Rector of LAD, Nabil Ayad, to join LAD in 2010, four years after its founding. Some accounts have Joseph Mifsud listed as LAD Director[188], some as *Honorary* LAD Director.[189] There is big difference. A director actually has a job responsibility. *An honorary director just has to lend his name to the organization. It is all part of being the "mysterious Maltese professor." Who was paying him and for what?*

Mifsud remained at LAD through the transition from LAD's affiliation with East Anglia University to University of Stirling in 2014. LAD continued its "affiliation" with Mifsud until it closed its doors in the spring of 2016. At that point, Mifsud was appointed a part-time teaching professor at the University of Stirling, the degree-granting arm of LAD.

In March 2017, Mifsud was installed as a full-time "Professional Teaching Fellow" at Stirling. After being hired full time, Mifsud did not make any appearance on the Stirling campus.[190] He resigned his position on November 23, 2017.[191] Also in the fall of 2017, Mifsud served as a visiting professor at the Link Campus University in Rome and left at the same time.

Again, the question is, *if Mifsud was a full time "Professional Teaching Fellow" and he never made an appearance on the Stirling campus, what was he doing? Who was paying him and for what?*

---

[188] Association of Mature American Citizens (Amac), *"Mueller Overlooked Mifsud's Contacts in Western Counterterror Circles"*, August 29, 2019

[189] BuzzFeed, *"These Are The Contradictions Surrounding The Professor At The Center Of The Trump-Russia Probe"* November 4, 2017

[190] Brig Newspaper, *"Questions remain over Stirling's role in Diplomatic Academy run by Russia-probe professor."* Warren Hardy, December 3, 2017

[191] Brig Newspaper, "Trump-Russia academic resigns from Stirling University" Craig Munro, November 30, 2017

In typically Mifsud style[192], he describes his "affiliation" with LAD in an exaggerated manner. According to Mifsud:

"In 2010, I took on a new challenge: to raise the profile of the London Academy of Diplomacy (LAD), a venerable institution located on Middlesex Street in the heart of London that's home to some 150 students hailing from 50 nations."

"LAD is considered one of the best diplomatic academies in the world. We form part of the International Forum on Diplomatic Training," Mifsud explained. "Besides teaching foreign languages, we teach how to be flexible in thinking, how to engage with the business community and how to act at different levels, from the highest level of diplomacy to more mundane people-to-people skills, as well as the ability to think strategically and geopolitically."[193]

What did LAD Do?

The London Academy of Diplomacy was a small graduate school catering to embassy officials living in the U.K. It is little known among experts in the field.[194]

The financial arrangements first between INTO and East Anglia University and second between INTO and Stirling University are unknown.

When Stirling announced their new "affiliation with LAD, they described their program as follows;

- The centers will provide a range of academic and English language preparation courses for international students, with teaching due to begin in September 2014.
- Programs offered at the Stirling campus include General English, Academic English, International Foundation, International Diploma and International Graduate Diploma courses, together with pre-sessional and in-sessional support.
- Students who successfully complete the preparation courses will be able to progress to undergraduate or postgraduate degree programs at the University of Stirling.

---

[192] See Appendix B, *"Who was Joseph Mifsud?"*.

[193] Washington Diplomat, *"Maltese Official Raises Profile Of U.K. Diplomacy Academy"* By Larry Luxner

[194] Wikipedia, *"Diplomatic Academy of London*

- Agreements already signed with affiliate partner institutions in Scotland, England and Northern Ireland will offer students additional options for progression.
- Students at INTO Stirling will have full access to all of the University's academic and support services as well as the full range of sporting and social facilities.

Professor Gerry McCormack, Principal and Vice-Chancellor of the University of Stirling, said: "INTO shares the University of Stirling's commitment to high quality education".

After INTO and University of East Anglia joint ventured LAD, East Anglia professor Nabil Ayad was named to head it in 2008. East Anglia sourced teachers and granted degrees and INTO marketed the school, recruited students and managed it. Ayad brought in Joseph Mifsud as "honorary director" in 2010.

Ayad stayed at LAD until November 2014. In November 2014, he left and started another "Academy of Diplomacy", the *Academy of Diplomacy and International Governance at Loughborough University London.* He served as the Director from November 2014 until October 2017.

Appendix G Steele Dossier

The Steele dossier played a central role in the Trump-Russia collusion investigation. Christopher Steele along with Joseph Mifsud provided the majority of the raw information used as a basis for conducting the Federal Bureau of Investigation (FBI) investigation. Most of the leads investigated by the FBI both before and after opening Crossfire Hurricane came from the Steele Dossier. As detailed below, the FBI investigation of these leads yielded little evidence of Trump-Russia collusion. In Christopher Steele's eyes, it was because the FBI botched the investigation. In other's eyes, it was because there was little real evidence.

Origin of the Steele dossier

Christopher Steele created the seventeen reports comprising his dossier because he was paid by Fusion GPS to produce them. Fusion GPS was on contract with the Clinton Campaign and the Democratic National Committee (DNC) to dig up dirt on Donald Trump and plant it inside the FBI. Fusion GPS hired Christopher Steele specifically to dig up dirt against Donald Trump from Russian sources. Steele's Russian guys delivered for him. Steele published the seventeen reports consisting of a total of 35 pages from the compiled dirt. Collectively the reports became known as the Steele dossier.

Steel's sources for dirt on Trump.

According to Steele, he talked only to two sources to get the contents of the seventeen reports comprising his dossier. The two sources were (1) Steele's "Primary Sub-source"[195], and (2) Michael Sussmann, a lawyer and ex Obama DOJ'er with the DNC/Clinton campaign law firm, Perkins Coie.[196] The Primary Sub-source provided the material for all the reports except report 112. Report 112 was provided by Sussmann. The only role for Steele on Report 112 was to plant it with the FBI.

The "Primary Sub source's" identity is Igor "Izzy" Danchenko. Igor is the 42-year-old who was hired by Steele in 2016 to deploy a network

---

[195] Realclear Investigations, *"Meet the Steele Dossier's 'Primary Sub-source': Fabulist Russian From Democrat Think Tank Whose Boozy Past the FBI Ignored"*, Paul Sperry, July 24, 2020,

[196] National Review, *"Steele Claims Clinton Lawyer Provided Tip about Trump Campaign Contacts with Russian Bank"*, Tobias Hoonhout, April 28, 2020

of sources to dig up dirt on Trump-Russia collusion. Danchenko's sources were his drinking buddies, according to Danchenko himself.

Danchnko was interviewed in January 2017 by the FBI. A summary of that interview was declassified on July 24, 2020 and it reveals that FBI agents learned that key allegations in the dossier, which claimed Trump engaged in a "well-developed conspiracy of cooperation" with the Kremlin against Clinton, were largely inspired by gossip and bar talk among Danchenko and his drinking buddies, most of whom were childhood friends from Russia. In the summary memo, the FBI notes that Danchenko said that he and one of his dossier sources "drink heavily together."

Igor's sub sources consisted of;

Source A   Senior Russian Foreign Ministry figure,
Source B   Former top-level Russian intelligence officer Vyacheslav Trubnikav,
Source C
Source D   Close associate of Trump, Sergei Millian. Also "person 1 in Horowitz Report,
Source F   Female staffer at the Ritz Carlton hotel,
Source E   Ethnic Russian close Trump associate Sergei Millian. Also Person 1 in Horowitz Report,
Source F   Company ethnic Russian operative, and
Source G   Senior Kremlin official, Vladislav Surkov.

The Horowitz report says that the FBI located Izzy Danchenko in January 2017. Izzy told FBI agents he was merely repeating Moscow gossip to Mr. Steele, not corroborated facts.[197] All of the documents and correspondence between Steele and his "Primary Sub-source" were "wiped" from Steele's computers in December 2016 and January 2017.[198]

Steele, the former British spy and dossier author told a State Department official during an Oct. 11, 2016 meeting that Trubnikov was Source B for the dossier.[199] Many of the sub-sources are believed to have unwittingly provided information to "Izzy."

---

[197] Washington Times, *"Former MI-6 operative Christopher Steele says his anti-Trump dossier records destroyed",* Rowan Scarborough, April 24, 2020

[198] The Blaze, *"Christopher Steele testified in court that his emails were "wiped", documents related to dossier no longer exist",* Paul Secca April 24, 2020

[199] Daily Caller, *"Steele Identified Russian Dossier Sources, Notes Reveal",* Chuck Ross, May 16, 2018

Report 112 was not treated the same as the other reports. Steele pushed it into the FBI through his back-up channel, Bruce Ohr.[200] Bruce Ohr sent it directly to the FBI. So the source of the Trump "dirt" documented in report 112 originated from the people who were paying Steele to find it. The veracity of that information would be highly suspect. As it turned out, that is exactly what the Mueller investigation determined, it was not credible.

The bottom line, the source of 90 % of the Steele dossier, the Primary Sub-source, is on record as saying that all the information he provided was just repeated gossip. The other 10% of the dossier, Report 112, was found to be flatly untrue by the FBI.

Steele's objective for the dossier switched from performing "work for hire" to saving the American people from Donald Trump.

In the process of gathering the dirt against Trump, Steele claimed he discovered that the Russian reporting was "so disturbing" Steele considered it his duty to share it not only with his sponsor, but with the FBI and the American people. Steele represented that the contents of the first report (Report 80) had national security implications and that the report therefore needed to be shared with the FBI.[201] Neither the FBI or an average American would find the dossier content nearly as "disturbing" as Steele did, even if some of it was actually true. In fact, the FBI implied that they didn't find Report 80, 86 and 94 disturbing at all when they said the reports were not used to open Crossfire Hurricane. They maintain to this day that despite having the reports in their possession on July 31, 2016, they were not used. Clearly, they didn't find the information contained in them nearly as significant as Christopher Steele did!

The proper channel for getting damning intelligence to the American people was through the FBI.

Chris had worked with the FBI before. In fact, Steele actually had an assigned FBI handler, an agent named Michael Gaeta. Chris knew that the FBI was a bureaucratic jungle and Michael might have trouble

---

[200] Washington Times, *"Hillary Clinton operatives pushed now-debunked Trump-Alfa server conspiracy, testimony reveals*, Rowan Scarborough, January 23,2019
[201] Horowitz Report Op. Cit. page 218

navigating the jungle to get his information, which Steele judged to have national security implications, to the right people.

Given the dirt was "so disturbing", Steele felt he needed a second channel into the FBI.

Steele needed a backup – a second channel just in case Michael Gaeta failed to get any attention in the FBI. Luckily, Mr. Steele had his old friend, Bruce Ohr in the Department of Justice (DOJ) who he thought could provide that second channel into the FBI. Chris enlisted Bruce Ohr to help.

As an added safety net, Steele developed a third channel into the FBI – right into the Director's office.

Simple redundancy wasn't good enough for Chris. Bruce Ohr couldn't be fully trusted to deliver the "disturbing" information on Trump either. Mr. Steele needed triple redundancy because of his concerns for U.S. national security. Apparently, Chris didn't feel he could rely on just normal FBI channels to take matters of national security seriously. Mr. Steele decided to use John McCain to personally deliver his reports to the Director of the FBI, Jim Comey. McCain did that, but by this time, Christopher was no longer doing this for the money, he was doing it either for US national security or simply to prevent Trump's election. Only Chris knows for sure.

Time ran out for Steele. The FBI wasn't going to release the dirt Chris found on Trump in time to influence the election.

Unfortunately, the FBI wasn't acting fast enough to fit Chris's schedule. Once Christopher had determined he was the chosen one to prevent Trump's election he needed a direct path to the American people to get the word out. It was getting too late. The election was coming up on November 9, 2016. Steele needed yet another channel that could bypass the FBI all together so the dirt could be given directly to the American people. It was the least he could do to save America. The FBI wasn't up to the task so Steele assumed the awesome responsibility himself.

Steele decided to use the press as a fourth and fifth channel to reach the American people directly instead of relying on the snail-paced FBI.

On September 23, 2016 Steele enlisted Michael Isikoff, an investigative correspondent at Yahoo news as the fourth channel. Michael Isikoff, published the first article. It is unknown what, if any reports were handed to Michael Isikoff. The Yahoo news item was limited to suspicions about Carter Page.

On October 31, 2016 Steele enlisted David Corn, a reporter at Mother Jones as the fifth channel to publish articles about the existence and content of Steele's reports. Mother Jones was given nine reports; 80, 94, 95, 97, 105, 111, 112, 134, and 136. The Mother Jones item covered all the aspects of the Steele reports. (Keep in mind, according to Christopher Steele, *"he had no intention that the dossier would ever become public."* Giving the dossier to two news outlets is not consistent with an intention that it would never become public. (Since he personally gave the reports to the press in unedited, unverified form, it raises questions as to what, if anything Mr. Steele says is credible.)

Steele informed Corn at Mother Jones that the FBI was also in possession of the reports. Corn published his story on October 31, 2016, just nine days before the election.[202] The article contained the essence of all the reports. The FBI cut their ties with Steele for violating the rules by leaking investigative material to the press.

Christopher Steele, as an agent of a foreign government had just colluded with a presidential campaign (Clinton campaign) to influence the outcome of an American presidential election. Hmmm. Wasn't that what he was investigating, but for the other political party? Christopher Steele should find that not only extremely troubling but "significant and disturbing." He should immediately recognize it as information that had national security implications. But he didn't.

Ultimately Steele wasn't successful in assisting a Clinton win over Trump. Trump won but Chris decided to pursue his quest to get Trump anyway, even if it had to be on his own money.

The Clinton campaign and the Democratic National Committee (DNC) had no interest in protecting national security, they were only interested in dirt against Trump to defeat him. Because national security was not a priority for the DNC or Clinton campaign, they stopped funding Fusion GPS and Steele.

---

[202] Mother Jones, *"A Veteran Spy Has Given the FBI Information Alleging a Russian Operation to Cultivate Donald Trump"*, **October 31, 2016.**

Steele still was driven to ensure our national security was protected so he self-funded digging for dirt and seeing that it got wide distribution. It wasn't too late to activate his third channel, John McCain. On December 9, 2016, after the election, John McCain hand delivered the Steele reports directly to Jim Comey. This set consisted of sixteen reports; 80, 86, 94, 95, 97, 100, 101, 102, 105, 111, 112, 113, 130, 134, 135, and 136. To further ensure that our national security was protected, Mr. Steele had McCain's aide, Dave Kramer also provide these sixteen reports to the Washington Post so the mainstream press could release the contents of the dossier even if that was not Steele's intent.

To further ensure that our national security was protected, Mr. Steele provided David Kramer the last report, Report 166. Over Christmas, 2016, Kramer handed Report 166 over to Ken Bensinger[203] at Buzzfeed for publishing (which Ken did on January 9, 2017), a move no doubt made in the interest of national security. Also, in the interest of national security, Steele asked Kramer to brief CNN's Carl Bernstein. Kramer complied. Besides BuzzFeed and CNN, Mr. Kramer briefed and/or provided dossier copies to Mother Jones' David Corn, The Washington Post's Tom Hamburger and Fred Hiatt, NPR's Bob Little, McClatchy news service's Peter Stone and Greg Gordon, ABC News reporter Brian Ross, The Wall Street Journal's Alan Cullison and The Guardian newspaper.

For someone who intended that these reports not be released, Mr. Steele certainly had a long distribution list of media personnel who might not be able to honor Steele's intentions of preventing release of the reports.

It is interesting that in his dossier Steele reported an "extensive conspiracy" between the Trump campaign and Moscow. In his London court declaration, Steele reported only of "possible coordination between the Trump campaign and Russia."[204] Even though he has maintained that some unidentified 70% of the dossier was true, when he was under oath, there was only "possible coordination" between the Trump campaign and Russia. If only that was the message he gave to the FBI, it would have saved $30,000,000 and nearly three years of investigation. It appears that "being under oath" has a chilling effect on honesty.

---

[203] AP News, "Christopher Steele, dossier author, led anti-Trump media push after 2016 election", Rowan Scarborough, March 18, 20

[204] Ibid.

We Americans are surely blessed to have an ex-UK intelligence agent more concerned about US national security than the FBI. If it wasn't for Christopher Steele taking such a patriotic position on behalf of the American people, we would not have been able to experience the Mueller investigation.

Importance of the Steele dossier to the FBI opening and conducting a full investigation of Trump-Russia collusion

The Steele dossier provided the FBI names of certain Trump team members and alleged evidence of their collusion with the Russians, so the dossier was important to the FBI in their investigation of those team members; Carter Page, Paul Manafort and Michael Cohen. Much of the Mueller investigation was consumed trying to validate the dossier "evidence" against these three people. The Steele dossier is recognized as being central to the conduct of the FBI and Mueller investigations. It was certainly used to get a FISA warrant on Carter Page.

The Steele dossier provided the FBI with certain claims about Trump being involved with prostitutes in a Moscow hotel in 2012. Steele identified this activity as potentially making Trump subject to blackmail. The FBI investigation delved into the veracity of this alleged incident, so in that sense, the Steel dossier was important to the FBI investigation of it.

The FBI adamantly denies that the dossier had any role in opening the investigation and IG Horowitz confirms that, saying, *Steele's reports played no role in the Crossfire Hurricane opening.*" At the time Crossfire Hurricane was opened, the FBI had in its possession three of the seventeen reports comprising the Steele dossier, Report 080, Report 086 and Report 094. The FBI is on record of saying the threat to our national security documented in the three Steele reports was so irrelevant that it wasn't even considered in making a case for opening an FBI investigation. It is easy to see why Christopher Steele was so concerned about the FBI not taking his reports seriously. His disturbing evidence didn't even make the screen at the FBI.

What the FBI and intelligence community knew about the veracity of the Steele report before and during the Mueller investigation.

The Horowitz report reveals that the FBI knew much of the Steele dossier was tainted because it consisted of bar room speculation, out-right lying sources, infiltration of Russian intelligence into the Steele "source network" and conflicting information about whether the Russians preferred Clinton or Trump.[205] Steele elected to go with the narrative that the Russians preferred Trump. As more footnotes from the Horowitz report are declassified, the more the American public knows about how the FBI skewed the investigation by ignoring exculpatory inputs. The good news – even with the skewed investigation the FBI couldn't find any evidence of collusion.

- Footnotes in the IG's report confirm that the FBI knew **Russian intelligence** was aware of Steele's contract to dig up dirt on Trump and that the Russians organized a set of "Russian sources" to feed Steele disinformation via Steele's Primary sub-source, Igor Danchenko. Before the FBI even began its investigation, they had reports in hand that their central piece of evidence was most likely tainted with Russian disinformation."
- Footnote 350 in the IG's report indicates that the FBI received a U.S. intelligence report on January 12, 2017, warning of an inaccuracy in the dossier related to Michael Cohen, and assessing that the material was "part of a Russian disinformation campaign to denigrate U.S. foreign relations." (All the evidence of collusion cited by Steele took place in a meeting in Prague. Michael Cohen never went to Prague.)
- A similar U.S. intelligence report arrived on February 28, 2017, undercutting a key allegation against Trump, noting the claims "were false, and that they were the product of the Russian Intelligence Service (RIS AKA SVR) "infiltrating a source into the Steele source network".
- Annex A to the January 6, 2017 Intelligence Community Assessment on Russian election interference noted that Christopher Steele had only "limited corroboration" regarding whether Trump "knowingly worked with Russian officials to bolster his chances of beating" Hillary Clinton and other claims.[206] The subsequent FBI and Mueller investigations did not provide any additional corroboration and in-fact disproved some allegations. In fact, in the recently declassified Footnote 347 to the IG report, it was revealed that one of contacts

---

[205] CBS News, *"Report footnotes show FBI knew Russians had early knowledge of Steele material" Catherine Herridge, April 17, 2020* (from IG Report footnote 347 - *"Individual in Russian Presidential Administration voiced (to Steele subsource) that he had strong support for candidate Clinton in the 2016 US elections. "*

[206] Fox News, *"Newly declassified intel document noted Steele dossier claims had 'limited corroboration"*, Brooke Singman, June 11, 2020. In fact footnote 347 in the IG report sites one example where the Russians voiced the opinion that they preferred Clinton

between the sub-source and an individual in the Russian Presidential Administration voiced strong support for candidate Clinton, not Trump. This statement of support occurred in June/July 2016. This brings into question who was Russia supporting, Clinton or Trump?

- Footnote 302 in the IG's report, references a document circulated among Crossfire Hurricane team members and supervisors in early October 2016, Person 1, (AKA Sergei Millian) had historical contact with persons and entities suspected of being linked to RIS. The document described reporting that Sergei Millian "was rumored to be a former KGB/SVR officer." In addition, in late December 2016, Department Attorney Bruce Ohr told SSA 1 (Joe Pietka) that he had met with Glenn Simpson and that Simpson had assessed that Sergei Millian was central in connecting Trump to Russia.

The only Steele dossier leads the FBI could collaborate were Paul Manafort-related.

As listed below, the Steele dossier contained five basic claims against the Trump campaign plus three each specifically against Carter Page, Michael Cohen, and Paul Manafort. The only claims the FBI could collaborate were those against Paul Manafort and they did not end up having any actual collusion implications.

The content of the Steel dossier is provided in attached, Appendix G1. Steele's *"evidence"* contained in the dossier and the FBI's documented lack of collaboration of it are:

1. *"Trumps conduct in Moscow included perverted sexual acts which have been arranged/monitored by the FSB."*
   a. The FBI could not collaborate the allegation.
   b. Christopher Steele could not confirm the allegation.
   c. The FBI has not been able to establish that Trump has been blackmailed.
2. *"Russian regime has been cultivating, supporting and assisting Trump for at least 5 years."*
   a. The FBI could not collaborate this.
   b. This is not a crime or evidence of collusion. The Russians and others have probably been cultivating and supporting and assisting many US politicians for at least 5 years.
3. *"In late July 2016, Source E, an ethnic Russian close associate of Republican US presidential candidate Donald Trump, admitted that there was a well-developed conspiracy of co-operation between them and the Russian leadership."*

a. The FBI could not collaborate this.
b. Christopher Steele could not confirm the allegation.
c. Source E was Sergei Millian who was not a "close associate of Trump" and was known to be unreliable, even to Christopher Steele.

4. *Source E claimed that Russian diplomatic staff in key cities such as New York, Washington DC and Miami were using the emigre 'pension' distribution system as a (money laundering) cover.*
   a. The FBI could not collaborate this.
   b. Christopher Steele could not confirm the allegation.
   c. The FBI did confirm however, that there are no Russian diplomatic staff in Miami.

5. *"Trump's previous (business) efforts had included exploring the real estate sector in St. Petersburg as well as Moscow but in the end, Trump had to settle for the use of extensive sexual services from local prostitutes rather than business success."*
   a. Since there is no crime in exploring business in Russia as a private citizen, there is nothing for the FBI to investigate, particularly when there was no deal.
   b. The FBI could not collaborate the sexual services allegation. (The statement, *"(Trump) had to settle for the use of extensive sexual services from local prostitutes"*) is clearly an accusation designed to smear Mr. Trump, not to present evidence. To an average American reading it, it just confirms that Mr. Steele is not a credible source for anything.

6. Evidence on Carter Page
   a. *"In July 2016, Carter Page holds secret meetings in Moscow with Sechin and senior Kremlin Internal Affairs official, Divyekin."*
      i. The FBI did not find this meeting as "secret." Carter Page readily admitted meeting Sechin.
      ii. Carter Page denied ever meeting with Divyekin. Page denied even knowing who Divyekin was. The FBI found no evidence that Page knew Divyekin.
   b. (The Trump campaign) *had a visceral dislike of Hillary Clinton and had the objective of swinging Bernie Sanders followers away from Hillary.* (The

objective) *had been conceived and promoted by Carter Page who had discussed it directly with Sergei Millian.*

      i. Really? The Trump campaign didn't like Hillary?! They wanted to swing Bernie voters to Trump?! How awful, but falling slightly short of rising to the importance of "having national security implications."

      ii. This "bombshell" finding didn't make it to the level of requiring investigation by the FBI.

   c. *"Carter Page was in Moscow in July 2016. The secret meeting (referred in (a) above) had been confirmed by a senior member of Sechin's staff, in addition to the Rosneft President himself. (The "secret" meeting) took place on either 7 or 8 July. In terms of the substance of their discussion, Sechin's associate said that the Rosneft President was so keen to lift personal and corporate western sanctions imposed on the company, that he offered Page the brokerage of up to a 19 per cent (privatized) stake in Rosneft in return. Page had expressed interest and confirmed that were Trump elected US president, then sanctions on Russia would be lifted."*

      i. Page confirmed he met with Sechin. The FBI never termed the meeting as "secret."

      ii. The FBI never confirmed that there was any discussion about Page getting any share of Rosneft, much less 19% in exchange for lifting sanctions.

7. Evidence on Paul Manafort

   a. *Sergei Millian, close associate of Donald Trump, admitted that there was a well-developed conspiracy of co-operation between them and the Russian leadership. This was managed on the Trump side by the Republican candidate's campaign manager, Paul Manafort, who was a foreign policy advisor.*

      i. The FBI concluded that Sergei Millian was not a "close associate of Trump" and was known to be unreliable, even to Christopher Steele.

ii. The FBI never confirmed there was a well-developed conspiracy of cooperation.

b. *Manafort had a corrupt relationship with the former pro-Russian (Ukrainian) regime.*

i. The FBI confirmed this to be essentially true.

c. *Ex-Ukrainian President Yanukovych confides directly to Putin that he authorized kick-back payments to Manafort, as alleged in western media. Yanukovych assures Russian President however there is no documentary evidence/trail.*

i. The FBI confirmed this to be essentially true.

ii. Manafort was convicted of 8 bank fraud charges and multiple conspiracy charges for a total of 90 months in prison.

8. Evidence on Michael Cohen

a. *Kremlin insider reports Trump lawyer Cohen's secret meeting/s with Kremlin officials in August 2016 was/were held in Prague.*

i. The FBI concluded that Cohen never went to Prague.

b. *A Kremlin insider provided further details of reported clandestine meeting/s between Republican presidential candidate Donald Trump's lawyer, Michael Cohen and Kremlin representatives in August 2016. Although the communication between them had to be cryptic for security reasons, the Kremlin insider clearly indicated to his/her friend that the reported contact/s took place in Prague, Czech Republic.*

i. The FBI concluded that Cohen never went to Prague.

c. *Cohen met officials from the (Russian) Presidential Administration (PA) Legal Department clandestinely in an EU country (Czech Republic) in August 2016. This was in order to clean up the mess left behind by western media revelations of Trump ex-campaign manager Manafort's corrupt relationship with the former pro-Russian Yanukovych regime in Ukraine and Trump foreign policy advisor, Carter Page's secret meetings in Moscow with senior regime figures in July 2016.*

> i. The FBI concluded that Cohen never went
> to Prague.

Despite the FBI and the Mueller Team spending three years investigating, they have been able to verify only a subset of Paul Manafort's record of bad deeds. Glen Simpson has a problem with that.

In his book, Glen Simpson blames the FBI and the media for *"failing to expose Trump."* Trump, the folks at Fox News and at the FBI don't agree with the assessment that the mainstream media and the FBI were protecting Trump.

According to Simpson and co-author Fritsch, *"the press failed to recognize that Moscow had potentially compromised a White House candidate."* Simpson and Fritsch are scathing about the FBI. On the election's eve the FBI told the New York Times there was "no clear Trump link to Russia. Simpson's response was, *"a misleading statement, even in an age of lies."*

Even today, the authors believe the dossier was mostly right. According to Steele's supporters, many of his allegations have been borne out or have proved "remarkably prescient", they argue. Others remain "stubbornly unconfirmed". A handful – including a claim that Trump's lawyer Michael Cohen met with Russians in Prague – "appear to be doubtful though not yet disproven."

Steele still claims to believe "at least 70 percent of the assertions in the dossier are accurate." Reviewing the scorecard itemized above it is hard to come up with more than 10 percent, and those are all Paul Manafort related.

Steele provided these examples;
- Russia really did intervene in 2016 to help Trump against Hillary Clinton. (Even this well accepted conclusion has now been called into question in the latest declassification of footnotes in the IG report.)
- Trump's then-adviser Carter Page really did travel to Moscow in 2016. As has been pointed out above, traveling to Moscow has never been debated, only what he did there. The FBI concluded that nothing Page did there was nefarious. One of the people Steele said Page met with, Page has never met in his life. Traveling to Moscow is not

germane to counting "accuracy" unless a claim of wrongdoing when there is made. The FBI could find no evidence of that.

- Page really had been in contact with Russian intelligence officers and was on the FBI's radar. (Page doesn't dispute that nor does the FBI. Being on the FBI's radar in the past is not germane to counting "accuracy" of the report.

Appendix G1 - Content of the Steele dossier

- **Report 080 June 20, 2016** - This report was delivered to FBI Handling Agent 1 on July 5, 2016.[207] It was also delivered to Mother Jones, late November 2016. Content:
    - "Russian authorities" had cultivated Trump "for at least 5 years", and that the operation was "supported and directed" by Putin. *(Evidence of "cultivation of Trump.")*
    - Trump accepted a regular flow of intelligence from the Kremlin", notably on his political rivals. (*Evidence of conspiracy, co-operation, and back channel communication.)*
    - Trump employed a number of prostitutes to perform a urination show in front of him. The alleged incident from 2013 was reportedly filmed and recorded by the FSB as compromising material and as a result Trump was vulnerable to blackmail from Russian authorities for paying bribes and engaging in unorthodox and embarrassing sexual behavior over the years and that the authorities were "able to blackmail him if they so wished." (*Evidence that Trump could be blackmailed.*)
- **Report 086 July 26, 2016** This was delivered directly to the FBI. Content:
    - It contained a synopsis Of Russian state sponsored and other cyber offensive (criminal) operations. *(Non-evidentiary to Trump collusion activity.)*
- **Report 094 July 19, 2016** – This was delivered to FBI Handling Agent 1 on July 19, 2016. It was also delivered to Mother Jones, late November 2016. Content:
    - Page was informed by Igor Divyekin, a senior Kremlin Internal Affairs official, "that the Russians had compromising information on Clinton and Trump, and allegedly added that Trump 'should bear this in mind'. (*Evidence of collusion.*)
    - During a July 2016 trip to Moscow, Page met secretly with Igor Sechin, Chairman of Russian energy conglomerate Rosneft and close associate of Putin to discuss future cooperation and the lifting of Ukraine-related sanctions against Russia. He also met with Igor Divyekin, a highly-placed Russian official, to discuss

---

[207] Horowitz Report, *Review of Four FISA Applications and Other Aspects of the FBI's Crossfire Hurricane Investigation (Revised)*, December 20, 2019 Page 95

sharing derogatory information about Clinton with the Trump campaign (see Report 94).[208] Sechin confided the details of a secret meeting with Page. Sergei Ivanov confided with a compatriot that Divyekin had met secretly with Page. (*Evidence of collusion.*)
- o Report 94 was one of 4 reports the FBI relied upon to support the probable cause in the Carter Page FISA applications.[209]
- **Report 095 (Date unknown)**- This was delivered directly to the FBI. It was also delivered to Mother Jones, late November 2016. Content:
  - o The Trump campaign and "Russian leadership" willingly exchanged information in both directions. This co-operation was "sanctioned at the 'highest level' and involved Russian diplomatic staff based in the US". The Trump campaign used "moles within the DNC as well as hackers in the US and Russia. (*Evidence of conspiracy, co-operation, and back channel communication.*)
  - o Trump had explored the real estate sectors in St. Petersburg and Moscow, "but in the end Trump had had to settle for the use of extensive sexual services there from local prostitutes rather than business success". (*Evidence that Trump could be blackmailed.*)
  - o Trump associates did not fear "the negative media publicity surrounding alleged Russian interference" because it distracted attention from Trump's "business dealings in China and other emerging markets" involving "large bribes and kickbacks" that could be devastating if revealed. (Evidence *that Trump could be blackmailed.*)
  - o Trump campaign manager Paul Manafort "managed" a "well-developed conspiracy of co-operation between the Trump campaign]and the Russian leadership", and he used Trump's foreign policy advisor, Carter Page and others, "as intermediaries". (*Evidence of collusion.*)
  - o Carter Page had "conceived and promoted" the timing of the release of hacked emails by WikiLeaks for the purpose of swinging supporters of Bernie Sanders "away from Hillary Clinton and across to Trump." (*Evidence of collusion.*)

---

[208] Horowitz Report, Ibid. Page vii
[209] Horowitz Report, Ibid. Page 98

- o Russian consular officials and diplomatic staff in Miami
     were making payments in order to facilitate a secret
     exchange of intelligence between persons affiliated with
     Trump and the Russian government. *(There is no Russian
     consulate in Miami.)*
  - o Page was an intermediary between Russia and the Trump
     campaign's then manager (Manafort) in a "well-
     developed conspiracy" of cooperation, which led to
     Russia's disclosure of hacked DNC emails to Wikileaks
     in exchange for the Trump campaign's agreement to
     sideline Russian intervention in Ukraine as a campaign
     issue (see Report 95*)[210]* *(Evidence of collusion but Page
     never met Manafort.)*
- **Report 097 Late November 2016** – This was delivered only to
  Mother Jones in late November. Content:
  - o Trump associates had established "an intelligence
     exchange [with the Kremlin] for at least 8 years". Trump
     and his team had delivered "intelligence on the activities,
     business and otherwise, of leading Russian oligarchs and
     their families in the US", as requested by Putin.
     *(Evidence of conspiracy, co-operation, and back channel
     communication.*
  - o The Kremlin had promised Trump they would not use the
     compromising information collected against him "as
     leverage, given high levels of voluntary co-operation
     forthcoming from his team". *(Evidence that Trump
     could be blackmailed.)*
- **Report 100 August 5, 2016 (Not Applicable to Trump)**
- **Report 101 August 10, 2016(Not Applicable To Trump)**
- **Report 102 August 10, 2016** – The recipients are unknown.
  Content:
  - o Carter Page had "conceived and promoted" the timing of
     the release of hacked emails by Wikileaks for the purpose
     of swinging supporters of Bernie Sanders "away from
     Hillary Clinton and across to Trump".
  - o Russia released the DNC emails to Wikileaks in an
     attempt to swing voters to Trump, an objective conceived
     and promoted by Page and others.[211]
- **Report 105 August 22, 2016** – This was delivered only to
  Mother Jones, late November 2016. Content:

---

[210] Horowitz Report, Ibid. Page vii
[211] Horowitz Report, Ibid. page vii

- **Report 111 September 14, 2016 (Not Applicable to Trump)**
- **Report 112 September 14, 2016.** Delivered only to Mother Jones, late November 2016. Content:
  - Alfa Bank allegedly had close ties to Putin. The Crossfire Hurricane team received Report 112 on or about November 6, 2016, from a *Mother Jones* journalist through then FBI General Counsel James Baker.
- **Report 113 September 14, 2016–** Content:
  - Witnesses to Trump's "sex parties in the city" had been "silenced" i.e. bribed or coerced to disappear. (Evidence *that Trump could be blackmailed*.)
  - Trump had paid bribes in St. Petersburg "to further his [business] interests". (Evidence *that Trump could be blackmailed*.)
- **Report 130 October 9, 2016 –** Content:
  - Russian government's support for Trump was originally conducted by the Ministry of Foreign Affairs, then by the Federal Security Service (FSB), and was eventually directly handled by the Russian presidency because of its "growing significance over time". *(Evidence of "cultivation of Trump")*
  - Putin and his colleagues were surprised and disappointed that leaks of Clinton's emails had not had a greater impact on the campaign; a stream of hacked. Clinton material had been injected by the Kremlin into compliant western media outlets like Wikileaks and the stream would continue until the election)
- **Report 134, Oct 9, 2016 -** Content:
  - A close associate of Rosneft President Sechin confirmed a secret meeting with Carter Page in July; Sechin was keen to have sanctions on the company lifted and offered up to a 19 percent stake in return. (*Evidence of a quit-pro-quo, but was judged to be disinformation.*)
- **Report 135 October 19, 2016-** Content:
  - "Cohen was heavily engaged in a cover up and damage limitation operation in the attempt to prevent the full details of Trump's relationship with Russia being exposed." (*Evidence of collusion and unlawful dealings.*)
  - Cohen had met secretly with several Russian Presidential Administration Legal Department officials; immediate issues were efforts to contain further scandals involving Manafort's commercial and political role in Russia and Ukraine and to limit damage from the exposure of Carter

Page's secret meetings with Russian leadership figures in Moscow the previous month. (*Evidence of a coverup to unlawful dealings.)*

- **Report 136 October 20, 2016**
- **Report 137 (Date unknown**) - Content:
  - Russian government's support for Trump was originally conducted by the Ministry of Foreign Affairs, then by the Federal Security Service (FSB, and was eventually directly handled by the Russian presidency because of its "growing significance over time" *(Evidence of "cultivation of Trump.")*
- **Report 166 December 13, 2016** – This report was delivered to David Kramer, McCain Staff Member in early January. Content: This report contained allegations that Trump attorney Michael Cohen had held secret discussions in Prague in late summer 2016 with representatives of the Kremlin and "associated operators & hackers," and that the "anti-Clinton hackers" had been paid by the "[Trump] team" and Kremlin. The FBI eventually concluded that these allegations against Cohen and the "Trump team" were not true. *(Evidence of collusion.)*

Appendix H Other Trump-Russia Collusion Books

Appendix H provides a review and analysis of eight books written about the Trump-Russia Investigation.

Three of the books conclude that Trump was unfairly targeted by a bad-intentioned investigation. These are, Appendix H2, *"Spygate"* by Dan Bongino and D.C. McAllister, Appendix H5. *"The Russian Hoax"* by, Gregg Jarrett, and Appendix H7, *"Deep State Target"* by George Papadopoulos. George Papadopoulos was one of those unfairly targeted Trump team members and thus provides a first-hand description of "what really happened."

Two of the books conclude that the investigation was well predicated and that the FBI was unfairly targeted by Donald Trump for conducting a witch-hunt and unjustly tarnishing the image of the FBI. These are Appendix H4, *"A Higher Loyalty"* by James Comey and Appendix H6, *"The Threat"* by Andrew McCabe. Both Jim Comey and Andy McCabe were two of the unfairly targeted FBI staff and thus provide a first-hand description of "what really happened."

The last three books conclude that not only was the Crossfire Hurricane investigation well predicated, but that despite the FBI investigation, Mueller Report and the Horowitz Report finding no evidence of collusion, Trump is guilty and should be removed from office even now. These are Appendix H1, *"Proof of Collusion"* by Seth Abramson, Appendix H3, *"Crossfire Hurricane"* by Josh Campbell, and Appendix H8, *"Crime in Progress"* by Glenn Simpson. Josh Campbell and Glen Simpson were insiders and like Comey and McCabe saw Trump as a bad person and a danger to the nation. Seth Abramson was an outsider but came to the same conclusion as Campbell and Simpson. Seth Abramson's book and Christopher Steeles books were similar in that they went back many years to create the foundation for Trump's misguided values.

Appendix H1 "Proof of Collusion -How Trump Betrayed America" – Seth Abramson 2018

Seth Abramson's, *"Proof of Collusion, How Trump Betrayed America"* is well documented and well written. In that sense, it is on a par with *"Spygate, The Attempted Sabotage of Donald J. Trump."* It covers much of the same ground as Glenn Simpson's book, "Crime in Progress."

The problem is that Abramson totally blew it on his interpretation of "evidence" of Russian collusion and its effect on Trump's governance effectiveness.

1. **What Abramson's *"Proof of Collusion"* covers that Rowe's *"Planted Evidence"* does not cover:**

    a. **Abramson** covers the history of Trump family connections with Russia prior to 2016,
    b. He covers Trump activities prior to the campaign in 2016, and
    c. He covers the Republican National Convention.
2. **What *"Planted Evidence"* covers that *"Proof of Collusion"* does not cover:**
    a. *"Planted Evidence"* covers the "creation" of "evidence" by Joseph Mifsud and Christopher Steele, the primary sources of evidence against the Trump campaign.
    b. It covers the planting of that evidence by the unsuspecting George Papadopoulos with the help of Alexander Downer and Erika Thompson and the direct planting of evidence by Christopher Steele with the help of Bruce Ohr.
    c. It covers the failure of the FBI to pursue the case to find out how all the evidence they were handed turned out to be phony. The FBI failed to look into who was paying Joseph Mifsud to create evidence of collusion.
3. **Examples of where *"Planted Evidence"* conflicts with *"Proof of Collusion"* coverage:**
    a. **Abramson** portrays George Papadopoulos as a key figure in arranging clandestine meetings between Trump and Putin. Seth actually believes that Joseph Mifsud was a Russian

agent helping Papadopoulos set up the meetings! **Seth** elevates Papadopoulos's role way beyond its true significance. **Seth** doesn't seem to realize that Mifsud never attempted to set up any meetings. All he did was (1) introduce George to "Putin's niece" who turned out to be a non-descript wine store manager in Moscow with no relation to Putin and, (2) electronically introduce George to Ivan Timofeev who could "help" George get a Putin meeting. **Rowe** points out that George never arranged one meeting. Papadopoulos only planted the paper trail implicating a collusion with Russia. George even failed in planting Mifsud's paper trail of Hillary dirt and emails in the Trump campaign. Joseph had to bring in Alexander Downer to plant that evidence of collusion. George never even talked face to face with a "real" Russian. **Rowe** portrays Papadopoulos as a "patsy" for the CIA to plant "evidence" of collusion in the Trump campaign. Instead of being a Russian Agent as Abramson claimed, connecting the dots shows he was an unsuspecting CIA patsy charged with sowing evidence of collusion in the Trump campaign.

   b.   **Abramson** portrays Michael Flynn, Carter Page, and George Papadopoulos as bad actors. **Rowe** portrays them as victims of John Brennan's evil plan, Jim Comey's ego, Peter Strzok's extreme bias and FBI lawyer, Kevin Clinesmith's criminal evidence tampering. **Rowe** portrays Flynn, Page and Papadopoulos as victims of FBI entrapment, blackmail and evidence planting. Both **Rowe and Abramson** have similar thoughts about the evil intents of Paul Manafort.

Critical critique of Seth Abramson's *"Proof of Collusion"*

Seth Abramson's book, *"Proof of Collusion, How Trump Betrayed America"* suffers from one major shortcoming – it doesn't offer any proof of collusion. It offers only a potpourri of miscellaneous "things" that happened in the life and business of Donald Trump. Abramson tries desperately to connect those dots, but ultimately fails. He and Glenn Simpson in his book *"Crime in Progress"*, used almost exactly the same set of "things" to build a case for collusion. Ultimately no collusion ever occurred. The underlying theory was that Trump colluded with Putin to benefit Russia and hurt America and eventually lead to financial gain for Trump. The "proof" of collusion is anything but. To date, "results" of this "collusion" have in no way benefitted Russia.

Seth Abramson fails to represent reality when it comes to Donald Trump's actions against Russia, particularly when compared to those of Barack Obama. With all the "evidence" of collusion "uncovered" by Mr. Abramson, one would expect that my now, the US and Russia would be walking down the aisle hand in hand with Russia getting the best part of the marriage. Since the exact opposite has happened, one would have to conclude that all that evidence gathered by Mr. Abramson was phony or hopefully just wrongly interpreted by Seth.

Mr. Abramson and all of America can rest much easier, now that Seth's interpretation of the "signs" of collusion have been shown to be bogus. Seth seemed to want his interpretation to be accurate not necessarily to hurt America, but to "get Trump." In retrospect, we should have been much more concerned about <u>Obama's</u> coziness with Russia and placed more credibility on the collusion inferences of pressing the RESET button at the start of his presidency.

Donald Trump not only has taken punitive measures against Russia's actions, but has taken proactive measures to prevent undesired results from Russian actions. Case in point is his action to prevent the building of the Russia-Germany pipeline which would result in Germany likely becoming dependent on Russia for its energy. Such a development would not be good for the western world. In contrast, Barack Obama took exactly no proactive measures to prevent any detrimental Russian initiatives. That kind of blows Abramson's theory of Trump and Tillerson cutting oil deals with Russia to get rich. It could lend credibility to the theory that Obama was trying to do a quid-pro-quo with Russia for a personal wealth payout.

As itemized below, Donald Trump has taken forty-nine reactive measures against Russia since being installed as president. He did that using a mixture of issued sanctions, export restrictions, military action and official statements. He has done this in just the first three years of his presidency. Barack Obama took four measures using three issued sanctions and one verbal warning. It took Barack Obama exactly eight years to be so bold. Clearly, Seth Abramson's concern about Trump-Russia collusion has been ill placed.

Seth Abramson's concern about Trump being susceptible to Russian "blackmail" has also not been something to worry about. It looks far more likely that Bill Clinton may be closer to being blackmailed over Clinton's cozy relationship with Jeffery Epstein and Harvey Weinstein.

The "friendliness" that Trump showed for Putin that Mr. Abramson pointed out as evidence of collusion paled in comparison to the much ballyhooed "RESET" button used by the Obama administration in 2009 in an effort to suck up to Putin. The reset button resulted in "friendly acts" by the Obama administration matched with "unfriendly acts" by Russia. Clearly, Russia saw Obama as weak and a pushover. Specifically, Obama;[212]

- Scrapped the 2009 missile defense plans for Poland and the Czech Republic as a signal of good will—Russia interpreted the move as a U.S. retreat from the European continent. Moscow pocketed the concessions and increasingly inserted itself in European affairs,
- Did nothing proactively to prevent Russia's invasion of Ukraine in 2014. Russia invaded Ukraine,
- Dismissed calls from Congress, foreign policy experts, and his own cabinet to provide lethal weapons to Ukraine that would have raised the costs on Russia and helped Kyiv defend itself against Russian military incursion into the Donbas,
- Did nothing proactively to prevent Russia's interference in the 2016 election. Russia interfered with the 2016 election.
- The Obama administration, not the Trump campaign, had invited the Russians back to the Middle East in an armed capacity, giving Moscow a role in that vitally important region that seven previous administrations, Democratic and Republican, had sought to deny,
- In a clear expression of a desire to collude with the Russians. Obama whispered to Russian President Dmitry Medvedev that he will have "more flexibility" to deal with contentious issues like missile defense after the U.S. presidential election, and
- Obama gave a huge boost to the Russian oil industry, which is the true source of power for Putin, by placing impediments to domestic American oil production. Fortunately, Trump has turned that around.

In terms of issued sanctions and executive actions, Obama on these dates;

- **March 2014 Obama issued sanctions in response to the Russian invasion of Crimea** – He issued economic sanctions

---

[212] Brookings Institute, *"Don't rehabilitate Obama on Russia"*, Haddad and Polyakova, March 5, 2018

prohibiting US oil companies or oil equipment companies from doing business with Russia, and US banks from issuing long-term loans to Russian energy companies

- **July 2014 Obama issued Sanctions in response to shooting down a Malaysia Airlines passenger plane-** He issued sanctions restricting transactions with Russian defense and energy firms and limited Russian banks' access to US economy.
- **September 2016 Obama gave Putin a verbal "warning" In response to reported Russian hacking of DNC emails** – Obama told Putin personally at the G20 Summit, to "Cut it out." The warning didn't seem to have any effect.
- **Dec 29, 2016, Obama issued sanctions in response to election interference-** Thirty-five Russian intelligence officers from the Russian embassy in Washington were expelled. In addition, four Russian individuals and five Russian entities were sanctioned. This action was ill-timed in that it set up a potential crisis with Russia that the new administration would have to deal with. It was not urgent to take this action.

In sharp contrast, specifically, Trump has taken these actions;[213]

- **Aug 2, 2017 Trump signed *"Countering America's Adversaries Through Sanctions Act"* (CAATSA) bill into law.** President Trump signed into law the *Countering America's Adversaries Through Issued Sanctions act* enacting new Issued Sanctions on Russia, Iran, and North Korea.
- **Oct 27, 2017 Trump released guidance on CAATSA Section 231(d)** - The Department of State issued public guidance on the implementation of Section 231 of the *"Countering America's Adversaries Through Issued Sanctions Act of 2017"*. The guidance specified 39 entities that the Department of State determined are part of – or are operating on behalf of – the Russian defense or intelligence sectors.
- **Dec 18, 2017 Trump released national security strategy -**The White House released its national security strategy, identifying Russia and China as adversarial to the United States.
- **Dec 19, 2017 Trump set export restrictions in response to Intermediate-Range Nuclear Forces (INF) Treaty violations-** The Department of Commerce announced new

---

[213] Brookings Institute, *"On the record: The U.S. administration's actions on Russia"*, Letas and Polyakova, December 31, 2019.

licensing and export restrictions on Russian companies Novator and Titan-Barrikady over production of a cruise missile prohibited by the Intermediate-Range Nuclear Forces Treaty (INF)

- **Dec 20, 2017 Trump issued sanctions in regard to Global Magnitsky Act.** Fifty two people and entities from Russia, Ukraine, Uzbekistan, and elsewhere were sanctioned for alleged human rights violations and corruption.
- **Dec 22, 2017 Trump issued an announcement regarding provision of lethal weapons to Ukraine** - The U.S. administration approved a plan to provide Ukraine with enhanced defensive capabilities to help it fight off Russia-backed separatists.
- **Jan 19, 2018 Trump released the national defense strategy** - The Department of Defense released its National Defense Strategy, identifying Russia and China as strategic competitors to the United States.
- **Jan 26, 2018 Issued Sanctions in response to Ukraine conflict** - 21 individuals and 9 entities were sanctioned in connection with the conflict in Ukraine and Russia's occupation of Crimea.
- **Jan 29, 2018 Trump released Russian *"Oligarch list"*** - The Department of the Treasury released a list of the most significant senior foreign political figures and oligarchs in the Russian Federation that could potentially be at risk of Issued Sanctions (114 senior political figures close to Russian President Putin and 96 oligarchs with a net worth of $1 billion or more).
- **Feb 7, 2018 Trump took military action in response to attack on U.S. - held base in Deir Ezzor, Syria** - U.S. troops killed hundreds of Syrian forces backed by Russian mercenaries (as well as Russian private military contractors). The American bombing was launched in response to a surprise attack on a U.S.-held base in the oil-rich Deir Ezzor region in Syria.
- **Feb 13, 2018 Trump issued a statement proposing sanctions on Latvian bank involved in illicit Russian-related activity -** The Department of the Treasury's Financial Crimes Enforcement Network proposed a new rule to ban ABLV Bank AS, Latvia's third-biggest bank, for its involvement in illicit Russia-related activity.
- **Feb 15, 2018 Trump made a statement in response to "NotPetya"** - The U.S. administration condemned the Russian military for launching a destructive cyberattack in June 2017,

also known as "NotPetya." "NotPetya prevents a PC from booting.

- **Mar 4, 2018 Trump made a statement in response to Russian and Syrian regime attacks on Eastern Gouta, Syria -** The U.S. administration condemned the military offensive that the Assad regime, backed by Russia and Iran, had been conducting in Syria's Eastern Ghouta region.

- **Mar 14, 2018 Trump made a statement in response to Salisbury attack -** The U.S. administration issued a statement expressing its solidarity to the United Kingdom over the nerve agent attack in Salisbury, and sharing its assessment that Russia was responsible for it.

- **Mar 15, 2018 Trump made a statement in response to Salisbury attack -** The United States issued a joint statement with France, Germany, and the United Kingdom strongly condemning the Salisbury nerve agent attack and suggesting Russia was responsible for it.

- **Mar 15, 2018 Trump issued an alert in response to Russian government cyber-activity -** The Department of Homeland Security and FBI issued a joint Technical Alert on Russian government actions targeting U.S. government entities, as well as organizations in the energy, nuclear, commercial facilities, water, aviation, and critical manufacturing sectors.

- **Mar 15, 2018 Trump issued sanctions in response to election meddling and cyberattacks -** Five Russian entities and nineteen individuals were sanctioned for conducting a series of cyberattacks and interfering in the 2016 U.S. elections.

- **Mar 25, 2018 Trump implemented expulsions of Russian intelligence officers in New York -** Twelve Russian intelligence officers from the Russian Mission to the United Nations in New York were expelled for actions deemed to be abuses of their privilege of residence.

- **Mar 26, 2018 Trump implemented expulsions of Russian intelligence officers in Washington and Seattle–** Forty-eight Russian intelligence officers from the Russian embassy in Washington were expelled, and the Russian consulate in Seattle was ordered to close, in response to the Skripal poisoning in the United Kingdom.

- **Apr 6, 2018 Trump issued sanctions in response to worldwide malign activity -** Seven Russian oligarchs and the companies they own or control, seventeen senior Russian government officials, and a state-owned Russian weapons trading company (and a bank it owns) were sanctioned for their roles in advancing Russia's malign activities – including the continued occupation of Crimea, engaging in cyberattacks, and supporting Assad's regime.

- **Jun 11, 2018 Trump issued sanctions in response to malicious cyber-related activities -** Five Russian entities and three individuals – all closely linked to Russia's Federal Security Service (FSB) – were sanctioned.

- **Jul 13, 2018 Trump issued indictments in response to malicious cyber-related activities -**Twelve Russian intelligence officers were sanctioned for their involvement in hacking the Democratic National Committee and the Clinton presidential campaign.

- **Jul 25, 2018 Trump made declaration – Secretary of State Mike Pompeo issued Crimea Declaration -** Secretary of State Mike Pompeo announced a formal policy reaffirming the U.S. rejection of Russia's annexation of Crimea. The announcement was released an hour before his scheduled testimony to the Senate Foreign Relations Committee.

- **Aug 8, 2018 Trump issued sanctions in response to Salisbury attack -** The U.S. administration announced it would restrict remaining sources of foreign assistance and arms sales to Russia, and deny U.S. credit to Russia, including through the Export-Import Bank. Restrictions would also prohibit the export of security-sensitive goods and technology.

- **Aug 21, 2018 Trump issued sanctions in response to malicious cyber-related activities -** Two Russian individuals, a Russian company, and a Slovakian company were sanctioned for helping another Russian company avoid Issued Sanctions over the country's malicious cyber-related activities.

- **Sep 6, 2018 Trump made a statement in response to Salisbury attack -** The United States issued a joint statement with France, Germany, Canada, and the United Kingdom, reiterating its outrage at the use of a chemical nerve agent in Salisbury and expressing full confidence in the British assessment that the suspects were officers of the Russian military intelligence service (GRU).

- **Sep 12, 2018 Trump issued Executive Order imposing issued sanctions for election interference -** President Trump signed an executive order imposing Issued Sanctions on any nation or individual who authorizes, directs, or sponsors meddling operations in U.S. elections. The order would allow for the freezing of assets and the limiting of foreign access to U.S.

financial institutions, as well as a cutoff of U.S. investment in sanctioned companies.

- **Sep 20, 2018 Trump issued sanctions in response to malicious activities** – Thirty-three Russian individuals and entities were sanctioned for their role in U.S. election interference and their involvement in supporting military operations in Syria and Ukraine. A Chinese entity and its director were also sanctioned for purchasing jet fighters and missiles from Russia.
- **Oct 4. 2018 Trump issued indictments in response to malicious cyber-related activities** - Seven officers of the Russian military intelligence service (GRU) were charged for their involvement in hacking Olympic athletes, anti-doping organizations, and chemical weapons monitors.
- **Oct 19, 2018 Trump issued indictments in response to attempted interference in U.S. political system** - A Russian woman was charged for her alleged role in a conspiracy to interfere in the U.S. political system, including the 2018 midterm election.
- **Nov 26, 2018 Trump made statements in response to a dangerous escalation in the Kerch Strait** - Secretary of State Mike Pompeo and U.S. Ambassador to the United Nations Nikki Haley condemned Russia's decision to intercept, fire on, and seize three Ukrainian navy vessels in the Black Sea.
- **Dec 4, 2018 Trump made statement withdrawing from INF Treaty** - Secretary of State Mike Pompeo said that the U.S. would withdraw from the 1987 Intermediate-range Nuclear Forces (INF) Treaty in 60 days if Russia did not return to compliance.
- **Dec 7. 2018 – Trump made statement in response to Russian false allegations on chemical weapons use in Aleppo, Syria** - The U.S. Department of State refuted Russia's and the Assad regime's false accusations that the opposition and extremist groups conducted a chlorine attack in northwestern Aleppo.
- **Dec 19, 2018 – Trump issued sanctions in response to Russia's continued disregard for international norms** - Eight Russian individuals were sanctioned for their involvement in a wide range of malign activities, including attempting to interfere in the 2016 U.S. election, efforts to undermine international organizations through cyber-enabled means, and the Skripal attack in the United Kingdom.
- **Dec 21, 2018 Trump made statement increasing security assistance to Ukraine's navy** - The U.S. Department of State

announced it would provide an additional $10 million in Foreign Military Financing to further build Ukraine's naval capabilities in response to Russian attacks near the Kerch Strait.

- **Jan 29, 2019 Trump released a Worldwide Threat Assessment of the U.S. Intelligence Community** - U.S. intelligence officials delivered their annual assessment of global threats to national security to Congress, identifying cooperation between China and Russia as their top concern.
- **Feb 1, 2019 Trump made statement withdrawing from the INF Treaty** – The U.S. administration announced it would suspend its obligations under the 1987 Intermediate-range Nuclear Forces (INF) Treaty because Russia was not complying with it.
- **Feb 27, 2019 Trump made statement on Russian occupation of Crimea** – Secretary of State Mike Pompeo issued a statement condemning Russia's illegal actions in Crimea and its continued aggression against Ukraine.
- **Mar 4, 2019 Trump issued notice on continuation of national emergency with respect to Ukraine** - President Trump announced the continuation for one year of the national emergency declared with respect to Ukraine.
- **Mar 11, 2019 Trump issued sanctions in response to dealings with Venezuela-** The United States sanctioned Evrofinance Mosnarbank, a Moscow-based bank jointly owned by Russian and Venezuelan state-owned companies, for attempting to circumvent U.S. issued sanctions on Venezuela.
- **Mar 14, 2019 Trump made statement in response to escalation of attacks against Idlib, Syria** - The U.S. Department of State condemned Russian offensive operations against northern Hama and southern Idlib in Syria.
- **Mar 15, 2019 Trump issued sanctions in response to Russia's continued aggression in Ukraine** -Ukrainian naval vessels in the Kerch Strait, the annexation of Crimea, and backing of separatist government elections in eastern Ukraine. These actions complement issued sanctions also taken by the European Union and Canada on the same day.
- **Apr 24, 2019 Trump made a statement in response to Russian assault on Ukraine** - The U.S. Department of State condemned Russia's decision to grant expedited citizenship to residents of Russia-controlled eastern Ukraine.

- **May 1, 2019 Trump made a statement on democracy in Venezuela** - President Trump denounced Russia's continued support for the Maduro regime in Venezuela.
- **May 16, 2019 Trump issued sanctions in response to human rights abuses** - A Chechen group and five Russian individuals were sanctioned under the Magnitsky Act over allegations of human rights abuses, including extrajudicial killings and the torture of LGBT people.
- **Aug 2, 2019 Trump issued sanctions in response to Salisbury attack** - The U.S. Department of State announced more Issued Sanctions against Russia over its use of a nerve agent in Salisbury in 2018. The Issued Sanctions fall under the Chemical and Biological Weapons Control and Warfare Elimination Act and mean the U.S. will oppose loans and assistance by international financial institutions, and restrictions on the export on Department of Commerce-controlled goods and technology.
- **Sep 26, 2019 Trump issued sanctions in response to Issued Sanctions-evasion scheme for Syria** - The Treasury Department's Office of Foreign Assets Control identified Moscow-based Maritime Assistance LLC as the head of a "Issued Sanctions evasion scheme" to deliver jet fuel to Syria.
- **Sep 30, 2019 Trump issued sanctions in response to 2018 election interference attempt** - Four entities and seven individuals, including Russian financier Yevgeniy Prigozhin, were sanctioned over attempted interference in the 2018 U.S. midterm elections.
- **Dec 5, 2019 Trump issued sanctions in response to $100 million bank hacking scheme** - A Russian-based cybercriminal organization called "Evil Corp" was sanctioned for using malware to steal more than $100 million from banks and financial institutions.

Clearly Seth was dead wrong on his suspicions of collusion. If there was collusion, Trump saw to it that America came out on the winning end at the expense of Russia. Many would like to think that Trump pulled that off. It is more likely that there was no collusion and Trumps actions independent of friendship or collusion just turned out to be effective. Mr. Abramson should be happy for America that he was wrong.

Appendix H2 "Spygate – The Attempted Sabotage of Donald J. Trump" – Dan Bongino and D.C. McAllister, October 18, 2018

Dan Bongino and D.C. Mcallister's *"Spygate – The Attempted Sabotage of Donald J. Trump* –is well documented and well written. In that sense, it is on a par with Seth Abramson's *"Proof of Collusion"* book. The thing that sets Bongino's book apart is that he does an infinitely better job defining the "real" dots and connecting those. Whereas Abramson takes the disinformation as facts and connects the dots around those. Bongino connects the dots around the corrected disinformation.

Critical critique of Dan Bongino's *"Spygate – The Attempted Sabotage of Donald J. Trump"*.

Dan Bongino and D.C. Mcallister have provided us an outstanding account of "Spygate." Anyone interested in a well-documented version of what happened needs to read this book. Where the authors extrapolated from the facts to complete the connection of the dots, they clearly point out their rationale.

Appendix H3 "Crossfire Hurricane – *Inside Donald Trump's War on the FBI*," Josh Campbell, September 17, 2019

Josh Campbell *"Crossfire Hurricane – Inside Donald Trump's War on the FBI" is* different in coverage to Dan Bongino's *"Spygate"*, Josh Abramson's *"Proof of Collusion"* and Rowe's *"Planted Evidence".* Instead it is similar to Jim Comey's, *"A Higher Loyalty"* and Andy McCabe's *"The Threat"* in that its theme is; "Donald Trump is a bad person and is highly critical of the FBI and that's unfair." Campbell's story is an inside account of the set of excuses used by FBI leaders to justify their actions regarding the instigation and execution of the FBI and Mueller investigations of Trump and his campaign staff.

Examples of where *"Planted Evidence"* conflicts with *"Crossfire Hurricane"* coverage:

1. **Campbell** remains disgusted by the debasement of law enforcement institutions by the president and his allies. Just as Comey did, he sees Trump acting as a "mob boss".[214] **Rowe** sees the FBI's own IG as laying the same criticism on Comey's FBI as Trump did.

2. **Campbell,** watching Trump suck up to Vladimir Putin in Helsinki in July 2018, concluded that Trump acted as if he were somehow compromised by the Russian strongman and "afraid of what Mueller might find". **Rowe** points out that Trump's 59 punitive actions against Russia in terms of sanctions, military actions export restrictions and other punitive measures dramatically illustrate Trump was not afraid of what Mueller would find.

3. **Campbell** rejects the notion of a "deep state." **Rowe** does not dismiss the possibility of a "deep state." Certainly, altering FISA applications and introducing 17 errors and omissions (all

---

[214] The Guardian, *"Crossfire Hurricane review: tale of Trump and the FBI is a gas gas gas"*, Lloyd Green, September 21, 2019

reflecting adversely on the Trump team) is significant evidence that a "deep state" may exist. Also Chuck Schumer's warning to Trump, *"Let me tell you, you take on the intelligence community, they have six ways from Sunday at getting back at you,"* provides bi-partisan recognition that there is a "deep-state."

Critical critique of Josh Campbell *"Crossfire Hurricane"*-.

The one common thread that comes from the books written by the three ex-FBI leaders including Josh Campbell is that Trump damaged the FBI's image. In all fairness to them, they wrote their books before their own Inspector General, Horowitz published his findings confirming the correctness of President Trump's views. In that light, Trump's criticizing the FBI was justified and any damage done was deserved and needed. The very people who accused Trump of doing harm to the image of the FBI were found by the DOJ IG to be the ones responsible for damaging it. *"Planted Evidence"* documents how those at the top of the FBI achieved this unintended consequence.

Like McCabe and Strzok, Campbell follows in the mold of Comey. He is an honorable person with a huge ego and a strong bias against all things Trump. All three consider themselves good "leaders". A common thread of pseudo leaders is that they strive to be leaders; they talk about leadership, and they read about leadership, but they frequently are not leaders. But Campbell came to the same conclusion as Comey, McCabe and Strzok; they were great leaders and chosen to lead. In Campbell's case, quitting the FBI and going to work for CNN was done for the greater good. The American people deserved his leadership. He could inform the American people as to exactly how bad Trump is.

The three ex-FBIers who wrote books about their leadership all had huge egos and anti-Trump biases. Fortunately, just average Americans get to choose our president and not FBI leaders like Jim Comey or Josh Campbell. That is what the founding fathers intended. That is what we American's want. Fortunately, Jim Comey's and Josh Campbell's assistance in trying to "save us" from our choice didn't work out for them. At least now Josh won't be helping choose our next president with the FBI aiding him directly.

Appendix H4 "A Higher Loyalty – Truth Lies and Leadership" – James Comey, April 17, 2018

James Comey's "*A Higher Loyalty – Truth Lies and Leadership*" is an excellent read. It is well written and provides great insight into James Comey the person. It is similar to Andy McCabe's "*The Threat*" in that it spends much ink on his person, his life experiences and uses that as a basis for explaining, (1) why he is a great leader and (2) why he has such disdain for Donald J. Trump.

Critical critique of Jim Comey's "*A Higher Loyalty – Truth, Lies and Leadership*".

Most of Jim Comey's book consists of an autobiography with only about ¼ of it discussing Trump and Trump's failings. Comey is someone who cares about doing the right thing. More accurately, Comey comes across is an honorable person with a huge ego and a strong bias against all things Trump.

This ego and bias prevented him from seeing that he was accomplishing what he was accusing Trump of, the degrading of the FBI. The DOJ Inspector General confirmed the extent of damage Comey managed to inflict on the reputation of the FBI. Comey's ego convinced him that Trump wouldn't fire him. Comey's ego got him fired.

The central themes Comey used to build a case against Donald Trump are the consequences of Mr. Trump's lies; and the corrosive effects of choosing loyalty to an individual over truth and the rule of law. "*We are experiencing a dangerous time in our country,*" Comey writes, "*with a political environment where basic facts are disputed, fundamental truth is questioned, lying is normalized and unethical behavior is ignored, excused or rewarded.*"

According to the IG, these are exactly the things that Comey did during the crusade to get Trump. He chose loyalty to his employees over truth and the rule of law. His unwarranted loyalty to his people allowed them to submit tainted FISA warrant applications whose accuracy and completeness were attested to by Comey. His unwarranted trusting loyalty allowed Kevin Clinesmith to actually alter a FISA application to reflect that there was no record of Carter Page having served as a CIA "asset" when the actual application said that Page had served as a CIA "asset."

Comey's unwarranted loyalty to his people resulted in the introduction of 17 errors and omissions, all designed to increase the chances of acceptance of the FISA application. This great leader blew it off as, "Oh, I must have been misled."

The rule of law dictates that all persons be treated equally under the law. Comey's FBI set George Papadopoulos, and Michael Flynn up for lying to the FBI, blamed them, sent George to prison and are still trying to nail Michael Flynn. Andy McCabe admitted lying to Congress under oath. He wasn't even charged. Christopher Steele handed the FBI a pack of lies in the Steele dossier, costing the FBI and Mueller's team $30 million to find that they weren't true and even the suggestion that Mr. Steele should be charged has not surfaced. Jim Comey accusing someone else of choosing personal loyalty over truth and the rule of law is the height of hypocrisy.

Mr. Comey does a good job of relating the many trials and tribulations of his early life and the things that made him a "great leader." In making the case for his great integrity and leadership, he unintentionally managed to explain how he developed such a giant ego.

Comey makes the case for himself that he is a good leader. A common thread among pseudo leaders is that they strive to be leaders; they talk about leadership, and they read about leadership, but typically they are not leaders. In Jim Comey's eyes, the American people needed his leadership. Great leaders are created by followers who decide who their leaders are, not vice-versa.

Unfortunately, self-anointed leaders are rarely the best leaders. Fortunately, just average Americans get to choose our president and not FBI directors. That is what the founding fathers intended. That is what we American's want. Jim Comey's book tries to convince us that he was the righteous one and the one who should correct the mistake of us electing the wrong president. He used his power and position as the Director of the FBI to aid and abet the unwarranted impeachment of Donald Trump. In other words, Comey was convinced he should be choosing our president, not the people. He doesn't see it that way, obviously. He sees that pursuing possible wrongdoing by the presidential candidate was his duty. Why was he taking notes of his conversations with Trump? It wasn't needed to investigate possible collusion. Jim needed the notes to nail Trump for obstruction of justice if Trump tried to fire him. Mr. Comey truly felt he had more power than the president.

Jim Comey's lack of true leadership skills led him to take notes of every communication he had with his boss, Donald Trump so that he could defend himself and help "bring Trump down" for obstructing justice if Trump tried to fire him. Comey admitted the President could fire him at any time, so why take notes to prevent it? If you have to disagree with your boss, do it but don't resort to "tattling to the teacher." This is the mark of a sniveling underling, not a great leader. Jim Comey's effort to "save us" from our choice for President, didn't work out for him.

James B. Comey calls the Trump presidency a "forest fire" that is doing serious damage to the country's norms and traditions. One man's "forest fire" is another man's "swamp that needs draining." Chuck Schumer's warning to Trump, "*You take on the intelligence community, they have six ways from Sunday at getting back at you.*" That warning from a political opponent is significant to the average American and further discredits the FBI and other members of the "community." One could take from this warning that there really is "a deep state" that in the minds of its members, is needed to keep politicians in check. If there is a deep state, Jim Comey is a member although probably not the leader.

Comey in his book does little but whine about how he was mistreated by politicians, while denying any responsibility for his own actions. That is the mark of a large ego. All the time Comey complains, he takes no blame for anything.

Appendix H5 "The Russia Hoax – The Illicit Scheme to Clear Hillary Clinton and Frame Donald Trump", Greg Jarrett, July 24, 2018

Greg Jarrett's *"The Russia Hoax – The Illicit Scheme to Clear Hillary Clinton and Frame Donald Trump"*–is a well written, though sparsely documented informative description of two FBI investigations, the Clinton email case ("Midyear Exam") and the Trump-Russia collusion case ("Crossfire Hurricane").

The Russia Hoax has less overlap with "Planted Evidence" than one might expect. For one thing, it covers the Hillary investigation as well as the Trump-Russia collusion investigation. Also, it addresses the Trump obstruction of justice investigation which this book does not address. Greg also discusses the errors Trump made in selecting his leadership team and although the author agrees with Mr. Jarrett, it was not part of the scope of this book.

"Planted Evidence" conflicts with Greg Jarrett's *"The Russia Hoax"*

Greg Jarrett omitted most of the discussion of the origin of the "evidence" used to open and sustain the Crossfire Hurricane investigation. Greg does not make a case about the planting of evidence against Trump and his organization or how Mifsud Steele, Downer and Millian figured into the creation and planting of evidence. He either doesn't agree with the analysis presented herein or just elected not to cover that aspect of the Trump-Russia collusion fiasco.

A significant difference between the two analyses, is that Jarrett blames "politics" as the motive for both the Clinton and Trump investigations and the way they were conducted. Jarrett supports his theory that it was an attack orchestrated at "the top" and that the FBI was behind the implementation. This book connects the dots in such a way that sees John Brennan as the instigator who planted the evidence of collusion and sucked the FBI into investigating it with selected knowledge fed to the Obama administration. Then FBI personal biases and Comey's ego and hate for Trump took over and did Brennan's bidding.

Jarrett claims there was "corruption" in the FBI that contributed to the targeting of Trump. *"Planted Evidence"* doesn't go that far. It portrays the FBI as well intentioned, but in this case its leadership got carried away because of huge egos and strong biases against Trump. This bias led to pushing the boundaries of their investigation of the Trump team beyond being objective. It was not FBI "corruption" on a general scale.

Critical critique of Greg Jarrett's *"The Russia Hoax* "

Greg Jarrett has provided us an outstanding account of "the Russia Hoax. Jarrett attempts to explain that the Russian hoax's objective was to frame Donald J. Trump for collusion. Jarrett believes that various parties worked together improperly to ensure that Trump was defeated. These people include Barrack Obama, and various individuals from the FBI. Subsequent to the election, the problem of "the Russian hoax" had escalated and Jarrett believed the issue was given unnecessary attention. To him, Trump had done nothing wrong in colluding with Russia

Appendix H6 "The Threat – How the FBI Protects America in the Age of Terror and Trump", Andrew McCabe, February 19, 2019.

Andy McCabe's book *"The Threat – How the FBI Protects America in the Age of Terror and Trump"*–is mostly an exceptional read about Andy McCabe and his interesting career in the FBI. As with Jim Comey's book, *"A Higher Loyalty"* Andy devotes about 25% of the book to describing his disgust with Trump the person and as our President. Mr. McCabe does not address the Trump-Russia collusion directly, so his book is not a description of the investigation, per se. *"The Threat"* is probably the best of the McCabe-Comey-Campbell trio of Trump expose' books.

Andrew McCabe gives a very in-depth look at how the FBI operates, and how they go about investigations. His account is fascinating. The majority of the book is about McCabe's career, first in going after Russian organized crime in the USA and then in counterterrorism after 9/11. He describes how the FBI finds and investigates terrorists in an "I can't put this book down" manner.

Critical critique of Andrew McCabe's *"The Threat"*

From an "average American's" perspective, McCabe articulates very well the frustrations that FBI leadership had with Trump. But as his narrative unfolds, McCabe's frustrations with Trump proved very similar to the frustrations that Trump must have had with FBI leadership – he did not like the false innuendos and charges he was accused of. (I think Trump called it a "witch hunt.") McCabe devoted 25% of his book to denigrating the president and the office of the presidency in an effort to communicate to the American public the frustrations he had with Trump and his management style. He did not like Trump deminish him or the FBI. After the FBI, Mueller and IG investigations, it appears that Trump was clearly smeared, but the FBI in general and Andy McCabe specifically didn't fare as well.

At this point, ALL of the charges against the Trump team regarding collusion have been determined to be false by both the FBI's and Mueller Team investigations. At this point, MOST of the charges regarding investigation abuses by the FBI have been determined to be true by the inspector general. Andy McCabe should reflect on that. Andy knows better than anyone that when a person is falsely charged for a crime, they know they didn't commit, they get angry. Andy should expect to be called out on conducting a witch hunt. Instead of a wake up-call, Andy complains about the IG who confirmed some of Trumps charges.

As you can imagine, the last quarter of the book is especially damning to Donald Trump. But, really, can you blame Trump for being offended after what the FBI did to him and his team? In the eyes of someone falsely accused of any misdeed, be it hiring a prostitute or collusion or whatever, and the person knows he is innocent, that person is going to see the accusing organization as corrupt and conducting a witch hunt. That is a normal response and is justified. That describes Trump's response.

When the shoe was on the other foot, and Andy was accused of benefiting from the $700,000 given to his wife's campaign by the Clinton organization, giving rise to the clear implication that Andy was corrupt he writes about how upset he was. What Mr. McCabe doesn't appreciate is that given the law enforcement role of the FBI, they have many tools available to "get someone" they want to "get." That was the essence of Chuck Schumer's comment to the effect that "the FBI has seven ways to Sunday to get you." That is what Donald Trump thought the FBI was doing to him. That's perhaps why he turned the tables on Andy McCabe. In McCabe's case his accusers were amateurs in "framing" him. They didn't have the "sources and methods" that McCabe had in his quest to "get" Trump.

McCabe points out the FBI has a right and obligation to investigate when a credible allegation that a government official is colluding with a foreign government. The lesson Andy hopefully has learned is, before the FBI does this again, they should have solid evidence before there are any leaks about an investigation. They should have real evidence of collusion, not just a series of reports of dirt from a political enemy and/or more than a secondhand rumor of collusion originating from an unknown source (Joseph Mifsud) who has an unknown sponsor, with an unknown motive. If there is more, we need to hear it.

Andrew McCabe is a decent person. Andy McCabe is an outstanding FBI Agent and boss. But Andy McCabe deserved to be fired. He deserved to be fired for playing the role he did to continue to drag Carter Page, George Papadopoulos and Michael Flynn through hell when he had evidence that they were likely not guilty of collusion, the "crime" he was allegedly investigating. He was a party to the missing exculpatory evidence and the altering of the Carter Page FISA application. McCabe seemed blinded by the herd mentality of Strzok, Lisa Page, Clinesmith, himself, Comey and others in the FBI to "get" Trump, innocent or guilty. We are saddened that Andy paid for it by losing his job and his retirement package. I hope he is just as saddened by what he did to the innocent members of the Trump team.

———

Appendix H7 "Deep State Target – How I got Caught in the Crosshairs of the Plot to Bring Down President Trump", George Papadopoulos, March 26, 2019.

George Papadopoulos's book *"Deep State Target – How I got Caught in the Crosshairs of the Plot to Bring Down President Trump"*–is a good read about the "Mifsud track" of the Trump-Russia collusion debacle. It is a unique, first-hand perspective of what happened.

George Papadopoulos gives a glowing account of his accomplishments and contributions. George's account is fascinating. Unfortunately, no one else seems to share his opinions about his accomplishments.

"Planted Evidence" conflicts with Papadopoulos's *"Deep State Target"*

Papadopoulos did not fully appreciate how he was used as a "patsy" to plant evidence of collusion inside the Trump campaign. Although he realized that Mifsud was trying to manipulate him, he didn't seem to understand how expertly he was manipulated.

Mr. Papadopoulos seems to almost understand what Alexander Downer and Erika Thompson's roles were, but he did not connect the dots that show those two Australians were actually tasked by Mifsud and the CIA to do what he failed to do - to plant evidence of collusion tied to his "knowledge" of emails and dirt on Hillary Clinton. He had suspicions about Downer and Thompson, but he didn't completely connect the dots. George did not see that Downer's and Erika Thompson's role was to get George to talk about his access to Hillary dirt so the Australian duo could provide an alternate path for planting that incriminating evidence of Russian collusion into the FBI.

Critical critique of George Papadopoulos's *"Deep State Target"*

George Papadopoulos is just an average guy but with a bigger than average need to be important. Appendix D describes George's background and explains how his background contributed to his need to make a mark in the world. Unfortunately, Mr. Papadopoulos, as of now has achieved notoriety, but not importance. At 33 George has a master's degree but has never held a real job. The closest he came was as a subcontract employee at the Hudson Institute in 2013 and 2014.

A couple of troubling things are raised in Papadopoulos's account of his part in the Trump-Russia collusion debacle; (1) his account of the Alexander Downer encounter doesn't make sense, (2) Why did the London Center of International Law Practice hire him and pay him to do nothing for the company?, (3) How could he afford to spend 2 1/2 months cavorting in Greece and other places with his girlfriend, Simona Manigiante, when he didn't have a job or any money?, (3) Why didn't he ever produce the $10,000 in "marked bills" that supposedly he gave to a lawyer in Greece?, and (4) Why did he lie about when and how many times he met with Joseph Mifsud?

George lived through the whole bizarre Mifsud incident, but never put it all together. Does he know something he is not telling or does he really not know who Joseph Mifsud is?

Appendix H8 "Crime in Progress: Inside the Steele Dossier and the Fusion GPS Investigation of Donald Trump", Glenn Simpson & Peter Fritsch, November 26, 2019.

Glen Simpson's and Peter Fritsch's book[215], *"Crime in Progress: Inside the Steele Dossier and the Fusion GPS Investigation of Donald Trump"*–is an interesting attempt to connect a long term history of Trump's business dealings with a recent collection of questionable Christopher Steele research to reach the conclusion Trump could be in the process of committing a crime.

Glenn Simpson has spent a lot of time researching Trump's business and banking deals going back to when Simpson was an investigative reporter for the Wall Street Journal. He should know much from such a long history of investigation, and he does. Where his book falls short is in connecting his knowledge of those business deals with any evidence of crime or collusion as it relates to Trump-Russian collusion in the campaign.

"Planted Evidence" conflicts with Simpson's *"Crime in Progress.*

Simpson concluded that *"there was ample evidence amassed over the past three years to show that the Trump campaign and the Russian government repeatedly <u>sought to work together</u> to swing the 2016 election and that they succeeded."* (Note the "wordsmithing"- ..."**sought to work together**"... i.e. **NOT "worked together"**...). This is an admission that Simpson never saw a "crime in progress" and that the parties only succeeded in **trying** to work together but never did. If he had found evidence that they **did** work together, it would be a valid supporting claim that there was a potential "crime in progress." Simpson didn't find this evidence. He only claims there was ample evidence to show that the Trump campaign and the Russian government repeatedly "**tried** to work

---

[215] Apologies to Peter Fritsch for referring to his and Glenn Simpson's book from this point on as "Simpson's Crime in Progress." This is not to slight Peter's contribution, but to make it easier to refer to the book.

together to swing the 2016 election," but according to Simpson, apparently never could.

"Planted Evidence" concludes that there was ample evidence to show that Simpson and a retired foreign MI.6 agent (Steele) did not only **try** to work together to swing the 2016 election, they **did** work together to achieve that purpose. The IG confirmed that Rowe was right. Simpson was wrong. (Note that one of the primary contributors to Simpson's "ample evidence" was the visit by Natalia Veselnitskaya to a meeting with Donald Trump Jr. and others to allegedly deliver dirt on Hillary. Ms. Veselnitskaya didn't deliver any Hillary "dirt" just as Mifsud didn't delivered any Hillary "dirt." However, Ms. Veselnitskaya succeeded in planting a record of Donald Jr. meeting with Ms. Veselnitskaya for the purpose of receiving dirt on Hillary. It is suspicious to an average American, that since Ms. Veselnitskaya visited Mr. Simpson just before the meeting with Donald Jr. and just after her meeting with Donald Jr, that THEY were the ones colluding to influence an election.)

Critical critique of Glenn Simpson's *"Crime in Progress:"*

Glenn Simpson was an investigative journalist at the Wall Street Journal before founding Fusion GPS along with Peter Fritsch. His first political hit job was against Mitt Romney. The second, according to Simpson was the initial effort to get dirt on Donald Trump. Paul Singer an anti-Trump Republican conservative hired Mr. Simpson to dig up dirt on Trump's business dealings. When Trump won anyway, Glenn shopped the deal to the Democrats. They bought it. Simpson wanted some Russian sourced "dirt" so he inked a subcontract with friend Christopher Steele who had much better Russian connections. (This sounds like the dreaded plot to collude with the Russians to get dirt on a political opponent, doesn't it?)

Simpson wrote in his book that after the investigation for Paul Singer was completed, *"There was now unanimity inside Fusion on the need to do what they could to keep Trump out of the White House and also unanimity as to why."*

The "why" may be legitimate, but without any evidence no one can judge. Examples of why Trump should be kept out of the White House according to the unanimous opinion of the whole Fusion GPS team were:

1. *"Trump's traits disqualified him for the job"* (that doesn't sound like a "crime in progress"),

2. *"Trump's political rhetoric was loathsome"* (that doesn't sound like a "crime in progress"),

3. *Trump's* (unidentified, unsupported) *ties to the criminal underworld* (not anything you could identify as a "crime in progress" without more definition),

4. *Trump's reliance on* (undefined, unsupported) *hidden flows of Russia money* (not anything you could identify as a "crime in progress" without more definition), and

5. *Trump's record of chicanery in business* (that doesn't sound like a "crime in progress".)

Simpson says he never intended that the work be leaked to the press, but it did. (Oh my god, the dog ate my homework!) Christopher Steele wanted to tell the FBI of the content of his work. Simpson and his employer even supplied their own "Trump dirt" for Christopher Steele to tell the FBI.

Steele was worried about the FBI not taking the Steele report seriously. So, he decided to leak it to John McCain and McCain talked to Jim Comey. Simpson needed an "insurance" policy to ensure the great "dirt" on Trump "didn't get swept under the rug."

McCain's guy leaked it to a journalist. It was published on January 10, a week before the inauguration. (SO cavalier!) Trump was justifiably upset. Simpson said, "this was very "unpleasant".

Simpson's reaction to the December 9, 2019 IG report that found, *"The FBI corrupted the secret court process for obtaining warrants to spy on former Trump aide Carter Page and it did so by supplying the court with false information produced by Christopher Steele, an agent of the Hillary Clinton campaign."* Glenn Simpson called the IG finding "total nonsense." The average American sides with the unbiased IG.

Simpson's had a negative reaction to the IG report that found, *"Bruce Ohr provided the information he received from Steele and Simpson to the FBI, which had already received much, but not all of the same information through its direct contact with Steele."* Ohr did not advise any of his supervisors in the Office of Deputy Attorney General (ODAG) about his contacts with Steele and Simpson, about his wife's work for Fusion GPS or about his acting as a conduit of this information to the FBI until the ODAG leadership confronted Ohr about his activities in late 2017." Glenn Simpson wrote in response that, *"Ohr was penalized for trying to uncover the wrongdoing.*" Ohr didn't try to uncover wrongdoing, he simply acted as a delivery boy for Simpson!

Mr. Simpson feels he has been treated unfairly. In that sense he feels like Donald Trump.

Index to Persons Mentioned